The *Twelfth Night* of
SHAKESPEARE'S AUDIENCE

Dalmatina, ò Schiauona.

AN ILLYRIAN LADY
From Vecellio's *Habiti*, 1608

The *Twelfth Night* of
SHAKESPEARE'S AUDIENCE

by John W. Draper

OCTAGON BOOKS

A DIVISION OF FARRAR, STRAUS AND GIROUX

New York   1975

Reprinted 1975
by special arrangement with John W. Draper

OCTAGON BOOKS
A DIVISION OF FARRAR, STRAUS & GIROUX, INC.
19 Union Square West
New York, N. Y. 10003

Library of Congress Cataloging in Publication Data

Draper, John William, 1893-
    The Twelfth night of Shakespeare's audience.

    Reprint of the ed. published by Stanford University Press, Stanford, Calif.

    Includes bibliographical references and index.
    1. Shakespeare, William, 1564-1616. Twelfth night.   I. Title.
PR2837.D7   1975   822.3'3   75-2242
ISBN 0-374-92277-2

Manufactured by Braun-Brumfield, Inc.
Ann Arbor, Michigan

Printed in the United States of America

☙ To Daniel, John, and Charles,
who studied *Twelfth Night* with me

~ Preface

THE scholarship on the major plays of Shakespeare has quite outgrown the scope of an edition; and scholarship in America, one hopes, has also outgrown the naïve interpretation of a masterpiece by mere guess without historical foundation. If one is to seek (in the words of the late Professor Schelling) *the* meaning, rather than merely *a* meaning, of Shakespeare's text, one should set forth with full and systematically marshaled evidence the reason why *this* interpretation, rather than any other, is indeed the one that Skakespeare meant and that his audience gathered from the performance: this holds true not only for short *loci* in the dialogue but also for larger matters of plot and characterization and theme. Even for a single play, so elaborate a scheme demands a monograph, and *ergo*, for Shakespeare's major plays a series of monographs, rather than mere editorial introductions. Some years ago, the present writer brought out, at Duke University Press, such an interpretation of *Hamlet*; now, in like manner, he offers *Twelfth Night* to the public.

Indeed, under this closer scrutiny, the comedy presents much greater scope and depth than is usually ascribed to it: Sir Toby and Sir Andrew, and Feste, and Maria, and Malvolio illustrate current types, and their situations and aspirations express current problems. The Countess Olivia's whole household is an Elizabethan household in transition from easygoing feudal paternalism, when crowds of retainers served their lords for mere board and keep, to the modern era of a more stringent economy. The change gave rise to hardships and uncertainties and fears, and all the major figures in the play—even the Duke and the Countess—are seeking on their several planes for some sort of social security. Many in Shakespeare's audience had reason to sympathize with them; and thus the pleasure of the comic ending must have had a large element of personal wish fulfillment. The characters of the piece, moreover, run a social gamut as wide as that of an Elizabethan audience, from nobility to servants, with an old soldier like Sir Toby and a professional fool like Feste. Such jocund company has the present writer been privileged to keep; he only hopes that his labors have given these merry friends of his a more authentic reality to the gentle reader of Shakespeare.

To his elders and betters in Elizabethan scholarship, on whose labors he has of necessity relied, he expresses the thanks that each generation owes its forebears, and also to his contemporaries who in one way or another contributed to this volume, to his students, who have been an inspiration and whose published work is occasionally cited, and especially to his friend, the late Arthur Dayton, of Charleston, West Virginia.

J. W. D.

May 1, 1948

Contents

‿Illustrations

∾Interpreting Shakespeare's
Twelfth Night

A great while ago the world begon,
  hey ho, the winde and the raine:
But that's all one, our Play is done,
  and wee'l striue to please you euery day.

THUS Feste's Epilogue concludes the comedy of *Twelfth Night*; and indeed the play effectually did "striue to please" its audience and well earned its subtitle of "What You Will." It was probably first given in January 1601; in January 1602 (N.S.) it was revived before the Middle Temple, presumably by request. The diarist Manningham enjoyed the performance; and many other revivals doubtless followed. At least twice it was given before James I; and, for more than twenty years, Shakespeare's company kept the piece from getting into print and so into the hands of rival players. In 1640, Digges testified to the continued popularity of Malvolio; and, shortly after the Restoration, Downes records its "mighty success."

In a less fortunate sense, *Twelfth Night* has been "What You Will" to a long line of critics, who have generally been so consumed with laughter at its gaiety and so charmed with its romance that they have ignored its Elizabethan background, and therefore have missed its significance of theme, blamed it for structural incoherence, and found it in effect the merest farce. Thus they condemn it *in toto* while they praise it in detail: they find it scintillating and disunified, imaginatively romantic and insignificant. They ignore, or give but formal recognition to, Shakespeare's vivid and subtle Elizabethan realism, despite Hamlet's advice to the players and despite the Preface to *Troilus and Cressida* (1609), which declared that

Shakespeare's "comedies . . . . are so fram'd to the life that they serve for the most common commentaries of all the actions of our lives." Perhaps this paradox of critical praise and blame arose from each critic's looking at the piece from the limited view of a monograph; or perhaps he was but summarizing vulgate doctrine together with his personal *aperçus* in the narrow compass of an introduction to the text. In either case, a systematic and well-documented interpretation could hardly be the result; and, indeed, no such ample treatment has yet appeared.

A thorough understanding of each character seems to be primary in studying any play that rises above the inconsequential level of farce or melodrama; for, in serious drama, character must motivate action and dialogue and theme. The clues to character interpretation must be sought partly in the text itself, interpreted in terms of contemporary life, and partly, external to the text, in early critical comment if any survive, in the author's treatment of his source, in his changes and revisions, and in the conditions and conventions of the contemporary stage. All of this evidence, as it bears on *Twelfth Night*, must be systematically gathered and weighed and applied to each individual figure in the piece before plot or theme can be adequately understood. Unfortunately, in this play, such external evidence is of little help. Seventeenth-century comment consists merely of the offhand praise of Manningham and Downes, and the offhand dispraise of Pepys—all too vague and general to indicate critical interpretation.

A study of the supposed sources is not much greater aid. The Elizabethan audience resented variations from a story that they knew; and therefore such changes as a competent playwright made usually arose from some major purpose, and so should afford a clue to the theme of the piece and the intention of the author. In *Twelfth Night*, however, the sources are so uncertain and seem to have supplied so little of Shakespeare's action that their light is seldom better than a will-o'-the-wisp. They relate almost exclusively to the Viola-Orsino plot, and give practically nothing of Feste or Malvolio or Sir Toby or

Sir Andrew or Maria. The addition of foolish suitors such as Malvolio and Sir Andrew may well have been inspired by Italian comedy; but most of the most comic parts of the play are Shakespeare's own, and so may well spring from extra-literary origins.

Some of these analogues of the plot were apparent to the Elizabethan audience, for Manningham in his *Diary* remarked that the play was "much like the Commedy of Errores, Menechmi in Plautus, but most like and nere to that in Italian called *Inganni*." This last, like Shakespeare, uses the name Cesare for the sister who disguises herself as a page. Somewhat closer in plot is the sixteenth-century comedy *Gl' Ingannati*, and it contributes the name Malevolti. The story also appears in Bandello and in Sidney's *Arcadia*; but the version nearest to Shakespeare is Riche's *Apolonius and Silla*, for it alone presents the shipwreck of Viola, the mourning of Olivia, and the cross-purposes-at-love of these two with Orsino. Of course, the stage conventions of mistaken identity and of a girl disguised as a page are commonplaces of Elizabethan drama, and Shakespeare works them out in general conformity to Riche's story. Furness, to be sure, considered Riche too "coarse" to be a source of Shakespeare's; but Riche is no cruder than some of his other sources, and Furness might well have borne in mind the couplet from *All's Well*:

> From lowest place when virtuous things proceed,
> The place is dignified by the doer's deed.

In *Hamlet* and in some other plays, the existence of one or more quarto texts makes it possible somewhat to trace the dramatist's conception as it grew; we can see him sharpening his main points and progressively bringing character and incident into focus to emphasize the theme that he wishes to convey; and this evolution helps to show his primary purpose. In *Twelfth Night*, however, the absence of quartos before the publication of the First Folio in 1623 leaves no evidence of such revisions as may have brought the piece to its present form and vitiates this method of approach. Luckily, the single text

3

that has survived in the Folio seems to be rather accurate, and the fact that it approximates the average length of an Elizabethan play—some twenty-five hundred lines—suggests both that it is probably complete and that it contains no extensive interpolations by other hands. Indeed, critics agree that the styles of both verse and prose are Shakespearean throughout. Thus a single good text survives, and only a single text, as the basis on which to judge the comedy.

The stage history of a play sometimes supplies a hint concerning the interpretation of a part. Certain actors, then as now, specialized in certain types of role; and, in a stock company such as Shakespeare's, the casting of the parts would largely be a matter of fitting the proper role to the proper actor. Indeed, Shakespeare must have written certain parts—that of Feste, for example—with certain actors in mind. Our theatrical records, unfortunately, for the reign of Elizabeth are rather scant and sketchy; but, even so, sufficient work has been done to make this type of background useful; for, if one knows the actor who played a part, one can somewhat infer from his other roles the traits of character that he most effectively expressed, and so the nature of the particular role in question. For example, the fact that the great Burbage seems to have played Orsino shows the importance of the Duke in Elizabethan eyes; William Sly, the "juvenile lead" who did the choleric Laertes and the romantic Fenton, apparently took the like part in *Twelfth Night* of Sebastian; and the casting of Robert Armin, who was famous as a professional court fool, in the part of Feste implies that this role realistically portrayed the professional fool in contemporary life. Of course, this type of proof is seldom definite and final; often only a few of an actor's parts are known, and sometimes they show little consistency in type. In a particular play, moreover, the actor may have tried an experiment, or he may have been accidentally miscast.

Elizabethan audiences were none too high in average intelligence—if one accepts Hamlet's estimate of the groundlings; and certain conventions of the stage were rather clearly calcu-

4

lated to assist their understanding of plot and character. Soliloquies and asides, for example, must always express the sincere belief of the speakers—even if these beliefs be wrong: Malvolio, for example, in the garden scene, speaks aloud his thoughts about Olivia's love for him; and, though he is evidently mistaken in his wishful thinking, yet his belief that she "did affect" him is obviously sincere, and forms the basis of the plot that brings on his ruin. The love of Viola for Orsino, likewise, early appears in an aside; and Olivia also expresses her passion for this youth who has made her as "mad" as Malvolio. This device is particularly useful to set forth feelings and motives that the characters would naturally conceal. In Elizabethan plays, moreover, with their several plots and many roles, a valuable convention decreed either that an important figure at his first entrance should show his social caste and relation to the others by dress or word or action—as the Duke does in the first scene, or that he be explained by others just before his entrance as Sir Andrew is by Sir Toby and Maria. Thus, the complicated pattern of the piece is carefully unrolled, and the exposition of the initial elements is clearly and quickly managed; if the groundlings did not understand, they would become noisy and spoil the play for the judicious.

Sometimes help can be found in the situations and the characters that the Elizabethan stage inherited from its Classical, Medieval, and Italian Renaissance forebears. How far is Sir Toby, for instance, a *miles gloriosus* in the long tradition that came down from Plautus? How far is Sir Andrew a gull, like those of the *commedia dell' arte*? And how much does Viola owe to the Elizabethan convention of the girl-disguised-as-a-page? Variations from the dramatic norm might well give a clue to Shakespeare's purpose; but, thus late in his evolution as a playwright, he was likely to treat such conventions rather freely, for he was no longer their servant but their master; and, in his maturity, he created characters rather than followed models The realism of his art, moreover, was so developed that truth-to-life might well account for such changes as he

5

made from his source or from the stock types of character that older drama supplied.

In short, the evidence on *Twelfth Night* external to the text throws but a pale and flickering light on interpretation: the sources are too doubtful and diverse; no trace remains of the evolution of the play in Shakespeare's mind; the casting of the parts is not always certain; and Shakespeare, as a great artist, treated conventional character and situation with such originality that it is not safe to suppose one of his fools just the usual stage fool, or his steward just the usual stage servant. Such evidence, however, though by itself inconclusive, cannot be ignored.

In this play, therefore, the text must serve as the chief basis for interpretation, not the text as the usual twentieth-century reader understands it, reading into it his own modern English, his own ideas and prepossessions, and his own social concepts, but the text as Shakespeare's audience must have experienced and felt it. To put ourselves back into this faraway locale is no easy matter, and to keep ourselves there requires a constant check of contemporary documents upon our every thought and feeling as we go through the play. Comedy, as an artistic medium, especially depends on contemporaneous background; for even the concept of what is funny varies from age to age, with the growth of new social prejudices and sympathies and with a quickening sense of the ironies of life. Tragedy takes its themes from greater, more universal laws and situations; but comedy satirizes current whimseys that change somewhat from year to year. A successful comedy like *Twelfth Night*, therefore, must of necessity clothe its universal theme in peculiarly Elizabethan, and therefore ephemeral, forms; and these habiliments of time and place must be mastered, in so far as that be possible, before one can understand even a minor character or a single situation and Shakespeare's way of handling it. Thus and only thus must the text be minutely and systematically scanned and shrewdly understood if it is to yield its secret of Shakespeare's purpose and his audience's reaction to the play.

6

Drama can be analyzed into its artistic elements: plot, character, setting, style, and theme. In serious plays, character is perhaps the point at which analysis should begin; for it reflects the setting, and from it grows the plot, and the interactions of plot and character express those fundamental patterns and principles of human conduct that constitute dramatic theme. With character, then, a systematic study may well start. Each figure in the play must be separately, thoroughly, and methodically explored, both in himself and in relation to the other characters and to the whole play. After exhausting such external material as appears in the source, in the casting of the role, and in theatrical convention and stock characters, criticism must examine all that the character says and all that is said about him, and must weigh his actions and the actions and attitudes of others toward him, so that it presents his inner psychology and his outer social relationships, his traits and life before the curtain rose (as far as Shakespeare tells them), his motives and doings in the play, and the situation in which the last act leaves him. All these must be presented clearly and in order, with pertinent quotation from the text and from other Elizabethan documents, so that we see this figure as the Elizabethans saw him.

The difficulties that inhere in such a plan are most considerable, even if one grant the rather large assumption of a perfect text. Since 1600, words have shifted not only in actual meaning but also in nuances of emotional coloring; the loose and somewhat ambiguous grammar and the idioms that English has since discarded are also constant pitfalls, and the fine distinctions like those of Continental languages, in pronouns of address, are not intuitive to the modern English ear. These subtle differences between *you* and *thou* in dialogue often imply the relative social class of the speakers, or show feeling, momentary or habitual, of scorn or anger or affection; and these finesses are the very stuff of drama. When Sir Toby, for example, addresses "Signior Fabyan" with *thou* and *thy*, he expresses, not the superiority of a knight toward a servant, but the intimacy of two gentlemen; and this gives the clue at

Fabyan's first entrance that he is not a menial but a "serving-man" of good family and, by birth, Sir Toby's equal; and, therefore, Fabyan, quite appropriately, joins with the gentles in gulling Malvolio. On the other hand Malvolio, as a steward, even when he berates his "masters" for their midnight revels, and when he plays "Count" to himself in the garden and admonishes an imaginary Sir Toby on his "drunkennesse," always employs the *you* of polite discourse, rather than the *thou* of familiarity or contempt. But Sir Toby expresses both his own social superiority and his personal scorn by regularly stigmatizing the upstart steward as *thou*. All such material must be carefully weighed and judged as evidence of caste in the nicely graduated social order of Elizabethan life, and also as evidence of personal feelings of the individuals concerned. The Elizabethans, like modern Spaniards or Italians, would know these things by feeling; we can know them only by careful study.

In many ways, not only the grammar but the style of the verse and of its delivery subtly reveal the characters. The many allusions are especially significant and include every sort of subject from a "Sheriffes post" that stood outside the dwellings of the city fathers to the "Sophy" of Persia, from Cressida of Medieval legend to the Tartars and "Catayans," and from Lilly's Latin *Grammar* to the "new Mappe with the augmentation of the Indies." Professor Spurgeon has recently used this conglomerate of references as an index to the poet's cast of mind; but, if a play is truly drama, should they not rather illustrate, when collected and systematically arranged, the character who is speaking—his education and interests and mental bent—and so furnish a clue to his motives and psychology and also to his former life, upbringing, and experience? Just so, Sir Toby's references to logic and rhetoric, to religion, law, and languages, and to contemporary pseudoscience define the scope and depth of his education and ideas; and just so, his references to sports and games and his apt quotations from current balladry imply the interests of his riper years. In like fashion, Feste's counterfeit classicism—Quinapalus and the Vapians—

shows how he debases his wit to the ignorance of some auditors; and Malvolio's plain speech, not only unadorned but brusque and even rude, accords with the limited horizon of a mere steward who must con "politic authors" to learn propriety— as certain moderns consult books on etiquette. A number of purely English references, moreover, to "Westward hoe" and to the bed of Ware give evidence, if evidence be needed, that Shakespeare wrote the play with Elizabethan England in his eye. Thus a wealth of allusion contributes not only to the poetic style but also to the characterization and setting, and so to the theme of the comedy; and, under each character and each major problem, these allusions must be collected and considered.

The verbal wit, moreover, presents a difficulty. The Elizabethans, in life as well as on the stage, delighted in persiflage and complicated wordplay that is often concealed from modern eyes by shades of meaning long since discarded; and modern editions are nowhere more remiss than in their failure fully to explain the rich scattering of puns and especially of double meanings that must have made the original audiences chortle. Sometimes a modern can hardly be quite sure whether a given passage has one of two meanings, or both, or even three; sometimes ambiguity of syntax can create a subtle innuendo; and sometimes dramatic irony, as in Viola's telling of her love to Orsino, who is at once her father-confessor and the unknowing object of her passion, gives double meaning a tragic seriousness. The Duke opens the comedy with a pun on "hart"; in Sir Andrew's company, Sir Toby is drunk "nightly" (and also "knightly" as a lord); and Sir Andrew is described as "tall," partly because his stature is altitudinous, and partly in the Elizabethan sense of *brave* because (by a fine irony) he is an arrant coward. Not only the amateurs, but also the professional wit, Feste, put sparkle in the lines. He declares that Olivia's orders that he be punished for his absence (and also her failure to value his fine wit) constitute "Misprison," in both its etymological and its legal senses. He is an artist at mistaking the word: Viola asks him whether he lives by his music, and he replies that he "lives

9

by the Church" because he lives next door to it. His talk is a fantastic anagram to be read in two or three directions. This is quite to be expected of a court jester who not only delighted the old Count but also charms the Duke Orsino, and whose quips can extort forgiveness from Olivia and cajole money from all and sundry. Feste's wit is part of his profession, and it must be understood, or the lines will lag and many fine points be lost. Such evidence of character in the piquant give-and-take of talk is elusive and not always sure, but it cannot be ignored.

The proper delivery of the lines is more often suggested in the meter than most critics and actors would seem to realize; and, in a given speech, tone and inflection and tempo are often expressive of character. Elizabethans when speaking slowly tended to pronounce certain syllables that have since grown silent, such as the *-on* in *-tion* and *-sion*; and, however the spelling, they slurred in rapid speech such phrases as *for't* and *on't*, and such words as *spirit*, *even*, and *never* into one syllable. Though most of *Twelfth Night* is in prose, the meter in some scenes reflects these slurs and so gives a clue to tempo. Ellipsis, of course, increases as Shakespeare's style evolves, but the amount of its use in a given passage also gives evidence of speed, for the omission of grammatical essentials suggests haste. The small size of the Elizabethan theater and the position of the actor out amidst the audience made possible great rapidity of speech. The tempo of the lines doubtless ran a wide gamut up to prestissimo, and changes in speed would suggest the speaker's emotional intensity and his reactions to the passing situation.

In the first scene, for example, Orsino's slurring of *spirit* and *even* into one syllable, in contrast to Valentine's *vailèd* and *remembrance* (in four syllables) suggests that the Duke is speaking, not in the languishing accents of a mere romantic lover who luxuriates in insincere affection, but with the quick intensity of actual love-melancholy; and other evidence bears this out. At the end of the scene, the tempo slows down to the final couplet as shown in the contrast between *affections*

10

(in three syllables) and *perfections* (in four). Likewise, the broken meter at the beginning of scene ii suggests the breathless fears of Viola just cast upon the shore. When the Duke reappears in the fourth scene, he begins with nervous haste: *know'st* and *unclasp'd* and *even* (pronounced according to the meter *e'en*); but he soon slows down for emphasis to *fixèd*; and Viola replies deliberately, as shown by *never* in two syllables. At the end of the scene her delivery is quicker, as evidenced in *I'll* and in the final ellipses. Quite as significant is Olivia's soliloquy near the end of Act I: her first three or four lines are spoken in the speed of passion, as appears in the slurring of *Gentleman* (in two syllables), *I'll, actions,* and *spirit,* and also the ellipsis of *that* before "thou art." Then, suddenly, her prudence asserts itself: "not too fast: soft, soft," she says, and pronounces *even* in two syllables, *perfections* in four, and adds a needless *to* in front of *creep.* Here change of tempo is a clear index of character: Olivia is at once consumed with love and yet afraid to bestow her hand on one unworthy. Since the spelling of the text in the prose passages was governed largely by the printer's convenience in justifying the right-hand margin, and since such a spelling as *never* is no evidence that the word was not pronounced in one syllable, meter is necessary to supply enough objective proof to show the tempo; and, therefore, this approach is possible only in such scenes and parts as use blank verse. Unfortunately, in *Twelfth Night,* these are rather few.[1]

Thus, from the lines themselves, their direct statements, and their subtler implications, the characters take form; but, before this palimpsest can properly be read, one should examine each character, not only in terms of his relation to his prototype, if any, in the source and to parallel stock figures of stage tradition, but also in terms of his prototypes in contemporary English life; for literary scholarship has concerned itself too

[1] See Appendix C, p. 264. In the tragedies, more of the crucial scenes are in verse; and in them, therefore, this approach is more revelatory. See J. W. Draper, "Patterns of Humor and Tempo in *King Lear*," *Bulletin of the History of Medicine*, XXI, 390 *et. seq.*; "Patterns of Tempo and Humor in *Othello*," *English Studies*, XXVIII, 65 *et seq.*; "Patterns of Humor and Tempo in *Macbeth*," *Neophilologus*, XXXI, 202 *et. seq.*

much with the influence of literature on literature and not enough with literature as an expression of contemporary life. Medieval and Renaissance society consisted of complex strata of more or less fixed classes, so distinguished from each other by law and custom and economic pressure that Chaucer could describe a monk or a squire per se as if all in a given class were stereotyped; and Elizabethan character-writers likewise could depict individuals by class and group, each one stamped by his life and environment in a set design, like graduates from certain colleges today. Orsino and Olivia are great nobles, and as such must speak and live and move. Like Falstaff, the two knights represent what knighthood had become in its decline. Fabyan and Maria are poor gentility earning bread and ale in the traditional way as servingman and waiting lady. Feste belongs to a profession of sorts, and Malvolio is a trusted and efficient upper servant. This is a wide social range, and the evidence for it all requires careful examination of the text in the light of current conditions attested by current writers. Thus each separate problem concerning each character must be seen in its Elizabethan setting; and the true Elizabethan setting must be determined, not by mere guess, but by the citation of contemporary documents. To achieve this, a mass of contemporary writings on the social classes and their relations and their attitudes toward one another must be explored and sifted. Material gleaned from plays, since it may reflect dramatic convention rather than actual fact, is not too reliable, and material from poetry is likely to be mere imaginative romance, and so is rarely useful; but current tracts on nobles and courtiers, on military life, on servants, and court fools take their rise from realistic observation. Above all, character-writers like Earle and Overbury give a wealth of evidence on manners and customs and contemporary social types. Such special situations, moreover, as the courtship of Olivia and the duel of Sir Andrew must be studied in relation to the actual conventions and the etiquette that governed such affairs. Incongruous contrast is perhaps the chief basis of the comic, and on the stage this incongruity arises not only between a Sir Toby and a Sir Andrew but also between each figure and its living prototype. This second sort of incongruity is lost on one who does not know Elizabethan society. We must carry constantly in our minds the noble, the gentleman, and the servant, the characteristic appearance and deeds of each in his appropriate milieu, or half the fun escapes us; for comedy of manners misses its point when the manners are not known. Such knowledge, moreover, helps the critic to infer, from mere scattered hints in the text—as the Elizabethans themselves inferred—the past and perhaps even the future of a full-drawn character, just as astronomy, from a few weeks' observation, can plot the whole orbit that a comet follows for many years in outer space. In short, social background is the most potent and revelatory index of the outer lives and the interrelationships of the characters in the play.

All living people have not only an outer social life but also an inner psychological experience that makes them what they are and that governs what they do; for thought and feeling are the soil from which grow word and deed. This inner life is subtle and complex, and the distinction between the higher types of drama—comedy and tragedy—and the lower types— farce and melodrama—is largely the fact that the two former take this inner life of their characters into account and thus show adequate motive for the doings in the plot, whereas the latter ignor it. Thus, tragedy and comedy are, as we say, "convincing" and true to life, because they reflect its inner complexities. All intelligent people in every age are bound to study human nature, to work more or less with their fellows and so try to understand them. The higher civilizations, from keen observation if not from laboratory experiment, have synthesized what they have learned into more or less coherent, systematic theories with a terminology of their own and with definite relationships to other fields of thought. Such a systematic theory of psychology, as an appendage to medicine, was developed in ancient times, and was integrated in the complex scheme of ancient science. It came down through Arabic and Medieval thought into the Renaissance, and, though somewhat variable and sometimes inconsistent in detail, its fundamental teachings were rarely questioned down to the middle of the seventeenth century when modern skepticism and new discoveries undermined Classical authority as the criterion of scientific truth. This time-honored tradition was buttressed by the great names of Hippocrates, Aristotle, and Galen; it had ruled European thought for some twenty centuries and woven itself into the folklore and the common understanding of the masses. Its terminology became common words, such as *sanguine, melancholy, jovial,* and *mercurial*—and the demand of the ordinary Elizabethan reader for such material produced numerous translations and summaries and popular handbooks.[2] Indeed, these volumes were so read to pieces that most of them rank as rarities today, and are to be found in only a few great libraries.

According to the theories that they set forth, the human body was under the astral influence of seven "planets"—Mercury, Venus, the sun, the moon, Mars, Jupiter, and Saturn—the earth being the center about which they all revolved. The body, furthermore, contained four fluids, or "humors"—blood, phlegm, bile, and black bile—their balance bringing perfect health, and the predominance of any one making a person sanguine, phlegmatic, choleric (wrathful), or melancholic (given to fits of depression and irritability). Each of these humors was associated, among other things, with a degree of heat and moisture, with a time of life, with characteristics of face and figure, and with a certain mental bent and certain experiences, activities, professions, and trades, with certain planets and constellations, with a certain degree of good or evil fortune, and with a time of the year and certain days and hours. Thus were integrated in one scheme the sciences of medicine, physiognomy, psychology, social organization, and astrology. So closely did the Elizabethans associate this astral science with practical life that kings and nobles kept in their regular pay mathematicians and crystal-gazers to calculate the horoscope of children at birth, to foretell the future, and to find the lucky time for commencing any venture. In order to fit together the seven

[2] J. W. Draper, *The Humors and Shakespeare's Characters* (Durham, N.C., 1945).

14

planets and the four humors, one astral complexion, the mercurial, was described as variable from one humor to another depending on the dominant environment; and two other humors, the phlegmatic and the choleric, were divided, each into two groups, the former under Venus or the moon, the latter under Mars or the sun; and the contrast of Sir Andrew and Sir Toby seems to be a contrast of these two phlegmatic types.

The matter, however, is even more complex than the foregoing explanation might imply. A man was thought to be born under a given planet and constellation and so with a given humor; but his time of life, the season, day, and hour, his profession or activities of the moment, his feelings such as anger, love, or jealousy, might modify or even overcome this innate bent; and thus Orsino—who, as a young man and by birth a duke, should have the sanguine temper that arose from too much blood and the corresponding joviality that showed the astral influence of Jupiter, and should be hot and moist with exuberant life—is actually, down to the fifth act, cold and dry and melancholy with black bile predominant and saturnine in astral influence. Of course, this revolution in mind and body rises from the recognized malady of unrequited love, and both his symptoms and his cure of this disease accord with the popular medical authorities of the day. In short, just as English social life must be explored to understand the outer lives of Shakespeare's characters, so also Galenic psycho-medicine and the astrology that had come down from ancient Babylon must be called into use, not only as former editors have used it, to explain a passing reference in the text such as *humor* or *Taurus*, but also to integrate this term in its proper current meaning and to use it in interpreting the play, for Shakespeare did not fling words about at random. He meant them to mean just what they meant to the Elizabethans of his time: *melancholy*, for example, was Elizabethan "melancholy" and not the modern Romantic conception of the term. Such semantic studies are intricate and elusive, but the interpreter has no choice but to pursue them.

For social background, dress would give immediate evidence on the Elizabethan stage, for the old sumptuary laws and customs still somewhat differentiated classes by this obvious means; but, perhaps because of the quickly shifting fashions among the wealthier sort, Shakespeare rarely gives more than the merest hint about clothing, such as Sir Andrew's "stocke" of much disputed hue. Therefore, nowadays, one must work backward and guess a character's clothes from his social standing, whereas the Elizabethan audience could usually guess at once his approximate standing from his clothes when he first entered. Shakespeare also gives little evidence of his characters' physiques, perhaps because of the difficulty in casting parts and the impossibility of keeping the same actor for all future revivals. The then-current science of physiognomy, moreover, was too full of disagreement to make matters of face and figure an unequivocal index of mental bent and humor. Sometimes, however, Shakespeare seems to use physique for comic contrast, as in the corpulent Sir Toby and his long and lanky friend, or the mountain of Falstaff's weight over against his diminutive page, Robin. The age, moreover, of some of these characters is matter for sheer guesswork, though their humor sometimes contributes some basis for the guessing: Orsino, according to Olivia, is a "youth"; and the violence of his love-melancholy suggests that he is of an age when such contageous blastments are most imminent. Olivia herself, therefore (some critics to the contrary), must also be young; and the twins, Viola and Sebastian, are also young. But what about Malvolio and Feste? For the producer of the play, these matters of dress and stature and age cannot remain in scholarly suspension; and some effort should be made to collect for his use such data as the text affords, not only in the direct dialogue but also as social and psychological implication may provide it.

Shakespeare, indeed, in the rich texture of his lines, has so fully reflected in a coherent synthesis every aspect of both inner and outer life as Elizabethan casual observation and Elizabethan popular science saw and understood it that whoever would study this life as the Elizabethans knew it can realize the deeper implications of the dialogue and not only solve with some certainty various vexed questions, but also present occasional new light on matters that have not heretofore engaged critical attention. Perhaps it is impossible finally to determine just what sort of stockings Sir Andrew thought most flattering to his calves, but a careful gathering of evidence establishes a sound presumption that he is phlegmatic under the influence of the moon with all that this implies, and that he is a callow *nouveau riche* whose father had perhaps raised himself to fortune and ill-fame by the hated wiles and extortions of usury. Malvolio by birth is surely no better than the yeoman whose noble marriage he cites as such consoling precedent. So with each of the others. They all speak and behave quite as an Elizabethan audience of wellborn tyro lawyers and young courtiers would have expected them and wished them to behave; and they come to ends that such an audience would have deemed appropriate; for Shakespeare, like a clever modern playwright, knew the feelings and tastes of his audience, not only in drama but in life, and, for that matter, doubtless shared them. Indeed, he shrewdly held the mirror up to very nature; but the great extent to which he did so cannot be comprehended until one knows "nature," both social and psychological, as he and his audience daily saw and understood it. To build in this missing background that the whirligig of time has shuffled off into obscurity is the present writer's purpose.

All of these types of evidence, external to the play and inherent in the text, closely entangled with one another, make the process of explaining even a single one rather like untwining and unknotting a fish net into its original strands. Age and physique and social class and mental traits depend on interlocking evidence, and a character may subtly change, as did Orsino's before the play began, so that his innate humor and true nature appear only by inference in the hints of others; or they may shift during the course of the action as with Malvolio's rising choler. Every part of the comedy, as in life, reacts on every other part, and can be fully understood only in these multiform relations. In the resolution of such a problem, a single unvaried plan for every chapter is hardly possible, but those chapters devoted to the analysis of each character in succession may well approximate some such arrangement as the following: first, a discussion of the place and importance of the role, a survey of the comment of some critics, and Shakespeare's introduction of the character at his initial entrance; then a review of the character's place in society—a matter generally fixed by birth—something of his education and past life, his psychological humor and astrological complexion, a survey of his chief actions in the play and his relation to the other characters whom his part touches, with some effort to see his motives and doings and reactions in the light of his inner and outer self as previously established, finally in conclusion, a hazardous suggestion of his future as an Elizabethan might suppose it, and some attempted explanation of Shakespeare's attitude toward him of praise or excuse or blame. Altogether, each chapter becomes a short biography so far as the play states or implies the facts. Such a review of all the major roles should prepare for a reasoned exposition of plot and then of setting and style and theme. Thus, in the end, the whole comedy, having been analyzed in detail as a product of the Elizabethan age, should appear before us, character by character, incident by incident, and element by element, so that the judicious reader, if he possess the patience to assimilate all these diverse materials and bring them to bear on a rereading of the text, can see in it something rather like what Shakespeare's audience saw, and what Shakespeare, as a master of his theater, must have intended them to see. The effort is great both for the present interpreter and for his reader; but despite the many pitfalls, it seems worthy of the trial.

~ Sir Toby Belch

THE interpretation of *Twelfth Night* might well begin, as do Chaucer's *Canterbury Tales*, with the characterization of a knight. Sir Toby Belch and his crony and gull, Sir Andrew Aguecheek, form one of those comic pairs, incongruous foils to each other, whose physiques and minds and characters parody the extreme vagaries of human nature. Sir Toby appears in ten of the eighteen scenes, and speaks some four hundred complete or partial lines—more than any other character. He is linked with all the currents of the action. He is the object of Maria's tender passion, the instigator of Sir Andrew's bootless wooing and mock duel, and a ready conniver in the gulling of Malvolio—the liveliest episodes in the comedy. He is mentor to Sir Andrew, uncle and self-styled protector to Olivia, and lord of misrule in her hall. His clothes, to be sure, are not as elegant or elaborate as those of the Illyrian gentleman pictured in Vecellio; they are merely "good enough to drink in"[1]—probably honest buff a bit the worse for wine stains and other contretemps. But for all his homely garments, Sir Toby does not recede into the background, for his lines are pungent with earthy wit, and his business should be brisk with hurly-burly horseplay. Thomas Pope, who apparently played Falstaff and Benedick, seems to have created the part,[2] and after the Restoration the famous Betterton himself assumed it.[3] Although closely integrated in the plot, Sir Toby, except for the merest hint in *Gl' Ingannati*, is mainly Shakespeare's own creation, and he seems to derive only in shreds and patches from the stock figures of the stage. Falstaff has long been

---

[1] *Twelfth Night* (ed. Furness var.), I. iii. 13.

[2] T. W. Baldwin, *Organization and Personnel of the Shakespearean Company* (Princeton, 1927), Plate III; also J W. Draper, "The Tempo of Shylock's Speech," *Journal of English and Germanic Philology*, XLIV, 281 *et seq.*

[3] See Downes quoted in *Twelfth Night* (ed. Furness), p. 378.

19

recognized as a sort of *miles gloriosus*,[4] and perhaps Sir Toby owes something to this type; but he never appears as a professional soldier, he never boasts of his prowess, and when he fights with Sebastian he does not whine about his hurt. His relations with Sir Andrew perhaps show a touch of the parasite type derived from Latin comedy,[5] and he may have something in common with the bravo of Italian *commedia erudita* and with the "rough, blunt soldier" of the contemporary English stage.[6] Sir Toby, moreover, along with his cronies, is involved in several situations listed by Forsythe as conventions of the Elizabethan theater: he joins with Sir Andrew in singing a comic song (No. 22); he takes part in eavesdropping on Malvolio in the garden (No. 30); and he repeatedly gulls the lily-livered Sir Andrew (No. 47). Of course, no dramatist can quite escape the stock characters and situations of the stage; but, in Sir Toby, so many of these echoes are woven into so complex a fugue that each separate one is hardly heard. Actually, Shakespeare would seem to have taken him, as he doubtless did Falstaff, not so much from theatrical tradition as from actual Elizabethan life. Indeed, most of these traits and actions derive as much from contemporary reality as from the shadow world of the stage: the roistering soldier who bilked callow, gilded youths was a common tavern type; Elizabethan gentlemen could, and did, commonly sing part songs; and every age has known eavesdropping and the gulling of fools. Sir Toby is truly of the earth, earthy, a very Teniers study in the genre.

As early as 1857, Halliwell declared Sir Toby "a genuine English humorist of the old school," and various critics since have noted his realism; but no one has placed him in detail in the Elizabethan social scene or sought out his haunts in the Illyrian counterpart of London, and no one has attempted to

[4] E. E. Stoll, "Falstaff," *Modern Philology*, XII, 211 *et seq.* Cf. J. W. Draper, "Sir John Falstaff," *Review of English Studies*, VIII, 414 *et seq.*; and "Falstaff, 'a Fool and Jester,' " *Modern Language Quarterly*, VII, 453 *et seq.*

[5] R. Withington, " 'Vice' and 'Parasite,' " *P.M.L.A.*, XLIX, 743 *et seq.*; E. P. Vandiver, "Elizabethan Dramatic Parasite," *Studies in Philology*, XXXII, 411 *et seq.*; also J. W. Draper, "Falstaff and the Plautine Parasite," *Class. Jour.*, XXXIII, 390 *et seq.*

[6] D. C. Boughner, "Sir Toby's Cockatrice," *Italica*, XX, 171–72; also R. S. Forsythe, *The Relation of Shirley's Plays to the Elizabethan Drama* (New York, 1914), No. 39, p. 101.

plumb his mind and motives in terms of his economic situation or of the Renaissance psychology of humors. Kenny, like Betterton, preferred him to Malvolio; Montégut called him "degraded and drunken"; and Furnivall referred to his "bibulous drollery." More recently, the Arden editors find him "a faint reminiscence of Falstaff"; and the Tudor editors, though admitting him a drunkard and something of a ruffian, think him witty and engaging. Mr. Priestley declares him neither a coward nor a fool.[7] Professors Quiller-Couch and Dover Wilson describe him as "Falstaff flattened out . . . . a derelict of the decaying feudal times";[8] but they do not explain his social background further. Drs. Mueschke and Fleisher suggest Ben Jonson's Young Knowell as his immediate source;[9] but Shakespeare need hardly have gone to Jonson for a character so clearly in his own great Falstaffian tradition.[10] In short, Sir Toby, for all his major role, has not been fully inventoried and anatomized, and the flowers of his rhetoric are still to be culled and docketed, lest one be lost.

Sir Toby first appears in the third scene after late comers to the theater have presumably pushed their way to their places and are ready for the fun. Quite unheralded, he rolls in with Maria, declaring that mourning does not become Olivia and her household. The lines that follow place him as uncle to the Countess, but a guest of doubtful welcome because of his "quaffing" and "ill houres," and apparently he is in no mind either to mend his ways or to take his leave. In fact, he shortly persuades Sir Andrew to remain another month. His colloquy with Maria goes on to explain that he has brought his foolish friend—whom he insists is not so foolish—to woo his niece. Maria disputes his panegyric on Sir Andrew, and then the subject of the argument enters and cuts it short. To chart Sir Toby's course in the comedy and calculate the meridian of his motives requires first a survey of his physical and mental traits,

[7] J. B. Priestley, *English Comic Characters* (London, 1925), p. 49.

[8] *Twelfth Night* (new Cambridge ed.), p. xxv.

[9] P. Mueschke and J. Fleisher, "Jonsonian Elements in *Twelfth Night*," *P.M.L.A.*, XLVIII, 722 *et seq.*

[10] Cf. Tucker Brooke, *Shakespeare's Principal Plays* (New York, 1914), p. 402.

21

and of his birth, education, and past life—matters that an Elizabethan would have read between the lines—and then one may attempt to evaluate his three chief actions in the stream of episode, his gulling of Sir Andrew, his taunting of Malvolio, and his marriage with Maria.

Like Falstaff, Sir Toby is a man of parts, especially about the girth; he tells Maria that his clothes cannot "confine" him any "finer,"[11] and his knightly revelry and wassail would indeed conduce to architectural amplitude. As uncle to Olivia, and as guide, philosopher, and friend to the hopeful Sir Andrew, he would seem to have attained at least his thirties, and the short life expectancy of the sixteenth century[12] made this middle age. Such a time of life should be choleric or sanguine; the merry month of May, when the play seems to take place, should also make him sanguine, and his profession as a soldier should go with choler. But Sir Toby's innate humor, however, is apparently so strong that it overcomes profession and age and season, for, indeed, his bulk and temper are clear tokens of the cold and wet phlegmatic type, something heavy in body and in wit but generally lucky in affairs.[13] This humor had two subdivisions: the duller, under the astral influence of the moon, and the more sprightly under Venus. Sir Toby, as matchmaker for Olivia and inamorato of Maria, is appropriately under Venus. Such persons were "luxurious, giuen to idleness and pleasures"[14] and very easygoing. As in the case of Falstaff, wine might impart an adventitious vigor, but Sir Toby generally prefers merely to take the goods the gods provide him and to bestir himself only when danger threatens his life of sedulous ease. Indeed, he is not a very hopeful scion of the noble House of Belch.

He must be a younger son, probably a brother of Olivia's father, for otherwise he would hardly have called her mansion

[11] *Twelfth Night*, I. iii. 12.

[12] J. W. Draper, *The "Hamlet" of Shakespeare's Audience* (Durham, N.C., 1938), pp. 47–48.

[13] C. Dariot, *Iudgement of the Starres* (tr. F. Wither; London, 1598), sig. D 4 r; T. Hyll [Hill], *Schoole of Skill* (London, 1599), leaf 10 v; J. W. Draper, *The Humors and Shakespeare's Characters* (Durham, N.C., 1945), chapter iii.

[14] Dariot, *loc. cit.*

22

"home" and presumed to take control of her affairs. In the Middle Ages, the younger son had looked to a career either in arms or in the Church;[15] but, with the decay of feudalism and the dissolution of the monasteries, these opportunities disappeared. The strong government of the Tudors had discouraged private warfare, and, consequently, knights and squires and servingmen were no longer needed for protection.[16] Thus, lacking a social *raison d'être*, they soon lost economic value. Despite the evil times, however, a conservative old family might still cling to the career of knighthood for its young cadets, though without much hope of their gaining honor or even a bare pittance by deeds of derring-do. The age bore hard on the landed gentry, who must make ends meet from the fixed incomes of their estates in spite of rising prices;[17] and the custom of primogeniture demanded that the eldest son must first be served. This left little for his younger brother, who was brought into the world "to be a gentleman," and yet had "nothing to maintain it."[18] As Oliver taunts Orlando, the cadet of the house must either serve his elder brother, or live by his wits, or turn highwayman and be hanged. Falstaff chose the second alternative, without the good luck of finding an heiress in a convenient Forest of Arden.[19] A younger son was obliged either to marry well or do something "notable" or "become a very Farmer, or Ploughman,"[20] for the English law of primogeniture gave "all to the elder brothers, lying sluggishly at home," and thrust "the younger brothers into the warres and all desperate hazards, and that in penury, which forcibly driueth the most ingenious dispositions to do vnfit things."[21] A younger brother might seek fame and fortune, without much prospect of either, in the Dutch wars;[22] or he

[15] J. W. Draper, "Orlando," *Philological Quarterly*, XIII, 72 *et seq.*
[16] *Idem*, "Falstaff's Robin," *Studies in Philology*, XXXVI, 476 *et seq.*
[17] *Idem*, "The Theme of *Timon of Athens*," *M.L.R.*, XXIX, 20 *et seq.*
[18] J. Earle, *Microcosmographie* (ed. princ., 1628), "A Younger Brother."
[19] J. W. Draper, "Sir John Falstaff," *Review of English Studies*, VIII, 414 *et seq.*
[20] *Cyuile and Vncyuile Life* (ed. princ., 1579; ed. Roxburghe Library, London, 1868), pp. 23–25.
[21] F. Moryson, *Itinerary* (1617), Part III, p. 98.
[22] Hist. MSS Comm., *MSS of the Marquis of Salisbury*, Part IV, pp. 4–5. Hereafter cited as *Salisbury MSS*.

might seek fortune and no fame by marrying a rich widow. Until the founding of Virginia he had no other hope, and the young men in Shakespeare's audience knew this very well, and many had suffered by it. Just where in this sordid picture did Sir Toby fit?

As a cadet of a great family, he had clearly been educated in accordance with his class. He had, therefore, been more or less exposed to the wide range of Renaissance arts and sciences. Dr. Kelso lists the approved subjects for a gentleman's education: logic and rhetoric, history, moral philosophy, poetry, theology, law, mathematics, astronomy and cosmology (doubtless including astrology and related pseudosciences), modern languages, drawing and heraldry; and, as dessert to this olla-podrida, he partook of a snack of travel, if not the full grand tour to Italy.[23]

Sir Toby, by passing reference if not more explicitly, shows some acquaintance with most of this congeries of knowledge. He has a patter of dialectic, and can scent a "false conclusion." In rhetoric, he is competent at wordplay and comic *non sequitur*,[24] and he can affect fine periphrasis so well that Viola (like Horatio with Osric) requires a translation.[25] Of religion he knows more than his way of life implies: he remembers Noah and enough of the Gospel according to St. Mark to retain the name of "Legion" for the devil.[26] Though hardly a theologian, he seems to be dimly conscious of the Protestant dogma of Justification by Faith.[27] Oddly enough, his relations with the law seem more casual than with religion, he makes but one legal reference,[28] and that of doubtful meaning. His science, like that of the Euphuists, is based on Pliny and other purveyors of pseudonatural history, whence is derived the belief in "Cockatrices."[29] He understands the physiology of cowardice,[30] and the danger of melancholy to long life,[31] and

[23] R. Kelso, *The English Gentleman of the Sixteenth Century* (Urbana, 1929), chapter vii.

[24] *Twelfth Night*, I. iii. *passim*.   [25] *Ibid.*, III. i. 75 *et passim*.

[26] *Ibid.*, III. iv. 89. Or possibly he had been reading Scot's conclusion to his *Discoverie of Witchcraft* (1584).

[27] *Twelfth Night*, I. v. 127–28.   [28] *Ibid.*, I. iii. 7.

[29] *Ibid.*, III. iv. 194. See also Boughner, *cit. sup.*

[30] *Ibid.*, III. ii. 61 *et seq.*   [31] *Ibid.*, I. iii. 4–5.

the ill effect on mental acumen from eating beef.[32] He knows some Latin—about as much as Don Juan's learned mother—for he can quote a sample sentence from Lilly's famous *Grammar*;[33] he has a smattering of astrology;[34] and he has picked up, perhaps in the Low Countries or perhaps from returned soldiers, a scrap or two of French and dubious Spanish.[35] Indeed, he has voyaged afar, or, more likely, talked to voyagers; he refers to England, a country rather remote from Illyria,[36] to Tartary and to India,[37] and to the Persian Sophy.[38] In short, Sir Toby is a repository of sufficient flotsam and jetsam of accepted fact and fancy to pass in some companies for a gentleman of liberal, not to say free-and-easy, education. Olivia is speaking with the exaggeration of anger when she calls him:

> Vngracious wretch,
> Fit for the Mountaines and the barbarous Caues,
> Where manners nere were preach'd.

In the sports and games recommended for young men of his class, he is somewhat less athletic than Renaissance tastes might wish. The chivalric tradition of bodily vigor still obtained, but one fears that Sir Toby's rotundity forbade running, leaping, wrestling, and tennis.[39] His use of "vppeshot" attests a knowledge of archery,[40] and he is versed in the lately fashionable etiquette of challenges and duels,[41] although military allusions are otherwise conspicuously absent. Does this mean that his career at arms had not progressed beyond the tavern door? He uses in passing a current term of falconry;[42] he knows the times and probably the steps of half a dozen dances,[43] though he is too stout, and perhaps too wise, to try (like Sir Andrew) to put this knowledge into use. He likes to sing,[44] and prefers "a loue song" to "a song of the good life,"[45] and he can interlard his talk with bits from broadside

[32] *Ibid.*, I. iii. 85. [33] *Ibid.*, II. iii. 4.
[34] *Ibid.*, I. iii. 128 *et seq.* [35] *Ibid.*, I. iii. 42 and 88.
[36] *Ibid.*, III. iv. 47. See Appendix A. [37] *Ibid.*, II. iii. 77; II. v. 16 and 194.
[38] *Ibid.*, III. iv. 278. [39] Kelso, *op. cit.*, chapter viii.
[40] *Twelfth Night*, VI. ii. 72–73. [41] *Ibid.*, III. ii. 42 *et seq.*
[42] *Ibid.*, II. v. 109. [43] *Ibid.*, I. iii. *passim*; V. i. 212. [44] *Ibid.*, II. iii. 60 *et seq.*
[45] *Ibid.*, II. iii. 21 and 39.

ballads.[46] He knows something of dogs, and likes a bear-baiting.[47] He has doubtless played cherry-pit[48] and diced at "tray-trip."[49] In fact, he surpasses in the accomplishments of the alehouse, and is a sort of alehouse gentleman.

As a younger son, he could not hope to inherit the lands and title, and so, by design or accident, he seems to have followed the feudal tradition and embarked, or pretended to embark, on a military career. Army life was sordid and corrupt, and many of his tastes that are infra dig may well derive from his days in camp, if not in the tavern. Gunpowder had not only unhorsed the knights and battered down castle walls, but had also eclipsed knight-errantry; and, in the Renaissance, only the fallen talus of chivalry remained. The social structure of lord and vassal with their feudal loyalties had crumbled, and professional troops, often foreigners for hire, waged the wars of Europe in place of the noble suzerain with his liege knights and tenants. In theory, this change should have made for better organization and discipline, but, actually, the bankrupt governments of the sixteenth century paid their soldiers so irregularly and with so much overt peculation that, even in wartime, the men had to steal or starve, and, in the piping days of peace, they were cast without pension[50] or recourse upon a tightly organized society that could not assimilate them in its economic structure. In such a case were the "young gentlemen" whom Sir John Smythe describes as trailing their pikes in Flanders.[51] Professional soldiers, like Riche and Digges, deplore this state of affairs; and Churchyard depicts the soldier's lot, and declares that, had he forty sons, not one should go to court or war:

> Lame lims and legs, and mangled bones,
> Wars bring a man unwares God wot,
> With privy pangs, and sighs and grones,
> Then come to court where nought is got.[52]

[46] Twelfth Night, II. iii. 101 et seq.
[47] Ibid., II. v. 7 and 10.   [48] Ibid., III. iv. 119.   [49] Ibid., II. v. 179.
[50] Elizabeth, for all her fine talk, did not pension veterans. See B. Riche, Fruites of Long Experience (London, 1604), p. 53.
[51] Salisbury MSS., cit. supra.
[52] T. Churchyard, Pleasant Discourse (London, 1596), "Churchyards Cherrishing."

26

Knaves and rapscallions passed themselves off as veterans, and a skeptic might inquire whether Sir Toby himself had ever smelled actual powder, but perhaps he should be given the benefit of the doubt. His knighthood must have been won on the field of battle, unless his father had bought it for him in childhood; he does not burgeon with brag and bluster like a mere impostor; and, in the fight with Sebastian, he seems no coward,[53] and takes his "bloody Coxcombe" like a good loser without whining about legal redress as does Sir Andrew. Sir Toby, in short, not only knew the etiquette of the duello, but also, for all his drunken "lethargie," could still play the soldier and the man—if not quite the gentleman.

Sometime before Act I, this worthy knight had sought surcease from his military labors, such as they were; or perhaps his lord had embarked upon a period of peace, and Sir Toby had hied him to the Illyrian counterpart of London to make his living as he could. The close organization of trades and professions, requiring long apprenticeships, closed most avenues of income, and those who had no "handycraft" could only "beg in the streats."[54] Like many a veteran from the Dutch wars, Sir Toby, accustomed to a roistering life, frequented the taverns to pick up what he could, and so picked up Sir Andrew. Their relation was a commonplace of the age; for, just as a knight of old had his page and squire, so the returned soldier commenced doctor-in-arms and gathered about him all and sundry who would learn the *joie de vivre* of soldiering; and this life was more likely to comprise wine, woman, and song, and a bit of brawling than a high-minded defense of the realm.[55]

Thus Sir Andrew became aprentice in the mystery of high living and, in return, supplied the means of high living for the two of them. It was a Renaissance variation of the ancient *rex* and parasite, with this notable change, that the parasite supplied not mainly amusement but worldly wisdom and protection, and

[53] *Twelfth Night*, III. iv. 316, and IV. i. 37 *et seq.*
[54] *Cyuile and Vncyuile Life*, ed. cit. p. 26.
[55] J. W. Draper, " 'This Poor Trash of Venice,' " *J.E.G.P.*, XXX, 508 *et seq.*

the *rex*—as callow fool extraordinary—supplied the amusement. The relations of Falstaff and the Prince[56] and of Roderigo and Iago reflect this same social usage. Just so might old soldiers "spoyle their friends and associates, yea their companions";[57] and a "roaring boy," according to the custom, "cheats young gulls that are newly come to town . . . . He is the supervisor to brothels. He will wear his gull threadbare e'er he forsake him."[58] Jonson, Stephens, and Breton depict this common type;[59] and Brathwait explains how broken gentlemen called "Censors" or "Moderates" acted as brokers between "Roarers" and "unseasoned Youth," so that the former may dupe the latter of their "late fallen patrimonie" and bilk their protégés by initiating them into the vices of the town.[60] Thus the relation between Sir Toby and Sir Andrew was a recognized practice of Elizabethan life: the eternal struggle between brains and money in which the brains were unprincipled and the money soon spent.

Indeed, indeed, Sir Toby had fallen in the world. Though his lines—cleansed perhaps when the Statute of Oaths was passed—do not contain much profanity, he had learned the value of "a terrible oath, with a swaggering accent,"[61] and he lapses into the obscene.[62] Moreover, he has known, doubtless from experience, the looks of a "bum-Baylie" who apprehended debtors.[63] Like Iago, he makes his fool his purse, and Sir Andrew is the fool. He importunes his gull to "send for more money";[64] and, casting himself in the role of *galeotto*, promises (like Iago) to reimburse him with a rich marriage. Even the sixpence with which Sir Toby tips the jester[65] doubtless originated in Sir Andrew's pocket. Falstaff is Shakespeare's guller gulled; Sir Toby is guller *in excelsis*, with all his tricks full blown as flush as May. He manages Sir Andrew's wooing

[56] *Idem*, "Sir John Falstaff," *R.E.S.*, VIII, 414 *et seq.*

[57] M. Sutcliffe, *Lawes of Armes* (London, 1593), p. 74.

[58] T. Overbury, *Characters* (London, 1614), "The Roaring Boy."

[59] J. W. Draper, " 'This Poor Trash of Venice,' " *J.E.G.P.*, XXX, 508 *et seq.*

[60] R. Brathwait, *English Gentleman* (London, 1633), p. 41.

[61] *Twelfth Night*, III. iv. 177–78.   [62] *Ibid.*, I. iii. 98.

[63] *Ibid.*, III. iv. 175.   [64] *Ibid.*, II. iii. 176–77.   [65] *Ibid.*, II. iii. 34.

in the most lucrative style, and later seems to turn the duel likewise to account; for, when Sir Andrew offers his horse to Viola to make peace, Sir Toby plans to take it for himself.[66] He does not boggle at a whole squadron of lies,[67] and, indeed, he shows no speaking acquaintance with the more exalted mores either of Medieval chivalry or of Renaissance gentility. His assumed superiority over Malvolio is a matter of little more than birth, for Sir Toby has become somewhat *declassé*.

Most of all, his wayward life appears in the "ill houres" and the "quaffing" to which Maria objects at their first entrance. Indeed, one fears that he is one of the "maltwormes" against whom Stubbes so vigorously inveighed. He sometimes prolongs his revels throughout the night,[68] and in the morning has a "Lethargie."[69] Feste remarks on these potations;[70] Olivia declares him "in the third degree of drink" even "early" in the morning;[71] and Malvolio plans, on becoming a Count, to admonish him anent "drunkennesse."[72] He calls for "a stoope of wine,"[73] and his cure-all for every tribulation seems to be "a cup of Canarie."[74] His very name of "Belch" suggests his valiancy at the pottle and the flagon. Like a gentleman born, he apparently prefers wine to the ale of the lower classes;[75] and surely he does not stop at stronger waters,[76] for, like Overbury's "Soldier," he knows the virtues of aqua vitae. Indeed, he is on the way to that final state described in Earle's "Drunkard": "His body becomes at last a miry way, there the spirits are clogged and cannot pass. . . . . All the use he has for this vessel of himself, is to hold thus much."[77]

The Arden editors say that Sir Toby is never "really sober";[78] and yet, one should add, he is never really drunk. After all, wine has no great proportion of alcohol, and Sir Toby's system had long been used to it. The Countess over-

[66] *Ibid.*, III. iv. 290. [67] *Ibid.*, I. iii. 26 *et seq.*
[68] *Ibid.*, II. iii. 183–84.
[69] *Ibid.*, I. v. 122–23. Cf. P. Barrough, *Method of Phisick* (London, 1590), p. 24.
[70] *Twelfth Night*, I. v. 26–27. [71] *Ibid.*, I. v. 134–35.
[72] *Ibid.*, II. v. 73. [73] *Ibid.*, II. iii. 16. [74] *Ibid.*, I. iii. 78.
[75] Cf. *Regimen Sanitatis Salerni* (London, 1575), leaf 55 r.
[76] *Twelfth Night*, II. v. 185. [77] Earle, *Microcosmographie*, "A Drunkard."
[78] *Twelfth Night* (Arden ed.), p. xvi.

states the case when she says that he is "drown'd,"[79] for he is not drunk enough to dull his senses or his wit or his pursuit of the main chance. Indeed, wine was thought to be a salutary corrective to the cold and wet phlegmatic humor, for its "heat dissolveth moisture,"[80] and so would artificially produce the more active, hot, dry, choleric temper, with something of truculence[81] and wit.[82] Corporal Nym seems to have assumed choler for his military profession; and Falstaff used wine to maintain his manly choler in spite of chilling age.[83] Sir Toby apparently used it to correct his natural phlegm.

He has certainly something of choleric wit. His puns, much admired in that day, do not suggest the sot "drown'd" in his cups; his use of *non sequitur*, in answers that do not correspond to his interlocutor's remarks, savor of clever evasion rather than drunken torpor. Just so he eludes Maria's embarrassing criticisms of Sir Andrew,[84] and tries to divert Olivia's interest from the handsome Cesario who waits at her gate. Sometimes, moreover, right after such a scene of seemingly drunken nonsense, he belies his condition and is quite sober when his interests require it: Maria lectures him on his unseemly carousal;[85] and he tipsily evades her; but, immediately after, on the entrance of Malvolio, he shows no signs of drink, and later, when Maria starts to explain her stratagem to gull the unlucky steward, he grasps it even before she has finished her explanation. In the Garden Scene, he realizes at once that Malvolio, on becoming Count, intends to quell his riot or drive him out of the house, and he is duly grateful to Maria for making Malvolio ridiculous and so ending the possibility of Olivia's marrying him.

[70] *Twelfth Night* (ed. Furness var.), I. v. 135.

[80] L. Lemnius, *Touchstone of Complexions* (London, 1576), leaf 118 r; also "Booke of the Vse of Sicke Men" appended to *Bvlleins Bulwarke* (London, 1579), leaf 22.

[81] Lemnius, *op. cit.*, leaf 23 v; Dariot, *op. cit.*, sig. D 3 r; N. Coeffeteau, *Table of Humane Passions* (London, 1621), pp. 544 *et passim*.

[82] This conception came down from Galen and appears in T. Elyot, *Castell of Helth* (London, 1541), leaf 2 v; *The Most Excellent Booke of Arcandam* (London, 1592), sig. M 2 r; T. W[right], *Passions of the Minde* (London, 1601), pp. 212–13; and J. Huarte, *Examen de Ingenios* (tr. R. Carew, London, 1594), pp. 57, 120, 203–4.

[83] J. W. Draper, "The Humor of Corporal Nym," *Shakespeare Association Bull.*, XII, 131–38; also Ruth E. Sims, "The Green Old Age of Falstaff," *Bull. Hist. Med.*, XIII, 144–57.

[84] *Twelfth Night*, I. iii. 20 *et seq.*   [85] *Ibid.*, I. v. 114.

Sir Toby, furthermore, manages the duel effectively enough, and talks good sense to Viola; and, indeed, if she had thought of him as drunk, she would hardly have believed his fearsome report of Sir Andrew. Then, when the officers come in, he has the discretion to lapse into the background; and drunkards are not likely to be discreet with officers. In short, Sir Toby, though less than half-educated and something less than a true gentleman, and not always or entirely sober, is yet no sottish fool. Feste says that he has "a most weake *Pia-mater*": apparently, the knight was clever enough to conceal his cleverness even from the fool, but, when the wind blew southerly, he knew a hawk from a heron.

Thus Sir Toby's past and his temper and character and habits are something conglomerate. Born or a noble family, he should have been sanguine like Romeo or choleric like Tybalt;[86] his time of life and the wine he drinks also should have brought on one of these humors; but instead he retains the phlegmatic temper of childhood—apparent in his stoutness and love of ease. He has been exposed to the rudiments of letters, and to the arts and sciences, has amused himself with sports, and taken naturally to games of chance. As a younger son, he could hardly expect his family to support him forever in the leisure of the landed gentry. Since he could not enter a monastery, he had little choice but to follow the wars—perhaps at a safe and politic distance, for this career was particularly unsuitable to his humor. Somehow, he achieved the accolade, and borrowed from wine and aqua vitae enough choler to pass, with such as Sir Andrew, for a gallant and a swordsman.[87] Perhaps he had befriended other gulls before a grinning Fortune presented him with Sir Andrew. At any rate, the conjunction of the stars was fortunate. He learned that his niece's father and brother were both dead. Apparently, Olivia had not hastened to inform him, for her father must have been gone a year and her brother almost as long[88] before this golden information reached Sir Toby in his haunts. Perhaps he had been abroad and was only just

---

[86] J. W. Draper, "Shakespeare's 'Star-Crossed Lovers'," *R.E.S.*, XV, 16 *et seq.*
[87] *Twelfth Night*, V. i. 204–6.   [88] *Ibid.*, I. ii. 38 *et seq.*

returned to rest upon his laurels. At any rate, with shibboleths of deep solicitude, he hastens to the side of the new Countess, and, as next of kin,[89] proposes to provide her, willy-nilly, with a protector and shortly with a husband. And here he is when the play begins, ensconced in her hall, eating and drinking, like Penelope's suitors, at her expense, and otherwise living off Sir Andrew—doubtless more phlegmatically idle and festively content than he had been for many a long day. His paunch was full, and he sang and rejoiced.

Sir Toby's relations with his dear niece, however, are far from satisfactory. As Maria repeatedly had warned him, Olivia resents his carousals in her house of mourning, and she will not even see his suitor. She assumes the headship of the family herself, and refers to him as "Rudesbey" and "Ruffian,"[90] and his appearance and manners do not gainsay such terms. Though he makes a point of their blood-relationship, and uses her health as an excuse for his much drinking,[91] yet he treats her feelings cavalierly: the noise of riot reaches even to her secluded chamber, and, when her back is turned, he does not stop at insolence.[92] To Maria's warnings he replies that he is "consanguineous," and he knows that, as his dismissal would create a scandal and perhaps a brawl, his niece is likely to endure him. In Elizabethan mansions, the old Medieval halls were generally deserted by the family itself[93] who sought greater privacy from their rabble of retainers in upper apartments, often newly added as at Penshurst, the seat of the Sidney family. As the custom of open house was passing, such uninvited guests as tradition obliged the family to entertain[94] forgathered in the hall. This custom, despite the threats of Malvolio, made Sir Toby feel secure as long as he had to deal only with Olivia and her underlings. Of course, her marriage would introduce a master of the house whom he must recog-

[89] For this, he had some legal right. See M. Bacon, *New Abridgment* (Philadelphia, 1811), III, 413; C. Viner, *General Abridgment* (Aldershot, n.d.), XIV, 166 *et seq.*

[90] *Twelfth Night*, I. v. 105; IV. i. 48 *et passim.*

[91] *Ibid.*, I. iii. 38–40.   [92] *Ibid.*, II. iii. 77 *et seq.*

[93] J. W. Draper, "Chaucer's Wardrobe," *Englische Studien*, LX, 238 *et seq.*

[94] P. Stubbes, *Anatomie* (ed. 1836), pp. 110 *et seq.*; *Cyuile and Vncyuile Life*, pp. 92 *et passim.*

nize, and twice he seems to show that he has this danger well in mind: when Maria tells him that he must reform, his reply appears to mean that Olivia must accept some suitor as her husband before she can effectively take exception to her uncle's ways;[95] and later, when Maria again warns him, he declares that his niece is a "Catayan,"[96] i.e., according to Theobald, "one who promised more than he could perform." Is he not "of her blood"—almost her legal guardian—so how can she dislodge him? In that boisterous age, a woman, especially a young unmarried woman, was at a disadvantage, and wellborn men-at-arms like Fabyan, who lived by the old system, would sympathize with Sir Toby's case, and so be loath to obey orders to cast him out. No wonder the knight is merry. This life of lordly leisure just fits his taste and nature. But if Olivia should marry anyone other than Sir Andrew, it all would quickly end. Fear for his security is the key to Sir Toby's actions in the play.

He has early ascertained his niece's intentions toward the Duke, and has learned, probably from Maria, that "she'l not match aboue hir degree, neither in estate, yeares, nor wit."[97] This luckily ruled out Orsino, who would undoubtedly have given Sir Toby short shrift. Olivia, moreover, will not admit the Duke's messengers. The way, therefore, seems open for a suitor of her own dear uncle's choice—a suitor who, as husband, will rule by legal right Olivia and her fortune,[98] and will rule them under Sir Toby's guidance. Sir Andrew is the perfect candidate. Surely his money and his knighthood make him the perfect lover, and his immaculate idiocy makes him putty in Sir Toby's shaping hands. All this must have been quite evident to any intelligent Elizabethan. Girls of wealth and good family were often married off by their fathers with little

---

[95] *Twelfth Night*, I. iii. 9.

[96] *Ibid.*, II. iii. 77. Cf. Y. S. Chang, *Studies in Philology*, XXXV, 203 *et. seq.*

[97] *Twelfth Night*, I. iii. 102–3.

[98] Elizabethan wives were acquiring great freedom, but law and religion in theory allowed them very little, and Sir Toby was old-fashioned; J. W. Draper, "Desdemona," *Revue de Littérature Comparée*, XIII, 337 *et seq.*; and W. Vaughan, *Golden Grove* (London, 1608), sig. O 4 *et seq.* In the thirteenth century, Common Law gave a wife's chattels to her husband's control. See W. S. Holdsworth, *History of English Law* (Boston, 1923), III, 526.

33

thought of their personal preferences or interests;[99] and the chivalrous Sir Toby, putting himself *in loco parentis*, assumes this happy office. Marriages, as reflected in Batista's betrothal of Bianca in *The Taming of the Shrew*, were rather mercenary matters; indeed, if parents had brought a girl into the world and gone to the expense of raising her and providing a dowry, should they not hope for some return on so costly an investment, especially in an age when the great families were hard put to it to hold up their heads and evade their creditors?[100] The records of the Court of the Star Chamber show how heiresses, even of low degree, were sedulously hawked about, and sometimes promised simultaneously by father and mother to two or more contestants,[101] as was Anne Page in *Merry Wives of Windsor*.[102] Girls not yet of age were sometimes sold to a prospective husband in return for his bond to deliver a moiety of their fortunes to the next of kin who made the match. In short, Sir Toby, like many an Elizabethan parent, under the guise of protecting an inexperienced niece, is actually providing himself with a future life of ease.

The wayward Countess, however, is not impressed, and treats Sir Andrew no better than she does the noble lord: she will not even listen to his suit. (Maria's report of him cannot have been too favorable.) Sir Andrew himself, moreover, grows restive under the goad of mounting costs, and he is barely persuaded to remain. Olivia is not only adamant to his suit, but receives with favor the handsome messenger from the Duke, and suddenly lays aside her sad serenity and is "much out of quiet."[103] Meanwhile, Sir Toby rejoices to see Maria's plot dash Malvolio's hopes by making him so ridiculous that Olivia thinks him mad; for the "ouer-weening"[104] steward must be defeated as a suitor. Not only is Malvolio a direct threat to Sir Toby's future plans, but also he is an outrageous social

[99] C. L. Powell, *English Domestic Relations* (New York, 1917), chapters ii and iv.

[100] J. W. Draper, "The Theme of *Timon of Athens*," *M.L.R.*, XXIX, 20 *et seq.*

[101] See C. J. Sisson, *Lost Plays of Shakespeare's Age* (Cambridge, 1936), pp. 14 *et seq.*

[102] E. J. Haller, "The Realism of the Merry Wives," *West Virginia Phil. Bull.* (1937), pp. 32 *et seq.*

[103] *Twelfth Night*, II. iii. 131.   [104] *Ibid.*, II. v. 31.

upstart; frayed gentility do not admire the *nouveaux*, and Sir Toby delights to remind him, "Art any more than a Steward?"[105] The plot against Malvolio, moreover, diverts the knight's attention from the new danger of the Duke's attractive messenger, and all at once Olivia falls head over heels in love with Orsino's young John Alden. Thus, while Sir Toby is guffawing at the steward, his own cause is really lost—a subtle irony that should not be ignored. When Sir Toby realizes Olivia's attraction for this youth, his efforts are too late. Doubtless, he hopes that the duel with Sir Andrew may scare Viola away, and perhaps he even still believes that Sir Andrew has a fighting chance. In Act III, however, when Olivia inadvertently encounters her lanky suitor, she utterly ignores him;[106] and Sir Andrew himself can only stand and gape at his courtly rival, whose fine talk he envies. Indeed, even Sir Andrew comes to realize that Olivia's "fauours" to Viola portend a hopeless issue to his own advances.[107] At all events, the duel not only amuses Sir Toby but also even if it does not help Sir Andrew, may keep Viola from returning, and so keep Olivia unwed a little longer.

The courtly code of the duello arose in southern Europe during the sixteenth century as a substitute for the casual fighting that had long been the curse of Italian city life,[108] and that often led to family feuds such as that portrayed in *Romeo and Juliet*. A rigid etiquette grew up around it: one gentleman must give the "lie" to the other, and so produce a quarrel that only blood could terminate. The result was a formal challenge delivered by a friend of the challenger, then the selection of time, place, and weapons, and finally the fight itself, with great ceremony and with seconds who were supposed to see that rules were duly kept. The drawing of some blood was usually necessary to "satisfaction." This custom came to London in the 1590's with the new Italian school of fencing, but it was resented as a foreign novelty by old-fashioned sword-and-

---

[105] *Ibid.*, II. iii. 112–13.
[106] *Ibid.*, III. i. 86–94.   [107] *Ibid.*, III. ii. 7–8.
[108] See F. Schevill, *History of Florence* (New York, 1936), pp. 103 *et seq.*

buckler Englishmen,[109] and was banned by the government, which insisted on regarding it as murder.[110] Shakespeare had already treated of duellos in *Merry Wives*, in *Much Ado*, and in *As You Like It*—always satirically[111]—and the duello in *Twelfth Night* is a romping travesty. Sir Andrew has not the least conception of the proprieties of "honor"; the two contestants had never met or spoken, and so the "lie" had never been given or received. Sir Andrew's challenge suggests that he has looked at current books of honor and arms enough to catch their phraseology, but not enough to understand it; and Viola apparently does not realize what Sir Toby means when he describes her antagonist as a "knight dubb'd with vnhatch'd Rapier, and on carpet consideration." Indeed, the whole affair is matter for a mad May morning.

Sir Toby manages it all with calm and consummate effrontery, lying to each principal in turn with the ease of inveterate practice. He first convinces Sir Andrew that his opponent is so terrible that the frightened knight offers his horse to patch up peace, and Sir Toby apparently grasps the opportunity to take the horse for himself. Then he convinces the knight that his opponent is so pusillanimous that his conquest will be easy, and so the fight and the fun begin again. But Sir Toby's well-laid plans miscarry; the second meeting is not with Viola, as it chances, but with her twin brother, Sebastian, a valiant youth and a good swordsman. Sir Toby has to intervene to save Sir Andrew in a way that no book of arms would tolerate, but Sebastian is not daunted and makes "hauocke with them." Thus the scheme of the duello comes to naught: it neither helps Sir Andrew, nor discourages Olivia's love for Cesario.

Sir Andrew, then, neither as lover nor as duellist, could give a solution to the solicitous uncle's plans, and other means at once must be devised to guarantee Sir Toby's footing in the household of his niece. Even as early as Act II, the knight had

[109] R. Kelso, *The English Gentleman of the Sixteenth Century*, chapter v.

[110] See *Cal. State Papers, Dom.* (London, 1858), p. 224; F. Bacon, *Charge Touching Duels* (London, 1614), pp. 12–13; and *Shakespeare's England* (Oxford, 1917), II, 391.

[111] See H. S. Craig, "Duelling Scenes and Terms in Shakespeare's Plays," *University of California Publications in English*, IX, 1–28.

remarked that Maria "adores me"; but a gentleman—especially a gentleman of Sir Toby's tastes and income—could hardly indulge in the quixotic luxury of marrying a girl who had no dowry. Indeed, Plutus had usurped the places of Cupid and of Hymen, and "almost all marie for couetousnes, not for the vertue, Chastity, or good report, which they beare of women and maidens";[112] and younger sons and poor knights especially had to wed rich widows to get support.[113] Elizabethan men, even the noble Bassanio, were not prone to sacrifice their freedom and the pleasures of promiscuous bachelordom without something to show for it. But circumstances sometimes alter cases: Maria had been a mighty fortress against Malvolio's efforts to curtail "Cakes and Ale" and the "meanes" for revelry, and her stratagem of making the steward appear mad had defeated his aspirations toward Olivia. Maria is clearly a sort of Nerissa, well entrenched in her lady's favor, close to her ear, and indispensable as Malvolio; above all, she keeps the key to the buttery, the abiding place of casks and bottles and their contents. Would not a match with her, dowry or no dowry, insure a limitless future of these necessities, even if the perverse and self-willed Countess insists on selecting her own husband? If Sir Toby could not marry Sir Andrew to Olivia's lands and fortune, could he not play the leech to them almost as well by marrying himself to the confidante and abigail?

As other plans fall through, he looks with growing favor on Maria. He calls her endearing names: "little villaine" and "Mettle of India," and "most excellent deuill of wit," and "youngest Wren." After the forged letter has befooled Malvolio, he declares (out of her hearing) that he "could marry this wench for this deuice," even without a dowry. When she enters a moment later, he intimates that he might gamble away his "freedom" and become her "bondslaue." The trumped-up duel between Sir Andrew and Cesario turns Olivia's anger full upon Sir Toby. She tells him to "be gone,"[114] and for once he

[112] P. de la Primaudaye, *The French Academie* (London, 1586), p. 492.
[113] A. Niccholes, *Discourse of Marriage* (London, 1615), p. 27.
[114] *Twelfth Night*, IV. i. 50 *et seq.*

has no answer. Malvolio on escaping from durance will doubt-less marshal every force against him. If Sir Toby means to remain in those purlieus of ease and luxury, swift action is re-quired, and Maria seems to be the only person whose intercession can avail. When he later enters with a broken head, Olivia, to be sure, repents her harsh dismissal, and orders him a surgeon and "to bed."[115] But, even so, his case hangs in the balance. He is a brave man and he takes the plunge, the last resort of an Elizabethan gentleman: he marries.

Sir Toby loses no time in applying this heroic remedy, and, indeed, some commentators have wondered how he could have gone through any wedding ceremony between the time that he left the stage to seek a surgeon at line 220, and the entrance of Fabyan who tells the happy news at line 298. The answer would be obvious to an Elizabethan. Neither Canon Law nor Common Law required any ceremony for a valid marriage, the former insisting on agreement and consummation, and the latter only on spousals *de praesenti*.[116] Such marriages were common enough,[117] and, indeed, Shakespeare himself may well have been wedded to Anne Hathaway in this informal fashion some time before the service in the church. Maria, at the news of his misfortunes, doubtless flew to the bedside of her wounded swain, and was doubly engaging in the role of devoted nurse. To make the trothplight legal, not even a witness was required, though probably Fabyan, who tells the news, and perhaps also the surgeon, overheard the binding words. Maria doubtless saw to it that somebody overheard them, and Sir Toby, with his ridicule of the local curate, was not one to wait on benefit of clergy. The affair cried haste, and speed did answer it.

Truly Sir Toby is a man of great parts, and a large figure in the comedy. His relations with all the chief characters show the actions and reactions of real life: with Sir Andrew, who fol-lows his behests but declines in his esteem from a prospective

[115] *Twelfth Night*, V. i. 220.
[116] See *Shakespeare's England* (Oxford, 1917), II, 407; Powell, *op. cit.*, chapters i and ii; R. Cleaver, *Godly Form* (London, 1598), pp. 106 *et seq.*; and especially H. Swin-burne, *Treatise of Spousals* (London, 1686), pp. 97 *et passim*. This work was written about 1600 (Powell, *op. cit.*, p. 251).
[117] See W. C. Bolland, *Selden Soc. Publ.*, Vol. XXXII, p. xxi.

suitor to a mere laughingstock; with Maria, who rises from being a dispenser of "Cakes and Ale" to a super-practical-jokester and thence to a wife; with Malvolio, who falls from being a serious threat to Sir Toby's easy life to being a mere gull; with Orsino, who drops quite out of Sir Toby's scheme of things; with Sebastian, who surely was magnanimous enough to think Sir Toby's broken head sufficient punishment for the misadventured duel; above all, with the lady chatelaine, the Countess Olivia, who, since her mourning and her wooing are now over, may well be more tolerant of not-too-much riot in her hall, and who has already repented of dismissing her con-sanguineous guest. Sir Toby now, moreover, is married to the indispensable Maria, and this marriage makes the play a comedy for him as well as for the others, for it seems to settle the pressing matter of his future life of ease—the only life for which his birth and training fitted him and which his phlegmatic nature could enjoy. Let us hope that he became in time as harmless a hanger-on of the establishment as Addison's Will Honeycomb, and his tales of his knightly prowess in the field doubtless grew with his girth and his nightly prowess at the trencher, a more Gargantuan epic year by year.

Sir Toby, though not the center of the play, has a major part in two plots, the marriage of Maria and the marriage of Olivia. In the former, he is the lucky bridegroom; in the latter, he is a force both for complication and resolution, for he proposes one candidate (Sir Andrew), helps to defeat another (Malvolio), and, by the duel, assists in the mutual recognition of Viola and Sebastian and in the final happy ending. He is woven more skillfully and fully into the major plot than is Falstaff in *Henry IV*, and so, not only furnishes amusement in both dialogue and intrigue, but also welds the parts of the play together. He and Sir Andrew, moreover, give variety to the types of comedy: Orsino and Olivia supply high comedy, Feste an effervescent mockery, and, in the two knights, wit verges on slapstick farce. Thus the economy of Shakespeare's art makes one figure serve many ends.

Sir Toby, for all the aspects of him that Shakespeare shows

39

us, has a singleness of motive that suggests a character in Molière, and he is as mindful of his economic needs as a figure in Augier or in Balzac. His whole concern, as with most of the human species, centers about the means of food and drink and lodging. He is, also as in Molière, a contemporary social type, not merely a drunken reveler and lord of gay misrule, but a calculating—sometimes miscalculating—younger son, who, like Bassanio or Orlando, though in a different way, provides for himself (as younger sons generally had to do) by a lucky marriage. He had at first tried to accomplish this by the spousal of Sir Andrew, and so save his own bachelor freedom; but, finally, he saw no other way but to immolate himself upon the altar of connubial bliss, and he rose to the occasion like a man. When he leaves the stage, his head is bloody but unbowed, and his end is surely happier than Falstaff's; for, even if Sebastian cast him forth, Sir Toby must have put aside some of the many ducats that he had looted from Sir Andrew, and Maria could be depended on to stretch them a long way. Indeed, he can hardly miss a ripe old age, doubtless like Justice Shallow, happy and respected for the great deeds he told of his valiant youth. Shakespeare's final disposition of his characters generally accords with the social judgments of his time, and the reason why Sir Toby in the end fares so much better than does Falstaff is that the audience despised the latter as a coward,[118] whereas Sir Toby has done nothing that the age would not condone: he only cheats an upstart fool, takes a natural interest in the marriage of his niece, puts a mere steward in a temporary madhouse, makes a travesty of the code of honor and arms, and finally takes a wife for the best prudential reasons. These were accepted peccadillos for an Elizabethan gentleman; and, if one must be censorious, let it be borne in mind that younger sons had little choice in a world arrayed against them. Sir Toby's character and way of life are far removed from Chaucer's perfect, gentle Knight; but times had changed, and knighthood no longer was in flower.

[118] J. W. Draper, "Sir John Falstaff," *R.E.S.*; and E. E. Stoll, "Falstaff," *Mod. Phil.*, XII, 197 *et seq.*

✒Sir Andrew Aguecheek

THOUGH Sir Andrew has a speaking part of only some hundred and eighty lines and appears in less than half the scenes, his role is probably the most obviously comic in this play of comic characters. Like Viola, he pursues Olivia's heart and hand beyond her gates into her very hall—even before the curtain rises—and his abortive duel with Cesario starts unwinding the conclusion of the plot. A long introductory dialogue heralds his first entrance. Such introductions in Elizabethan plays usually consisted of a mere adjective or a telling phrase as the actor picked his way among the gentlemen that crowded the sides of the stage; and they were essential in apprizing the audience of the nature of the role and of its relation to the other parts; but, instead of a mere phrase, Maria and Sir Toby give Sir Andrew a prologue of some twenty lines. Their talk reiterates three facts: he is, though a knight, a coward; though rich, a spendthrift; and, *ergo*, above all, a callow fool. Maria first mentions him as "a foolish knight" whom Sir Toby has brought into the household as Olivia's unwelcome wooer. Then follows his name; and "Aguecheek" is as suggestive of his cowardice as "Belch" is of Sir Toby's predilection for the bottle. Thrice Maria objects to this empty-headed suitor, and thrice Sir Toby defends his protégé by a comical illogicality that, in effect, admits the charge. He first declares that Sir Andrew is as "tall" as any man in Illyria: "tall" in Elizabethan speech commonly referred to bravery as well as to height, but is never used by Shakespeare to denote intellectual capacity. Thus Sir Toby shifts ground instead of meeting the charge—a case of *non sequitur*, rank and gross in nature. He tops off this fallacious answer with the meaningful remark that his candidate has an income of three thousand ducats a year. Maria replies with the retort courteous, repeating her objection and at the same

41

time rebutting Sir Toby's defense: "but hee'l haue but a yeare in all these ducates: He's a very fool and a prodigall." This attack Sir Toby counters by declaring his friend a great linguist and a musician, two patent lies that match his previous "tall" talk. For a third time, Maria declares Sir Andrew a "foole," and adds that he is also "a great quarreller" but a "Coward." Sir Toby is finally driven to cover in mere vituperation, and declares that those who call him so are "scoundrels and subtractors." This show of heat impresses Maria not a whit; she carries the war into Africa by remarking that rumor also has it that Sir Andrew is "drunk nightly" (also knightly?) in Sir Toby's company. He at once defends their conviviality by declaring that they are drinking healths to his niece Olivia, and roundly dubs anyone "a Coward and a Coystrill that will not drinke to my Neece." The desultory argument has fulfilled its function and given a panorama of Sir Andrew's frailties—which his love-making and his duel will illustrate in action—and of Sir Toby's valiant championship of his friend's three thousand ducats a year. Now the abridgment of the argument enters in the person of "Sweet Sir Andrew"; such prologue for the omen coming on!

The role of Sir Andrew appears to have been created by Richard Cowley who regularly took the parts of "naturals" and zanies such as Gobbo and Slender.[1] One may well suppose that the worthy Cowley made up for the paucity of his lines by his ridiculous appearance, byplay, and vacuous expression. Indeed, Sir Andrew, though he might perhaps be spared from the plot, could not be spared from the comedy. He is, moreover, Shakespeare's own addition to the story and no mere fossilized form retained only because it was embedded in the original. Strangely enough, however, critics have generally passed him by on the other side or given him but casual remark as Sir Toby's "comrade" or as an obvious and egregious fool. Dr. Johnson found him "drawn with great propriety," but felt that his "natural fatuity" kept him from being "the proper

[1] T. W. Baldwin, *Organization and Personnel of the Shakespearean Company* (Princeton University Press, 1927), Plate III.

42

prey of the satirist."[2] The Elizabethans, of course, were not inclined to suffer fools gladly, and showed little Christian charity toward innate weaknesses. Even so, as in the case of Shylock,[3] their dislike of Sir Andrew may also have derived from current conditions that made this type especially fair game; and the present chapter, in due course, will look into this matter. Nineteenth-century critics enjoyed his pretty wit more than they analyzed his character. Lamb's brief remarks on Aguecheek are really a comment on the actor Dodd, whom he saw play the part. Halliwell thought the tall knight who is "always enjoying a joke, and never understanding it," even more "richly comic" than the captivating Belch. Conrad rather obviously notes that the duel reveals the "pusillanimity of Sir Andrew." The Arden editors summarize the knight in a short paragraph as the "ideal butt," and "perhaps the most perfectly foolish personage ever presented on the stage"—indeed, "an embryo Justice Shallow."[4] Mr. Priestley compares him to "a monkey which presents us with a parody of human life."[5] Mr. Schell points out his importance as "a binding agent of plot elements" and notes that he fits into the stock situations of a gull;[6] and Mr. Lothian finds his source in Aretino.[7] Drs. Mueschke and Fleisher suggest Sir Andrew's kinship to the "old amorous fool in Italian comedy"; but Sir Andrew is not old, and is not exceptionally amorous. Their article discusses him at length as a borrowing from Jonson's comedy of humors: "Shakespeare's treatment of Andrew exemplifies to the fullest extent the Jonsonian conception and treatment of the gull and his relationship to his victimizer."[8] But with London full of dolts and gulls ready to hand for any sharper, Shakespeare need hardly have snatched a grace from Jonson's art; and the

---

[2] *Twelfth Night* (ed. Furness var.), p. 378.

[3] J. W. Draper, "Usury in *The Merchant of Venice*," *Mod. Phil.*, XXXIII, 37 *et seq.*

[4] *Twelfth Night* (ed. Innes and Pierce), p. xvi.

[5] J. B. Priestley, *English Comic Characters* (London [1925]), p. 62.

[6] J. S. Schell, "Shakespeare's Gulls," *Shakespeare Bulletin*, XV, 28–29.

[7] John Lothian, "Shakespeare's Knowledge of Aretino's Plays," *M.L.R.*, XXV, 416 *et seq.*

[8] P. Mueschke and J. Fleisher, "Jonsonian Elements in *Twelfth Night*," *P.M.L.A.*, XLVIII, 722 *et seq.*

parallels to Stephen and Sogliardo cited by Mueschke and Fleisher were doubtless commonplaces of contemporary life. Despite all this, Jonson may have given Shakespeare the hint for using in comedy this common type; but the master dramatist was certainly no mere follower of his younger contemporary. Even more recent is the comment of Mr. Granville Barker, who seems to stand alone in defending Sir Andrew's pretensions to gentility.[9] In short, the criticism of two centuries on Sir Andrew is generally desultory and somewhat contradictory.

Shakespeare was not primarily a bookish man like Spenser and Milton, and scholars, who generally are bookish folk, suffer under a disadvantage in studying his plays. Though serious literature and popular stories contributed to his plots, the lifelike characters he drew derive this very lifelike quality, not in the main from the printed page, but from life itself, as Shakespeare and his audience observed it. But as a man of the theater, he was aware of the long tradition of drama that stretched back to Classical times, and, especially in some of his early plays, he borrowed from it freely. One might, therefore, wisely ask how much Sir Andrew derives from the Latin stage, how much from the comedy of the Italian Renaissance, and how much from Tudor drama. Plautus and Terence supply a number of profligate youths—like Philolaches and the *Mostellaria*, Chrinus in the *Mercator*, the title roles of the *Adelphoe*, Antipho in the *Phormio*, and Chremes in the *Eunuchus*— but not one of them is a fool like Sir Andrew, for ludicrous fatuity in Latin comedy was the appurtenance of fawning parasites or of doting age. The *commedia dell' arte* of Renaissance Italy likewise associated gullibility with age, as in Shakespeare's Thurio in *Two Gentlemen of Verona*, and its common type of the grotesque lover is a person of inferior social status, a ridiculous schoolmaster like Holofernes in *Love's Labour's Lost*,[10] or a physician like Dr. Caius in *Merry Wives of Wind-*

[9] *Twelfth Night* (ed. Granville Barker), p. viii.

[10] O. J. Campbell, "*Love's Labour's Lost* Re-studied," and "*The Two Gentlemen of Verona* and Italian Comedy," in *Studies in Shakespeare, Milton and Donne* (Ann Arbor, 1925).

44

sor, or perhaps a lawyer. The Medieval Vice with his dagger of lath, and the braggart fool of the Old French *sotties*[11] came down into the Tudor theater and mingled with the fool of the morality plays, who, unlike his French analogues, was regularly the butt of scorn. This morality type has the weakness and ignorance of Sir Andrew[12] and so is susceptible to avarice, bragging, and vanity in dress; but these characters remain more moral abstractions than living men, and thus they could have furnished only a skeleton to which Shakespeare gave the actuality of flesh and blood. With the tradition of the court fool, well exemplified in Feste, Sir Andrew has little in common; but he may owe something to the "gull or foolish suitor" type, usually under middle age and often a man of rank, who during the 1590's gradually "usurps the function of the clown of earlier drama."[13] Several of these figures, such as Ralph Roister Doister, and Don Armado in *Love's Labour's Lost*, have also something of the braggart coward, and characters of the sort appear, not only in Jonson, as Mueschke and Fleisher suggest, but also in Greene and elsewhere. Perhaps the most notorious specimen is Falstaff in *Merry Wives*, who, like Sir Andrew, plays the prodigal as much as he can, the lover as much as he dare, and the boaster as much as he will, without regard for fact or future circumstance. Sir Andrew, therefore, belongs to an established tradition of the Tudor stage that may owe something to Classical, Italian, and earlier English drama, but, like Sir Toby, seems to be mainly derived from actual Elizabethan life.

Sir Andrew, in fact, is conceived realistically as an Elizabethan with clearly implied origins and past. In this he resembles Chaucer's Knight, but it is the only similarity. As Shakespeare's knowledge of social types grew broader and more precise, and as his *vraisemblance* developed accordingly, he glimpses for us more and more not only something of a char-

[11] Barbara Swain, *Fools and Folly During the Middle Ages and the Renaissance* (New York, 1932), chapter vi.

[12] *Ibid.*, pp. 158–59.

[13] R. S. Forsythe, *The Relations of Shirley's Plays to the Elizabethan Drama* (New York, 1914), p. 108.

acter's past but also, for those versed in Elizabethan life, a sort of biography—something of his parents' place in the rather strict social hierarchy, and something of his own education, attainments, and vicissitudes. In an age that endeavored to fix the social classes, and that tended to set each man's activities, personality, and even dress, according to his "degree,"[14] in an age when the vogue of "character" writing suggests how greatly economic and political pressure had stereotyped the professions and trades, a knowledge of a man's place among his fellows implied much more than it does today, when occupations are less confining and society less exacting in its demand for conformity to class.

The rise of the monarchy on the ruins of the feudal system had centered everything in London where were concentrated the opportunities of mercantile wealth and of political power. Youths of good county family, come up to court or to the great law clubs of the metropolis—the elder sons to seek rich wives, the younger to seek their fortunes in countinghouses or the law courts or in civil service—such youths, gilded or tarnished according to their birth and lands, composed a large part of Shakespeare's audience, especially for a play given, as *Twelfth Night* was, under the legal auspices of the Middle Temple. Not without reason does Shakespeare depict this class of young men always with sympathy. He has a bit of merry banter, to be sure, at the expense of a Mercutio; but generally this class supplies the Romeos and Bassanios, Orlandos, Benedicks, Hamlets, and Ferdinands. But Sir Andrew is most unflatteringly portrayed, and one therefore suspects that the youthful gentles of the audience would not have accepted the knight as one of themselves. Where then did he belong? Sir Andrew, though not the sort to accumulate wealth himself, is clearly rich, and doubtless in that age of primogeniture is an eldest son. Whether he came from a good county family is highly questionable; mere wealth did not bring social rank, which was based rather on heredity. Sir Andrew definitely lacks the martial prowess that the rural nobility, who still

[14] *Troilus and Cressida*, I. iii. 83–136.

46

thought in terms of chivalry, generally instilled into their sons. His very wealth, moreover, suggests another explanation. Sir Toby, who had good reason to inform himself, declares his protégé to be possessed of an income of three thousand ducats a year. A ducat was a gold coin of Naples, Venice, and other countries, varying in value from eighty-three cents to almost three dollars. Calculated on the basis of the average, Sir Andrew's income then would have been almost six thousand dollars a year, which would mean more than ten times as much in modern purchasing power. Such wealth was "tall" indeed. The decay of feudalism and the rising prices consequent upon the recent flood of gold from Mexico and Peru, the jealousy of the upstart Tudors who preferred to the few lucrative positions their own creatures rather than the old nobility, and the cost of keeping traditional open house, had all combined to sink most ancient families in debt—a situation that Shakespeare deplores in *Timon*.[15] Sir Andrew's affluence, therefore, like his character, does not suggest a highborn lineage. While the old aristocracy declined, mercantile enterprise and the extortions of usury were creating an opulent *bourgeoisie* whose sons climbed to preferment—such figures as Osric and Roderigo.[16] Sir Andrew then, like Malvolio, appears to be a social upstart; and, though his wealth has bought him a somewhat higher status than the steward's, he is still of questionable place, and indeed he has no conception of the proprieties of duelling or of courtship. This would explain why Shakespeare and his audience considered him a subject for satire and why Fabyan, who is a wellborn servingman and understands the duello, joins with Maria and Sir Toby in putting him through his paces as an ass.

The social revolution that Shakespeare expresses in Sir Andrew was widely noted and commonly deplored. Persons of yeoman stock were growing rich "in so much that many of them are able and do buy the lands [the only conservative investment by which to save their fortunes] of unthrifty gentle-

[15] J. W. Draper, "The Theme of *Timon*," *M.L.R.*, XXIX, 20 *et seq.*
[16] *Idem, The "Hamlet" of Shakespeare's Audience* (Durham, N.C., 1938), chapter v.

men," and so became gentlemen of a sort themselves.[17] In 1594, Churchyard complained that the whole social order was topsy-turvy: "Thus kartars and cloyns can courtiers now teach."[18] Stubbes disapproved of the efforts of the lowborn to achieve gentility,[19] and Nashe had only contempt for the "obscure vpstart gallants [who] without desert or seruice, are raised from the plough to be checkmate [equal] with Princes."[20] Ben Jonson in the first scene of *Every Man Out of His Humor* explained the steps by which these *nouveaux* gentlemen rose in the social world. Sir Thomas Smith, glancing at Elizabeth's open sale of knighthoods, sardonically remarked that gentlemen "be made good cheape [at bargain prices] in England."[21] Lodge declares: "Purchased arms [coats of arms] now possess the place of ancient progenitors, and men made rich by youth's mis-spendings doe feast in the halls of our nation's young spendthrifts."[22] Ferne mentions no less than a dozen grounds on which one might apply to the College of Heralds for an escutcheon,[23] payment of sundry fees being the actual *sine qua non*. Rowlands expresses his disgust by listing among those worthy to be stabbed "Gentlemen of base broode."[24] According to Sir Toby, his friend is "a knight dubb'd with vnhatch'd Rapier, and on carpet consideration,"[25] that is, a knight by purchase, and Earle's character of "An upstart country knight" is a very picture of Sir Andrew: such a one

is a holiday clown, and differs only in the stuff of his clothes, not in the stuff of himself, for he bare the king's sword before he had arms to wield it [i.e., his knighthood was bought for him when still a child]; yet being once laid o'er the shoulder with knighthood, he finds the

[17] W. Harrison, *Description of England* (London, 1587), Bk. II, chapter v.

[18] T. Churchyard, *The Mirror of Man* (London, 1594).

[19] P. Stubbes, *Anatomie of Abuses* (1583) (ed. Furnivall), *New Shakespeare Society Publication*, p. 29.

[20] T. Nashe, *Works* (ed. McKerrow), I, 173.

[21] T. Smith, *De Republica Anglorum* (London, 1589), sig. E 3.

[22] T. Lodge, *Chrestoleros*, Publication of the Spenser Society, No. 47 (1888), p. 44; cf. Jonson's Sogliardo in *Every Man Out of His Humor*.

[23] J. Ferne, *Blazon of Gentrie* (London, 1586), sig. F 3. See also A. H. Nason, *Heralds and Heraldry in Jonson's Plays* (New York, 1907), chapter vi.

[24] S. Rowlands, *Look to It* (1604), (ed. Hunt. Club, 1872), VII, 16.

[25] *Twelfth Night*, III. iv. 234–35.

herald his friend. His father was a man of good [respectable?] stock, though but a tanner or usurer; he purchased land [doubtless by entangling an old family with usurous rates of interest], and his son the title. He has doffed the name of a country fellow, but the look not so easily and his face still bears a relish of churn-milk [pale and cowardly?].

The hopeful heir goes in for fine clothes, extravagance, and drink:

In sum, he is but a clod of his own earth, or his land is a dunghill and he the cock that crows over it: and commonly his race is quickly run, and his children's children tho they scape hanging, return to the place from whence they came.[26]

Sir Andrew's way of life certainly does not suggest that he will leave much for his "children's children."

The very names of some of Shakespeare's characters, especially his more comic figures, are often suggestive of their class and personality: Costard, who had no "head," at least for thinking; the tiny Moth; the inconstant Proteus; Nym, who "takes" what and when he can; the thrasonical, brawling Pistol; and, most obviously, Sir Toby Belch, whose all-day-long potations might well produce a queasy stomach. If the term *merry Andrew* was in use at so early a date—a matter of question in the *New English Dictionary*—then the knight's first name would signify a clown such as helped a mountebank. His family name, moreover, of Aguecheek—jocosely varied by his friend to Agueface—suggests the incontrollable shakings associated with palsy and with fear. Fear was no proper feeling for a knight, and dull, phlegmatic persons under the influence of the moon were thought to be subject to "palsies" of various sorts.[27] Breton in *The Goode and the Badde* (1616) associates "palsy" with cowardice, and cowardice also jibes with the womanish humor of phlegm. Indeed, Sir Andrew's very name implies a foolish mind and womanish fears. Thus the social background of the age seems quite to settle the all-important matter of Sir

[26] J. Earle, *Microcosmographie*, No. XVIII. Cf. H. Peacham, *Coach and Sedan* (London, 1636), sig. D.

[27] C. Dariot, *Iudgement of the Starres*, tr. F. Wither (London, 1598), sig. E r.

49

Andrew's ancestry: his lack of gentlemanly attainments combined with his wealth, his knighthood that sets upon him like a giant's robe upon a dwarfish thief, his very cognomen, all suggest an origin incongruous with his present gracious state.

Sir Andrew's physique is also a matter of some importance, not only because it would affect the casting of the part and because it doubtless contributed to the merriment of his role, but also because an unusual number of details seem, as in Chaucer's characters, to bring out, in terms of the current pseudoscience of physiognomy, certain traits of his mind and aspects of his social relationships. Indeed, his very bodily appearance obliquely infers the incongruity between his humble origins and the high station that he is trying to assume. As one of the ruling class, he should either show the balanced temperament of perfect health, or be dominated by the dynamic humor of choler (under the astral influence of the sun), or display a predominance of the humor blood, which made one sanguine and magnanimous and handsome. "Base trades," on the other hand, were generally linked with melancholy; and stupid, weak, and craven types with waterish phlegm.[28] Sir Andrew's humor, as implied in his physique, certainly does not suggest either knighthood or the social origins from which it was thought to spring; for, according to the Renaissance, knightly virtues were hereditary.[29] This theory constituted the prime argument in defense of an aristocracy of birth; and birth is what Sir Andrew did not have.

Sir Toby, apparently playing on *tongues* and *tongs* (i.e., curling irons), declares that the use of the latter would improve Sir Andrew's hair; and he adds that "it hangs like flax on a distaffe."[30] In fact, it is straight and yellow. According to the current science of physiognomy, "hair right downward" belonged to "simple" men;[31] and soft hair, which would tend

[28] Dariot, *op. cit.*, sig. D 2 *et seq.*

[29] B. Castiglione, *Courtier* (tr. Hoby, ed. Rouse and Henderson), pp. 32 *et seq.*; James I, *Political Works* (ed. McIlwain), p. 31; J. Newnham, *Nightcrowe* (London, 1590), p. 6; and J. W. Draper, "Bastardy in Shakespeare's Plays," *Shakespeare Jahrbuch*, LXXIV, 173 *et seq.*

[30] *Twelfth Night*, I. iii. 93 *et seq.*

[31] "Phisiognomie" appended to *The Booke of Arcandam*, tr. W. Warde (London, 1592).

to lie flat, betokened one of dull and phlegmatic temper.[32] White and pale colors,[33] especially of the hair,[34] also characterized the phlegmatic type. Sir Toby, furthermore, seems to call Sir Andrew "a thin fac'd knaue";[35] and, though some critics doubt to whom he is aluding, the terms of the reference seem to fit: a small head and especially a long, high forehead reflected both impudence, such as must actuate a too-persistent wooer, and the "dull witte"[36] of phlegm that Sir Andrew ubiquitously displays. Strangely enough, for one of cold, moist humor, the knight's hand is described as "dry";[37] but Maria, whom he has just attempted to "accost," seems to mean merely that, for all his proffered devotion both to her and to Olivia, he has in fact only the dull debility of a simpleton[38] rather than the warm, moist, sanguine temper of a true nobleman[39] or an accepted Romeo.[40] In another matter also, Sir Andrew does not run true to his phlegmatic type: phlegm was usually associated, as in Falstaff and Sir Toby, with flabbiness and fat;[41] but Cowley, who apparently took the part, also seems to have played Slender in *Merry Wives*, and Sir Toby calls Sir Andrew "tall"[42] and compares him to a "distaffe"[43] and a "Clodde-pole."[44] His legs, moreover, seem to have been well developed in length, if not in muscle: he envies Feste's,[45] but takes pride in clothing his own to conspicuous advantage.[46]

Of course, the sight of this loose- and long-limbed creature, a trifle the worse for drink, contorted spider-like in a "caper" or convulsed in his superlative "backe-tricke," must set not only Sir Toby but any audience laughing. In the actual theater,

[32] T. Hyll [Hill], *Schoole of Skill* (London, 1599), leaf 10 v.

[33] Dariot, *op. cit.*, sig. E 1 r; T. Vicary, *Anatomie*, E.E.T.S., Ex. Ser. LII, 41; W. Vaughan, *Directions for Health* (London, 1633; ed. princ., 1584), p. 128.

[34] L. Lemnius, *Touchstone of Complexions*, tr. T. Newton (London, 1576), leaf 146 r.

[35] *Twelfth Night*, V. i. 219.

[36] *Arcandam, loc. cit.*; Hyll, *op. cit.*, leaves 28 and 31 v.

[37] *Twelfth Night*, I. iii. 71.

[38] Cf. *Much Ado About Nothing*, II. i. 112.

[39] Dariot, *op. cit.*, sig. D 2 v.

[40] J. W. Draper, "Shakespeare's 'Star-Crossed Lovers,'" *R.E.S.*, XV, 16 *et seq.*

[41] Dariot, *op. cit.*, sig. D 4 r.   [42] *Twelfth Night*, I. iii. 21.

[43] *Ibid.*, I. iii. 97.   [44] *Ibid.*, III. iv. 187.   [45] *Ibid.*, II. iii. 23.

[46] *Ibid.*, I. iii. 126–27.

furthermore, Sir Andrew's attenuated frame would look incongruous beside his tubby friend. This build, however, seems to have had more point than merely giving a thin actor a chance to clown in contrast to a fat one, for long legs denoted the owner to be "dull of capacite,"[47] and so they seem to be a characterizing element in the part. Sir Toby, moreover, declares that both he and his crony were born under the astral sign of Taurus,[48] and he humorously intimates that this constellation of the zodiac was associated with "leggs and thighes"[49] —a joke, like his pun on "tall," that would be pointless unless Sir Andrew had long legs and so, presumably, the dull wit that went with them. In short, straight, yellow hair, a thin face, and an elongated frame, all suggest, if not a phlegmatic temper, at least the flaccid heaviness of a knight who is neither *sans peur* nor *sans reproche*. So full a use of physiognomy for characterization is unusual in Shakespeare, but finds parallel in Falstaff's mountain belly, which expressed his weakness, cowardice, and sloth,[50] and perhaps in Lady Macbeth's "little hand" and "fair" complexion.[51] Sir Andrew, having a paucity of initiative and intellect and will, and so a small speaking part, had to be characterized largely by the dialogue of others and by his own physique.

Just how the knight arrayed his disproportioned length is matter for wonderment. Shakespeare gives only two clues, both somewhat ambiguous: the Folio text makes Sir Andrew take complacent pleasure in a "dam'd colour'd stocke"[52] which some editors emend to read "flame colored," or "dove-colored"; the second reference is Fabyan's apology to Viola for Sir Andrew's "forme," and this may apply to his dress as well as to his figure.[53] Of course, for the original performance, Shakespeare himself might select the proper—or improper— garments; but, unfortunately, the wardrobe records of the troupe have not survived, and so hypothesis must replace certainty. Upstart prodigals, especially on courtship bent, de-

[47] Hyll, *op. cit.*, leaf 123 v.   [48] *Twelfth Night*, I. iii. 128 *et seq.*
[49] Dariot, *op. cit.*, sigs. D 3 v and D 4 v.   [50] Hyll, *op. cit.*, leaf 5 v.
[51] J. W. Draper, "Lady Macbeth," *Psychoanalytic Rev.*, XXVIII, 479 et seq.
[52] *Twelfth Night*, I. iii. 127.   [53] *Ibid.*, III. iv. 263–64.

Giouanetti.

A YOUTH IN VENETIAN COSTUME
From Vecellio's *Habiti*, 1608

lighted in extravagant habiliments—extravagant both in cost
and in design. Even the wellborn Bassanio required a great
sum for just this purpose, and Antonio recognized his need.
The young profligates in *Muld Sacke* "decke themselues vp in
effeminate fashions";[54] even a vulgar roarer was "daub'd thicke
with gold Lace";[55] Breton's "Effeminate Fool" is at once a
fashionable lover and a Lord Foppington;[56] Earle's "Upstart
country knight" is deeply concerned with his attire, and his
"Gallant" is "a kind of walking Mercers Shop." A gentleman
on courtship bent would be all the more extreme and such
sartorial display would have made a gross contrast with Sir
Toby's "cloathes [that] are good enough to drink in." Indeed,
Shakespearean Costume (1889) arrays Sir Andrew like a very
Osric. In that case, however, as with Osric, one should find in
the text some satire of his love of dress; but none is there.
Sir Andrew clearly has not climbed to Osric's studied elegance
in language, etiquette, or knowledge of swordplay; and, as he
seems to be but new commenced in the career of prodigal, perhaps the super-fashionable tailors had not yet found him out
—and Sir Toby would hardly encourage wastrel expenditure
on any but himself. A wooer, moreover, attired in plain travel-
stained buff, as in the case of Petruchio, would seem an incongruous and comic figure. Possibly, therefore, Sir Andrew's
stock was "dun colored"[57] like Sir Toby's serviceable leather,
or "dam'd"—i.e., black—as the Folio text reads. At all events,
Sir Andrew should be attired in one extreme or t'other to contrast either with Sir Toby or with his marital intentions. Venice
was the center of gaiety and fashion, and, if Sir Andrew is to
be so portrayed, the accompanying illustration from Vecellio's
Habiti (1608) might approximate his attire.

Sir Andrew's name and origins and physique suggest that
Shakespeare conceived him as having a phlegmatic tempera-

---

[54] *Muld Sacke* (London, 1620).

[55] *The Wandering Jew*, quoted by Bryne, ed. Massinger's *Maid of Honour* (London, 1927), p. 90.

[56] N. Breton, *The Goode and the Badde* (London, 1616).

[57] See *Twelfth Night* (ed. Quiller-Couch and Dover Wilson), I. iii. 137. "Graphic" evidence supports this emendation.

ment. Phlegm was considered a dull and waterish fluid that adulterated the blood[58] and so deadened the sensibilities:

The Flegmaticke humor is of colour white, somewhat brackish, like unto sweat, and properly placed in the kidneyes, which draw unto themselves the water from the bloud, thereby filling the veines, instead of good pure bloud.[59]

Vicary preferred to locate the humor in the lungs;[60] and Elyot imputed its formation to the digestive tract. "Natural Fleume," he says, is "engendred by insufficiēt decoction in the second digestion of the watry or raw partes of the mattier decoct called Chilus, by the last dygestiō made apt to be cōuerted into bloud. In this humour, water hath dominion most principall."[61] Sir Andrew's phlegmatic humor is not of Sir Toby's genial sort which was under the influence of Venus, but the duller and more vapid type under the astral influence of the moon: it was appropriate to women, fools, travelers, and lackeys,[62] and was characterized as "fearefull, faynt-hearted, prodigall . . . . delighting in iourneis and variety of life. . . . ."[63] Sir Andrew is just such a man. Elyot likewise describes the phlegmatic type as slow, dull, and cowardly,[64] and adds that the humor was strongest from the third hour of the night to the ninth of the same night;[65] and possibly this accounts for Sir Andrew's markedly phlegmatic silliness in his belated revels with Sir Toby. Batman declared the humor "heauie and slow" and cowardly.[66] Lemnius adds "rechlesse unheedynes"[67] and a craving for "bellycheere."[68] Walkington suggests that poor health makes such men "dull of conceit . . . . faint hearted . . . . mild of nature, seldom incēsed with anger . . . ."[69] In short, a composite

---

[58] T. Walkington, *Optick Glasse of Humors* (London [1631 ?]), chapter xi.
[59] Vaughan, *op. cit.*, p. 128.   [60] Vicary, *op. cit.*, p. 69.
[61] T. Elyot, *Castell of Helth* (London, 1541), leaf 8.
[62] Dariot, *op. cit.*, sigs. D 4 r and E 1 r.
[63] *Ibid.*, sig. E 1 r.   [64] Elyot, *op. cit.*, leaf 2.   [65] *Ibid.*, leaf 71 v.
[66] *Batman upon Bartholome* (London, 1582), leaves 31 v and 32 r.
[67] Lemnius, *op. cit.*, leaves 23 v and 81 r.
[68] *Ibid.*, leaf 111 v. See also leaves 86 v and 107 v *et seq.*
[69] Walkington, *op. cit.*, chapter xi.

of the accepted psychology of the phlegmatic comes close to being an analysis of Sir Andrew's character, and seems to account, not only for various accidentals but especially for his three major traits, prodigality, dullness, and cowardice. His astral type of phlegm, moreover, under the influence of luna, like half-wits and lunatics, stands out in sharp contrast to Sir Toby's astral type under the happier influence of Venus. Sir Andrew's phlegm made him too stupid to act effectively; Sir Toby's made him too lazy to act at all, except in defense of his lazy life. The contrast of these two phlegmatic natures must have been to intelligent Elizabethans even more telling than the superficial contrast of their physiques, their talk, and perhaps their clothes. It reminds one of the contrast of choleric types in *Othello*.[70]

Such being the ancestry and station and natural bent of Sir Toby's precious crony and nephew-in-law-elect, it remains to inquire into his education and accomplishments, though truly, Nature had given little on which to edify a structure. Sir Toby declares that his friend "speaks three or four languages word for word without booke"—a statement that apparently means only that Sir Andrew has memorized odds and ends from a popular phrase book,[71] rather than learning the ancient languages at college and the modern by travel as a true nobleman would.[72] He himself later admits that he has neglected "the tongues";[73] and "Dieu vou guard Monsieur" is apparently all the French he knows, for, when Viola answers him in the same language, he beats a quick retreat into English.[74] His Latin is quite as rudimentary, for he cannot construe even a sample sentence from William Lilly's *Grammar*[75] that every schoolboy conned, and that even Sir Toby could quote (inaccurately) by heart.[76] Surely Sir Andrew is a far cry from the comic school-

[70] J. W. Draper, *The Humors and Shakespeare's Characters* (Durham, N.C., 1945), chapter iv.

[71] L. B. Wright, *Middle Class Culture in Elizabethan England* (Chapel Hill, 1935), pp. 357 *et seq.*

[72] R. Kelso, *The English Gentleman in the Sixteenth Century* (Urbana, Ill., 1929), chapter iv.

[73] *Twelfth Night*, I. iii. 90.   [74] *Ibid.*, III. i. 72 *et seq.*   [75] *Ibid.*, II. iii. 4–6.

[76] See Sir J. E. Sandys in *Shakespeare's England* (Oxford, 1917), I, 225–26.

master of the popular Italian theater and the pedant of Classical comedy. Even in the niceties of penmanship, he does not seem far advanced, for he apparently does not understand Malvolio's remarks on Olivia's handwriting.[77] Indeed, Sir Andrew has neglected not only the "tongues" but all the "Arts" in which a gentleman was supposed to excel; and he seems to be letter-perfect in the "polite and finical ignorance"[78] ascribed by Earle to the "Mere [utter] Gull Citizen." In courtly English he is not adept: he cannot even "accost" Maria, and he envies the polished elegance of Viola[79] and hopes to filch some of her golden words to spend them as his own— doubtless the first step in making himself an Osric. He boasts that his wit is more "naturall" than Sir Toby's;[80] but, unfortunately, "natural" commonly referred to a "natural born fool." Sir Andrew cannot even follow Maria's rapier-like repartee, and is touched in every bout.[81] He is so completely witless that he cannot tell wit from nonsense, and he tips Feste for mere counterfeit badinage.[82] He boasts of his prowess in a light, fantastic "caper,"[83] but the "caper" that he cuts dissipates all illusions. Sir Toby says that he "playes o'the Viol-de-gamboys,"[84] an ancestor of the modern cello; and Sir Andrew fancies himself at part singing,[85] but his envy of Feste's voice[86] and Maria's description of the round in which he sings as "catterwalling"[87] do not imply a high artistic level. Witty talk and competent part singing[88] were *de rigeur* for any Elizabethan who hoped to cut a figure; but Sir Andrew, apparently, can hardly cut even a "caper."

The thin knight lacks not only the graces but the elementary instincts and mores of an Elizabethan gentleman: he stoops to envy the voice and leg of a mere court jester; he makes the shocking *faux pas* of offering to challenge Malvolio, a mere steward; and his crass misconception of the duello appears when

[77] *Twelfth Night*, II. v. 89.   [78] *Microcosmographie*, ed. cit.
[79] *Twelfth Night*, III. i. 88 *et seq.*   [80] *Ibid.*, II. iii. 83–84. Cf. I. iii. 28–29.
[81] *Ibid.*, I. iii. 69 *passim.*   [82] *Ibid.*, II. iii. 24 *et seq.*
[83] *Ibid.*, I. iii. 113 *et seq.*   [84] *Ibid.*, I. iii. 26.   [85] *Ibid.*, II. iii. 63–64.
[86] *Ibid.*, II. iii. 24.   [87] *Ibid.*, II. iii. 74.
[88] See W. B. Squire in *Shakespeare's England*, ed. cit., II, 20 *et seq.*

he suggests that he "challenge" Malvolio to fight and then "breake promise with him, and make a foole of him."[89] A gentleman's promise was much too sacred to be flung away thus lightly.[90] Of course, the challenge that he later writes to Viola is a mere chop-logic of phrases from contemporary books of arms, so strangely conglomerate as to be in Fabyan's words, "exceeding good sence-lesse";[91] and naturally Sebastian routs him in actual fight. Apparently, this was the meager net result of all the time that Sir Andrew says that he had given to "fencing."[92] The tavern roisterers of the day were wont to use, as a convenient substitute for swordplay, various fancy oaths, as recondite as their learning would allow, and so shocked the hearer into a ready compliance. Sir Andrew boasts of his proficiency in swearing,[93] but he generally uses only petty oaths such as "by my troth" and "faith," or minced oaths such as "marry" or "Odd's lifelings"; and, even when he rushes in with a broken head, the best that he can do is a vain repetition of "For the love of God." In that age of rich, round profanity, such oaths show neither force nor elegant eccentricity; Sir Andrew is neither gentleman enough to command respect, nor man enough to resent the lack of it. Clearly, he has nothing of the courtier's, soldier's, scholar's, eye, tongue, sword; he is the perfect opposite of Hamlet and Bassanio and Romeo and the rest. Such was the merry-andrew whose craven cowardice and doltish word and deed belied his knighthood.

Sir Andrew's aptitudes ran rather to high living and plain thinking. He delighted in "Maskes and Reuels";[94] and "Reuels" apparently meant dancing.[95] At a "beare-baiting," furthermore, he shines, doubtless at a safe distance from the bear. He is his best, however, at the table, or at the "Buttry barre," where only "Canarie" can put him down. He is a great eater of beef, which, he seems to think, has made him beef-witted;[96] and he roundly declares that life "consists of eating and drinking"[97]—especially the latter—for, like Falstaff, his cure for

[89] *Twelfth Night*, II. iii. 124–25.
[90] Kelso, *op. cit.*, chapter v.
[91] *Twelfth Night*, III. iv, 159.
[92] *Ibid.*, I. iii. 90.
[93] *Ibid.*, III. iv. 181.
[94] *Ibid.*, I. iii. 106–7 and 127.
[95] *Ibid.*, I. iii. 108 *et seq.*
[96] *Twelfth Night*, I. iii. 83–84.
[97] *Ibid.*, II. iii. 13–14.

hunger is "to drink."[98] Indeed, he is Overbury's "Improvident Young Gallant":

There is a confederacy between him and his clothes, to be made a puppy: view him well, and you'll say his gentry sits ill upon him, as if he had bought it with his penny. He hath more places to send money to, than the devil hath to send his spirits; and to furnish each mistress, would make him run besides his wits, if he had any to lose.

He "studies impudence," pretends to be a "scholar," but actually gives his time to cockfights, horse racing, and the like.[99] Of course, he is a pillar of the social system that lets such as he live as they list: he hates conspirators and Brownists[100] and every sort of Puritan[101]—so much so that he will not even sing a moralistic song.[102] Indeed, he is a monument, not of solid but of stolid conservatism, a very Dogberry raised to the empyrean sphere of knighthood.

Everyone calls him fool and treats him so. He even overgoes Earle's "Weak Man" who is "discoverable in all silliness to all men but himself";[103] for Sir Andrew's follies have been noted to his face, though still he regards them not. He naïvely says, "many do call mee foole,"[104] and some, "knave,"[105] but still he can only accept these soft imputations. The present study has repeatedly set forth his likeness to the gulls and fatuous prodigals depicted by the character-writers and pamphleteers of the age; but a dramatist like Shakespeare must show his puppets, not merely in general terms, as the character-writer does, but actually dallying in the action and reaction of the plot: his figures must live and move. The foregoing survey, therefore, of Sir Andrew's ancestry, appearance, and humor, and of his education and accomplishments (or their lack), must lead to a discussion of his doings in the comedy and his relations with each of the other characters: his alliance with Sir Toby, and their optimistic plan to ensnare Olivia's heart, the progress of that plan, and its conclusion in the fight

[98] *Twelfth Night*, II. iii. 124.
[99] T. Overbury, "Characters," appended to *The Wife* (London, 1614).
[100] *Twelfth Night*, III. ii. 31–32.   [101] *Ibid.*, II. iii. 137.
[102] *Ibid.*, II. iii. 40.   [103] Earle, *op. cit.*, "A Weak Man."
[104] *Twelfth Night*, II. v. 81.   [105] *Ibid.*, II. iii. 69–70.

with Sebastian and Sir Andrew's part in the fooling of Malvolio. All these must be reviewed in the light of what Sir Andrew was and what he aspired to be.

A flagon of canary in some not-too-choice Illyrian—or should we say English?—tavern had doubtless begun and sealed the fellowship between Sir Toby and Sir Andrew. The former stood in need of a docile husband for his rich and unprotected niece; the latter would do as a husband. Thus Sir Toby could attend to the protecting of both Lord and Lady for a price. Sir Andrew stood in need of a rich and titled wife to solidify his shaky social status and to continue the glorious line of Aguecheeks; and Sir Toby was of course the perfect *galeotto* to tutor him in the guiles and wiles of love, and even to produce the very lady. Thus the two knights, as supplements to each other, flew to mutual embrace like atoms oppositely charged. Sir Andrew seemingly had but late come into his inheritance, and he takes his fling at what he thinks high life as a prelude to the serious business of providing a son and heir.[106] Sir Toby was not one to palter at a mere matter of expense, and speeds his crony on the primrose path to such good effect that Maria declares that the whole fortune will last but a twelvemonth. Such gulls as Sir Andrew feathered the nests of many a rare bird in Elizabethan London. Just so Earle's "Brainless" readily "makes friends over supper and loses them with loans to them."[107] Just so, Hall's "Unthrift" gives his days and nights to "idle pastime," and "knows not to govern either his mind or his purse."[108] Indeed, contemporary realistic writings teem with Aguecheeks; and, though Sir Andrew could not take Olivia to wife, he and his archetypes begat a numerous progeny in letters.

Of necessity, the alliance with Sir Toby was one-sided, for Sir Andrew is the very picture of a "Novice" or a "Weake brain'd Gull,"[109] and he is "Like waxe to vice"[110]—Sir Toby

[106] H. Peacham, *Coach and Sedan* (London, 1636), sig. D 1 *et seq.*
[107] Earle, *op. cit.*, No. 42.
[108] J. Hall, *Characters* (London, 1608), "The Unthrift."
[109] John Stephens the Younger, *Essays and Characters* (London, 1615).
[110] L. Bryskett, *Discourse of Civill Life* (London, 1606), pp. 103-4.

being the Vice. Sir Andrew's stupidity, his cowardice, and his inexperience make him indeed putty in sophisticated hands; and this relationship of mentor and gull appears in the use of pronouns: though both are knights, he politely calls Sir Toby *you*, whereas Sir Toby calls him *thou* as if he were a pupil or inferior. In thought and action, his mentor is his pattern: he tips when Sir Toby tips;[111] again and again, he echoes Sir Toby's very words,[112] often with no sense of their meaning; and, even when Sir Toby promises to wed Maria, Sir Andrew makes a like promise as if he were repeating the patter of a song.[113] No wonder that Sir Toby has already extracted so rich a plunder from this pliant disciple that the latter, though both are living on the bounty of Olivia, is even now "a foule way out"[114]—indeed, "some two thousand strong or so."[115] When the play opens, Sir Andrew has but recently arrived, for he has to be introduced to Maria; but already the Countess has made it clear that she will not see him. He is discouraged, and will "home to-morrow." He balks at further outlay to no purpose, and yet quickly succumbs to Sir Toby's blandishments—even more quickly than the scatterbrained Roderigo does to Iago's. Olivia's "fauors" to Viola later daunt him so that, he declares, he will "not stay a iot longer."[116] He even rises to the intellectual height of accusing Sir Toby of making "an Asse" of him; but still he stays.[117] Sir Toby plays the snake, and he the fascinated bird.

Indeed, Sir Andrew as a lover, though he declares himself experienced in being adored,[118] is hardly a success. His methods are most unconventional[119] without being brilliant or astute. Noble marriages, like Juliet's or Bianca's were arranged by the girl's father. The death of Olivia's father and brother had apparently left Sir Toby next of kin, but she would not grant him such prerogatives, and his officious haste in bringing the

---

[111] *Twelfth Night*, II. iii. 36.   [112] *Ibid.*, I. iii. 62–63; II. iii. 58 *passim*.
[113] *Ibid.*, II. v. 171 *et seq*.   [114] *Ibid.*, II. iii. 178–79.
[115] *Ibid.*, III. ii. 55–56.   [116] *Ibid.*, III. ii. 1.
[117] *Ibid.*, III. ii. 14 *et seq*.   [118] *Ibid.*, II. iii. 175.
[119] C. L. Powell, *English Domestic Relations, 1487–1653* (New York, 1917), pp. 3 *et seq*.

chosen wooer as his guest to her house and then in reveling with him at her expense was hardly likely to win her favor. Sir Toby and Sir Andrew clearly did not realize that Elizabethan women were no longer docile as of yore;[120] the knights at once proceed to take the Countess by storm, but she eludes them. Sir Andrew agrees to spend another month,[121] but his hopes are not of the brightest. His efforts (whatever they were) to charm the lady are not displayed before us; she simply will not receive him. Shakespeare, however, does depict the tall knight's attempt to "accost" and "board" Maria, and she puts him down without ado: if the lady-in-waiting could repulse him so, he stood small chance with the noble mistress. Olivia doubtless had report of him from Malvolio and from Maria, and perhaps she had herself looked down at him through one of the "peeping windowes for Ladies to view what doings there are in the Hall."[122] At all events, she soon made up her mind; and, when in Act III the two meet upon the stage, she pointedly ignores him; and, though he sees her "do more fauours" to Viola "then euer she bestow'd vpon mee,"[123] he is so overcome by his rival's courtly address that he cannot say even a word for himself. Indeed, Sir Andrew as a lover is neither conventional, nor astute, nor impetuously ardent, and his lassitude in the pursuit of both Maria and Olivia shows his phlegmatic temper. If he had really been in love at all, his rejection would have caused symptoms of melancholy, and none appear. The tender passion also was thought to stimulate the liver;[124] and even Sir Toby at last has to admit "For *Andrew*, if he were open'd and you finde so much blood in his Liuer, as will clog the foote of a flea, I'le eate the rest of th'anatomy."[125]

[120] J. W. Draper, "Desdemona," *Revue de Littérature Comparée*, XIII, 337 *et seq.*

[121] *Twelfth Night*, I. iii. 105.

[122] D. L. Lupton, *London and the Country Carbonadoed* (London, 1632). Such a peep-window still exists high in the wall of the hall at Penshurst, the seat of the Sidney family in Kent.

[123] *Twelfth Night*, III. ii. 7–8.

[124] J. Ferrand, 'Ερωτομανία, *or a Treatise of Love* (Oxford, 1640; ed. *princ.*, Paris, 1624), pp. 25–26, 67–68; and A. Laurentius, *Discourse of the Sight* (London, 1599), p. 118.

[125] *Twelfth Night*, III. ii. 61 *et seq.* Cf. III. ii. 21.

By degrees, Sir Toby seems to make up his mind that his "tall" and talented candidate is no longer in the running, and he drops the role of publicity agent, and admits Sir Andrew a "clodde-pole" and compares him contemptuously to a "bum-Baylie."[126] Surely, he has no faith that the stratagem of the duel will make Olivia accept such a lover. He is merely amusing himself and at the same time keeping up the hopes of his dupe. In short, he makes his fool his purse. Fabyan joins in persuading Sir Andrew once more to assail the Countess "by some laudable attempt, either of valour of policie";[127] and Sir Andrew, on the horns of this dilemma, chooses valor. Shakespeare carefully prepares for the duel scene that makes up the latter half of Sir Andrew's stage career. Even before he entered, Maria called him coward when Sir Toby boasted that he was "tall." As in the matter of his dancing and his oaths, the knight rather fancies himself in fencing;[128] and yet a mere steward can abash him into silence; and, when Malvolio rebukes the revelers, he keeps discreetly quiet. He later admits that his idea of making a fool out of a person is to make a poltroon out of himself.[129] Maria and Sir Toby call him bad names to his face,[130] and he suffers these slurs without word or deed: truly, he is a recreant knight. The duel was the prime convention that protected a gentleman's honor, and a duel with Sir Andrew as a principal could only be the veriest travesty.

That Shakespeare should depict it so was quite in the current tradition; for most Elizabethans still preferred a good old-fashioned brawl with sword and buckler, and disliked such newfangled Italianate doings[131] as the duello. For example, the "Dedication" to *The Boke of Honor and Arms*[132] (1590) apologizes for its very subject; the law accounted duelling mere murder,[133] and King James, who disapproved the custom,[134]

---

[126] *Twelfth Night*, III. iv. 175 *passim*. [127] *Ibid.*, III. ii. 19 *et seq.*
[128] *Ibid.*, I. iii. 90–91. [129] *Ibid.*, II. iii. 125–26.
[130] *Ibid.*, II. iii. 164; III. iv. 175, etc. [131] Kelso, *op. cit.*, p. 102.
[132] Probably by R. Jones. See R. Kelso, *M.L.N.*, XXXIX, 33 *et seq.*
[133] *Cal. State Papers Dom.* (London, 1858), p. 224.
[134] James I, *Political Works* (ed. McIlwain), p. 28.

later issued a special edict to suppress it.[135] Doubtless its unpopularity among the more conservative accounts for the fact that all of Shakespeare's duels are treated comically. The first step in such an affair should be a quarrel in which one party gives the other the lie. No such meeting had taken place; but Sir Andrew, egged on by his associates, proceeds at once to the challenge, and the expression of this challenge is indeed "excellently ignorant."[136] He thinks that he has put "vinegar and pepper"[137] in it, but it is such a conglomerate of misapplied phrases as to be a mere parody. Sir Andrew seems to have learned them by rote or borrowed them hit-and-run from some vade mecum of honor and etiquette:

Youth, whatsoeuer thou art, thou art but a scuruy fellow. Wonder not, nor admire not in thy minde why I doe call thee so, for I will shew thee no reason for't. Thou comst to the Lady Oliuia, and in my sight she uses thee kindly: but thou lyest in thy throat, that is not the matter I challenge thee for. I will way-lay thee going home, where if it be thy chance to kill me, thou kilst me like a rogue and a villaine. Far-theewell, and God haue mercie upon one of our soules. He may haue mercie upon mine, but my hope is better, and so looke to thyself. Thy friend as thou usest him, & thy sworne enemie, Andrew Ague-cheeke.

This is as gross and palpable as the lies of Falstaff. To give a gentleman "the lie," especially "in his throat," made a duel unavoidable;[138] and, in the bravado of the moment, Sir Andrew even threatens to "way-lay" his enemy as if he were the merest highwayman; and yet, when he hears that Viola may actually put up a fight, he cravenly offers to settle the nonexistent dispute by giving away his horse! What a merry round of laughter for the young gentles in Shakespeare's audience.

The actual meeting of the opposing parties occurs in two sections, or, more properly, it does not occur at all, for the first encounter ends before the swordplay begins; and the second is not between Viola and Sir Andrew but between Sebastian and Sir Andrew and then Sir Toby. Sir Toby at first represents

---

[135] *A Publication of His Ma'ties Edict and Severe Censure against Private Combats* (London, 1613).
[136] *Twelfth Night*, III. iv. 186.   [137] *Ibid.*, III. iv. 147.
[138] Kelso, *op. cit.*, pp. 100–101; and L. Bryskett, *op. cit.*, p. 64 *et seq.*

Viola as a young fire-eater who insists on fighting "for's oath sake";[139] and, indeed, "many" men did "thrust thēselves rashly into quarrels . . . . upō fantasticall points of honor, as if they were weary of their lives."[140] As both contestants stand blenched and mammering, Antonio's arrest interrupts, for none dares duel before officers. The arrest being made and the arms of the law withdrawn, Sir Toby assures his gull that Viola is really a coward; and Sir Andrew's fine fury at his rival's lack of spirit is a fit climax to the scene. Sir Andrew pursues Viola and meets her brother Sebastian, whom he mistakes for her, makes a pass at him, and is struck himself. Sir Toby, fearing for the precious life that connects him with three thousand ducats a year, intervenes in a way that no code of honor would allow. Indeed, all this is a mere brawl. Sir Toby, perhaps because he is "in drink,"[141] fares no better than Sir Andrew, and so ends the duel that was supposed to establish on the basis of his valor Sir Andrew's claim to his lady's hand. He has not even the sporting sense to take his bloody coxcomb in wise (if painful) silence, and, like a poor craven, threatens to "haue an action of Battery" against his opponent "if there be any law in Illyria."[142] Indeed, the duello amply illustrates his cowardice as the earlier scenes display his fatuous prodigality: he is like Breton's "Coward" the "shame of manhood, the disgrace of nature, the scorn of reason and the hate of honour."[143] He is the very living picture of Earle's "Coward":

. . . . commonly most fierce against the coward, and labouring to take this suspicion from himself; for the opinion [reputation] of valor is a good protection to those that dare not use it. No man is valianter than he in civil company, and where he thinks no danger may come of it . . . . wonderful exceptious and choleric where he sees men are both loth to give him occasion, and you cannot pacify him better than by quarrelling with him . . . . and you threaten him at last into a very honest quiet man.[144]

---

[139] *Twelfth Night*, III. iv. 294–95.

[140] Bryskett, *op. cit.*, p. 215.   [141] *Twelfth Night*, V. i. 205.

[142] *Ibid.*, IV. i. 34–35. See F. F. Heard, *Shakespeare As a Lawyer* (Boston, 1883), pp. 30–31.

[143] Breton, *op. cit.*, "A Coward."   [144] Earle, *op. cit.*, No. LXXIII.

Sir Andrew got more than threats, but he got no less than he deserved.

Of the tall knight's actions in the play, it remains only to note his minor part as applauder of the gulling of Malvolio. Just as his own cowardice made him especially delight in playing on the cowardice of Viola, just so his own doubtful status as a social climber made him especially indignant at the pretensions of the pushing Malvolio, who had not the advantage of a rich father to buy him knighthood. To the *nouveaux*, the social aspirations of others is the very height of vulgar outrage. With an insistence almost pathetic, Sir Andrew includes himself in the plot against the hapless steward.[145] He clings to the genteel companionship of Sir Toby and the rest, for truly how could he live or move or have his knightly being were they not there to prompt him? He is neither man enough, nor gentleman enough to stand alone. In return for this almost canine loyalty, the others gull him into a nayword with the duel as they had gulled Malvolio with the forged love letter. Indeed, Malvolio, Sir Andrew, and perhaps Osric represent three stages of the genus social climber that the age abounded in and particularly detested: Malvolio is the mere aspiring servant; Sir Andrew is the son of a rich merchant or usurer whose money can purchase a title but nothing else; Osric has even commenced courtier and studied politic arts to such effect that he dresses beyond the dreams of ultrafashion and commands the most superfluous elegancies of speech, so that even the Crown Prince can hardly understand him. In this scale of ascending airs and graces, Sir Andrew is the happy medium. The young bloods who crowded the galleries and the stage would have hated him for his very wealth, and been quite content to see him cheated out of it. Sir Toby is at least a man of sorts, if hardly a gentleman; Sir Andrew is not either.

If his repeated folly and failures in the play are any indication, and if we may trust Maria's prediction[146] and Sir Toby's efficiency as a leech, Sir Andrew's affluence was not for long. The comedy leaves his future, like Malvolio's, somewhat

---

[145] *Twelfth Night,* II. v. 196.   [146] *Twelfth Night,* I. iii. 24–25.

undetermined. Perhaps, however, Earle's "Idle Gallant" inferentially supplies the lack: Earle's character lives an empty life in the extreme of fashion, runs through his money and is ruined—doubtless by the very usurious practices that originally built up Sir Andrew's inheritance—and finally dies "in the gaol or the country," that is, in gaol for debt, or living as a poor pensioner on the estate of some rich relative. Or perhaps Sir Andrew, like the seventeenth Earl of Oxford, became a sort of beachcomber of the London taverns, finally to die in obscurity and want. Sir Andrew verily could not live by his sword, by his swagger, and indeed not by his wits!

Sir Andrew, by his probably bourgeois origins, belongs to the weak phlegmatic type incapable of the courtly arts of love and war. He is a study in both social and psychological maladjustment, like Kate whose choler must be cured before she could truly be a wife,[147] like Falstaff and Nym who pretended to a marital choler that neither had by nature,[148] like the unstable Macbeth whose mercurial temper unfitted him for the choleric role of king.[149] If the essence of comedy be incongruity, Sir Andrew represents the very *summa* of the comic both in body and mind and in his social status: physically he is incongruously tall and incongruously complacent of his broomstick legs; mentally, his phlegmatic stupidity is incongruous, especially after Sir Toby's panegyric, for he does not know wit from nonsense and, in his challenge to Viola, cannot put two sentences coherently together; spiritually, his knightly title and his clownish courtesy and sense of honor, his bragging and his craven cowardice cry out at one another. His relations with the other characters reflect this mad disparity: a chivalrous knight who forces his way into his noble lady's hall and lives upon her even when she will not see him; the son of a usurious tradesman who aspires to a Countess; a fledging noble who cannot even comprehend the laws of honor and arms and must learn them from such as Fabyan and Belch, and must even

<hr/>

147 J. W. Draper, " 'Kate the Curst,' " *Jour. Nerv. Ment. Dis.*, LXXXVI, 757 *et seq.*

148 *Idem*, "The Humor of Corporal Nym," *Shakespeare Bulletin*, XIII, 131 *et seq.*

149 J. W. Draper, "Macbeth 'Infirme of Purpose,' " *Bulletin of the History of Medicine*, X, 16 *et seq.*

68

depend on the latter in the fight with Sebastian. Gull, prodigal, and coward, he is the *reductio ad absurdum* of a man. In chivalry, he is the perfect foil to His Grace, the Duke Orsino; in arms, to the brave Sebastian; in wealth, to the impecunious Sir Toby. He is cousin germane only to the despised Malvolio, for both are social upstarts—and both have their reward.

Sir Toby and Sir Andrew are a far cry from Chaucer's "worthy knight," and for good historic reason: in the Renaissance, among the old families, chivalry had so declined that it could support its lackland followers only as ragtag hangers-on of their landed relatives, living in time of peace at home on charity or by theft and chicancery in London, and in time of war by theft abroad. The Falstaff plays depict this vividly.[150] Of such stripe also was Sir Toby. Or, among the bourgeois newly rich, knighthood was merely an outer gilding, a title and a few empty prerogatives hastily donned to flaunt before the vulgar and give a spurious show of gentle birth: of such was Sir Andrew. Thus the two knights are contrasted not only as two types of the phlegmatic humor with contrasting physiques and characters, but also as two social types, both of which reflect the decay of chivalry, the gilded upstart and his mentor, the tosspot knight. With all these differences, however, both are actuated by the same human motive, the urge for security in a mutable world and a transition age: Sir Toby wants the economic security of future years of "Cakes and Ale"; Sir Andrew, the social security of a titled wife and a son and heir. Sir Toby seems to achieve his lofty purpose, but Fate in the person of Shakespeare has drawn a kindly curtain over Sir Andrew's future: the world punishes fools more harshly than it does shrewd knaves, and Sir Andrew's wealth and knighthood and pre-eminent folly made him a shining mark. So, in the end, he follows Sir Toby out to have his head bound up, and such slight impression had he made on friend and foe and chosen fiancée, that no one troubles to make inquiry or remark. Sir Andrew is just one of those persons that simply do not matter.

[150] J. W. Draper, "Sir John Falstaff," *R.E.S.*, VIII, 414 *et seq.*

❧ Mistress Mary

THE object of Sir Toby's tender passion is the shrewd and frolicsome Maria — frolicsome, but shrewd enough to bait the gin that snared even as great a fly as the Countess Olivia's uncle. Across the panorama of the comedy, she trips an eccentric course with both eyes fixed on the main chance; and, like a hummingbird, she flutters, a sparkling fleck, sportive and seemingly insouciant, but actually bent — quite as a hummingbird is — on the serious business of providing for herself. Most critics have admired the gay plumage of her wit without too much perceiving the purpose of her manifold gyrations and the fine technique with which she accomplishes her ends. Indeed, although she is Shakespeare's own creation and speaks a hundred and seventy lines very much to the purpose of the plot, yet scholars have generally passed her by with brief conventional formality, much as a caller passes a servant at the door. Montégut describes her as a "sly waiting woman," and says that she is not "exempt from the folly of which she accuses Malvolio," for she pursues "the same ambitious dream of making a match with Sir Toby"; but her gentle birth and Sir Toby's poverty spoil his analogy. Winter, in like fashion, calls her "a pert chambermaid." The Tudor editors realize that she is a "gentlewoman" and term her the "arch-intriguer" of the comedy, but impute her intrigues merely to "sheer delight in a practical joke": they find her "clever," but do not see the purpose of her cleverness. The Arden editors, like Montégut, seem not to realize her gentility, though they gauge her motives more astutely. Mr. Priestley describes her as a "dainty rogue";[1] and the new Cambridge editors — unspeakable *faux pas!* — derive her character from the notorious Dame Quickly. Indeed, the critics have hardly been her friends.

---

[1] J. B. Priestley, *English Comic Characters* (London [1925]), p. 43.

Just as Sir Toby is somewhat allied to the *miles gloriosus* and Sir Andrew to the gull, so Maria shows some affinity to the stage types of the wily young woman and the maid who woos her lover or at least confesses her love to him,[2] a type already apparent in *Sir Clyomon* and in *The Arraignment of Paris*; but, like Sir Toby and Sir Andrew, she so far transcends the mere conventions of the theater that one is constrained rather to seek her source and inspiration among the real ladies in waiting and younger daughters of the age; for truly Shakespeare's comedies "are so framed to the life that they serve for the most common commentaries" of Elizabethan men and women. Indeed, although Maria's type was less celebrated in contemporary pamphlets and character books than the roarer or the gull, and so is harder for the modern scholar to define, yet the surviving evidence would seem to show that she closely conforms to current actuality. A survey of her physique and character, of her past and present social status, and of her relations with the other figures, as the plot unfolds, supports the conclusion that in motive and action and in the outcome of the piece she is in fact "framed to the life" that Shakespeare's audience knew. Thus she contributes not only to the witty style and to the comic intrigue but also to the realistic verisimilitude of the play.

Maria's physique suggests her humor and her character. Sir Andrew calls her "faire"[3]—doubtless referring to her blond complexion and consequent good looks, for Elizabethans preferred blondes. Persons with "faire eyes" belonged to the phlegmatic type under the influence of Venus; like Maria, they were feminine and, again like Maria who at last wins the hesitant Sir Toby, they might look for "lesser [good] fortune."[4] According to this, her humor would be the same as that of her spouse; but it was more appropriate to "damsels" than to men, least of all to soldiers. Maria, moreover, is repeatedly de-

[2] R. S. Forsythe, *The Relation of Shirley's Plays to the Elizabethan Drama* (New York, 1914), pp. 65, 102.

[3] *Twelfth Night* (ed. Furness var.), I. iii. 47. On the characteristics of the phlegmatic humor, see J. W. Draper, *The Humors and Shakespeare's Characters* (Durham, N.C., 1945), chapter iii.

[4] C. Dariot, *Iudgement of the Starres* (London, 1598), sig. D 4 r.

scribed as very small, a "beagle,"[5] a "little villaine,"[6] a "youngest Wren,"[7] and Viola ironically calls her Olivia's "Giant."[8] As Warburton suggests, Samuel Crosse, who apparently played the part,[9] perhaps required some excuse for his small stature; but the lack of such excuse in his other roles throws doubt upon this theory. At any rate, Maria's size accords with her humor and her mental bent: those of small body who were "of a colde and moyste qualitye" (i.e., phlegmatic) were supposed, on the authority of Aristotle, to be "apt to conceyue, and readiley to descerne," whereas choleric persons of small body were described as stupid.[10] The diminutive Maria is certainly "apt to conceyue"; she is a "most excellent diuell of wit";[11] she originates the stratagem against Malvolio at a moment's notice;[12] and she puts down even Feste at repartee and wins a compliment from him.[13] Thus Maria's phlegmatic disposition, implied in her sex, her fortune, and her fair complexion, accords also with her slight stature and her ready wit. Indeed, a small body even implied that one was "Wise";[14] and, if a main part of wisdom be lively understanding of character and motive, then Mistress Mary had pretensions even to wisdom. On short acquaintance, she summarizes Sir Andrew's three outstanding frailties, and sees at once the hopelessness of his suit; she shrewdly warns Sir Toby that this gull is a valueless ally; and she understands Malvolio so well that she can calculate her plot to his defects. In short, Maria, in both mind and body, fits a definite and recognized subdivision of the phlegmatic type; and Shakespeare gives her truth to life, as he did so many of his characters, in terms of the accepted physiology, astrology, and psychology of the age. She and Sir Toby and Sir Andrew form a phlegmatic trio; but Sir Andrew, being under the influence of the moon, has a different astrological

[5] *Twelfth Night*, II. iii. 173.   [6] *Ibid.*, II. v. 15.
[7] *Ibid.*, III. ii. 67.   [8] *Ibid.*, I. v. 204.
[9] T. W. Baldwin, *The Shakespearean Company* (Princeton, N.J., 1927), Plate III.
[10] T. Hyll, "Art of Phisiognomie," appended to *Contemplation of Mankind* (London, 1571), leaf 125.
[11] *Twelfth Night*, II. v. 194–95.
[12] *Ibid.*, II. iii. 150 *et seq.*   [13] *Ibid.*, I. v. 26–27.
[14] Hyll, *op. cit.*, leaf 110 [210] v; *Booke of Arcandam*, tr. Warde (London, 1592), sig. M 3 r *et seq.*; and T. Churchyard, *Mirror of Man* (London, 1594).

72

complexion, and Sir Toby's being a man and a soldier makes his phlegmatic humor of Venus work out in speech and action quite differently from the same humor and astral influence in Maria.

The play contains no direct statement of Maria's age, but she cannot be either a mere girl or an old woman. She is clearly old enough to betroth herself without her parents' consent; but, as Church and State variously set this age as seven, twelve, and sixteen,[15] it helps but little. Indeed, Maria is certainly not an Ophelia or a Juliet: she nicely weighs the character and motives of each member of the household; and, with the realistic outlook of maturity, she grasps her own position, and lays befitting plans. On the other hand, she must be young enough to attract Sir Toby. In short, she may well be in her middle twenties, and, among Elizabethans, who were generally short-lived,[16] this would verge on middle age. Such a time of life would accord with her undowered spinsterhood and also with her position as lady in waiting to the Countess. The period of betrothal was well passed,[17] and Lord Gilbert Talbot, after careful inquiry, employed a "sober maiden" of twenty-seven to attend his youthful wife.[18] Moreover, Crosse, who apparently took Maria's part, seems to have played Gertrude, not Ophelia, in *Hamlet*, and Mistress Quickly in the Falstaff plays;[19] such a casting would imply that he took the roles of mature women rather than of girls. In short, Maria, though by no means old, is not as young as she once was.

Mistress Mary is a gentlewoman, and her position in the Countess' household quite accords with the customs of the age. Her birth is unimpeachable: not only does a stage direction in the folio[20] but also Olivia and even Malvolio call her "Gentlewoman,"[21] and her duties in the household suggest responsi-

[15] D. Pickering, *Statutes at Large* (Cambridge, 1763), VI, 104 *et seq.*; C. L. Powell, *English Domestic Relations, 1487–1653* (New York, 1917), p. 6.

[16] J. W. Draper, *The "Hamlet" of Shakespeare's Audience* (Durham, N.C., 1938), pp. 47–48.

[17] W. S. Davis, *Life in Elizabethan Days* (New York, 1930), p. 93.

[18] M. S. Rawson, *Bess of Hardwick* (New York, 1910), p. 100.

[19] Baldwin, *op. cit.*, Plate III.

[20] *Twelfth Night*, III. i. 85.   [21] *Ibid.*, I. v. 162–63.

bility and position rather than menial servitude: she is entrusted with the key to the wine cellar;[22] she fetches and carries for Olivia's personal wants;[23] and Olivia consults her on the love affair with Cesario.[24] Indeed, she conforms to Overbury's picture of "a *waiting, gentle-woman*,"[25] a constant and indispensable attendant on her mistress. Had she been a mere "Chamber-maid" as Sir Toby once calls her,[26] possibly for a joke, her base degree would have fitted her more properly to be his mistress than his wife.[27] The system of putting out well-born children, both boys and girls, to service under one's feudal overlord was a survival from the Middle Ages;[28] and, since Mistress Mary was in the household of a Countess, her father was doubtless a baron or a knight or at least a squire who in those times of financial stress could not afford her a dowry.[29] Perhaps, moreover, like Orlando and Sir Toby, she was not the eldest child. At seven or nine, children were sent from home to do "service"[30] and supposedly "to learn better manners"[31] and with luck perchance make a good marriage.[32] Thus "My Mistress" might well have "had her education vnder a great countesse."[33] Such a position, dependent on the whim of my Lord and Lady and on their financial and political stability, was sometimes arduous and often insecure. England was indeed the "Purgatory of Servants,"[34] and it was well said that "service is none heritage."[35] Thus Maria, by aiding and abetting Sir Toby's untimely revels in a house of mourning and by risk-

[22] *Twelfth Night*, II. iii. 117 *et seq.*   [23] *Ibid.*, I. v. 165.
[24] *Ibid.*, III. iv. 3 *et seq.*   [25] Sir T. Overbury, *Characters*, "A Very Woman."
[26] *Twelfth Night*, I. iii. 51.   [27] Overbury, *op. cit.*, "A Chamber-maid."
[28] J. W. Draper, "Falstaff's Robin and Other Pages," *Studies in Philology*, XXXVI, 476 *et seq.*
[29] *Twelfth Night*, II. v. 170 *et seq.*
[30] G. Markham, *Gentlemanly Profession of Servingmen* (*ed. princ.*, 1598), in *Inedited Tracts*, ed. Hazlitt (London, 1868), p. 110.
[31] *A Relation of the Island of England* (c. 1500), ed. Camden Society (London, 1897), pp. 24–25.
[32] W. Powell, *Tom of all Trades*, quoted in G. B. Harrison, *England* (London, 1928), pp. 81–82.
[33] John Stephens, *Essayes* (London, 1615), p. 302.
[34] F. Moryson, *Itinerary* (*ed. princ.*, 1617), (ed. Furnivall, New Shakespeake Society), p. 271.
[35] William Harrison, *Description of England* (ed. Furnivall), p. 13.

ing the displeasure of a mistress already "much out of quiet,"[36] was in danger of losing her livelihood, a danger that her warning to Feste[37] shows her to have realized. Places were few, and servants plentiful, and dismissal meant starvation; but Maria seems to have felt secure in Olivia's high favor, and furthermore, the stake she played for was worth a risk.

Mistress Mary, for all her native shrewdness and her gentility of birth, had the limited outlook and education of most Elizabethan girls; for only a few noble bluestockings received from tutors anything like the wide Classical training that the great public schools gave to their brothers. Traditional opinion and economic pressure combined to deny much book learning to women,[38] and parents were said often to neglect even their sons' education.[39] Girls of the upper middle class, to be sure, were generally able to read and write, at least after a fashion;[40] but their literary pabulum seems to have consisted mainly of devotional works, housewifery, cooking, farm matters, and medicine, including astrology as dispensed in the almanac and pharmacy in the herbal.[41] The metaphor and allusion of Maria's speech closely follow just these subjects. She refers to the "fiend,"[42] and calls Malvolio a "Heathen" and "a verie Renegatho":[43] religion has at least taught her some terms of opprobrium. From housewifery she draws the allusion to the "brissle" of a brush;[44] and she speaks of the "points,"[45] or laces, by which Elizabethans fastened their clothes.[46] She is countrified enough to refer to a horse,[47] and ass,[48] and a "Trowt."[49] In medicine, she shows the commonplace knowledge of the humors.[50] Despite such works as *The Academy of Compliments*, which aimed to teach courtly language to "wait-

<hr/>

[36] *Twelfth Night*, II. iii. 131.   [37] *Ibid.*, I. v. 5 *et seq.*

[38] Davis, *op. cit.*, p. 92; *Cyuile and Vncyuile Life*, in *Inedited Tracts*, ed. *cit.*, p. 66; and Sir T. Overbury, *The Wife*.

[39] H. Peacham, *Compleat Gentleman* (London, 1622), pp. 31 *et seq.*

[40] L. B. Wright, *Middle-Class Culture in Elizabethan England* (Chapel Hill, 1935), pp. 103 *et seq.*

[41] *Ibid.*, pp. 108–9.   [42] *Twelfth Night*, III. iv 95.

[43] *Ibid.*, III. ii. 70.   [44] *Ibid.*, I. v. 4.   [45] *Ibid.*, I. v. 24–25.

[46] M. C. Linthicum, *Costume in Shakespeare* (Oxford, 1936), pp. 209 n. and 282.

[47] *Twelfth Night*, II. iii. 162.   [48] *Ibid.*, II. iii. 123 and 164.

[49] *Ibid.*, II. v. 23.   [50] *Ibid.*, I. iii. 67 *et seq.*; II. iii. 166.

ing Gentlewomen," her speech is generally simple and straight-forward, and her wit dry and homely, a sharp foil to Sir Toby's Castilian graces, and good enough to put down Sir Andrew and match even Feste. This leaves only two nautical references, to "hoyst sayle"[51] and to "the newe Mappe, with the augmentation of the Indies,"[52] the latter of which she may have caught from Sir Toby's geographical predilections.

Miss Spurgeon, in a late, illuminating study, has taken Shakespeare's imagery as a reflection of his interests, experiences, and subconscious mind; but the present writer finds that this material, as it should in the greatest drama, reflects rather the interests and background of the characters in his plays— and so is it with Maria. In short, she shows the intellectual limitations of her sex, her social status, and her phlegmatic humor. Her feet are so much on the ground that her head does not reach up into the rarefied atmosphere beyond every-day experience and ideas. The scattered hints that Shakespeare gives of her physique and character and age, of her ancestry and livelihood and education, are at once consistent with her social group and highly individualized. The Elizabethans would have recognized her at once, not only as a mere general type, but as a characteristic living individual that belonged to it. These hints, which become significant to us only by research, were obvious to them, and fitted into a well-known social and psychological scheme. Great drama, however, requires more than this. It is not a static art like sculpture or painting; and time and event should turn toward the beholder various facets of the character depicted—if not actually impress their changes upon it. The portrayal of a personality by the expository method in a psychological novel constitutes perhaps the easiest and least artistic means, for it is the least vivid and the farthest removed from living actuality. Description in the concrete of the "character" is more vivid and telling, but it can hardly show action and change. The fullest and liveliest but most difficult method of portraying the human individual is that of drama in which the word and deed of a man and his

[51] *Twelfth Night*, I. v. 202.   [52] *Ibid.*, III. ii. 79–80.

reply and reaction to the word and deed of others express his inner self, quite as in real life we show ourselves by what we say and do in given circumstances. A good play, in short, shows us the puppets dallying; and the following paragraphs will therefore discuss Maria in her relations with Malvolio, with Fabyan and Feste, with Sir Andrew, with Olivia, and finally with Sir Toby—the six persons who most concern her.

The organization of a great household could not but breed a certain rivalry, if not professional jealousy, among the servants and retainers. Maria, having unexpectedly risen from the comparative obscurity of lady's maid of a daughter of the house to the commanding position of factotum to its titled mistress— Maria would be a shining mark for ill feeling and jealousy. In her former status, only a few months before, she must have occupied a place less important than that of Malvolio, and doubtless it was then that she had flattered him with the thought that Olivia "did affect" him.[53] She had dealt with Malvolio, and knew him of yore as an "affection'd Asse."[54] Then she had played upon his foibles from necessity; now she could afford to do so for amusement and revenge. Malvolio, not too keen of comprehension, is somewhat slow to realize this turn in Fortune's wheel; and, when Maria displeases him, he takes, from mere force of habit, his accustomed high-and-mighty tone, threatens to bring her into her mistress' disfavor,[55] and under provocation even calls her "Minx."[56] As a lady born, she naturally resents such impudence from one of base degree; and, partly for this reason, partly to please Sir Toby, and partly to indulge her own "sportfull malice,"[57] she sets in motion the plot against the overweening steward. Having accused him of being "a kinde of Puritane,"[58] she ironically urges him to pray to cure his supposed lunacy;[59] and, to assist the deviltry, she brings in Feste disguised as the local curate. She has no sympathy for Malvolio, and callously remarks that if he were truly mad, "The house will be the quieter."[60] Mal-

[53] *Twelfth Night*, II. v. 25-26.   [54] *Ibid.*, II. iii. 143.
[55] *Ibid.*, II. iii. 119 *et seq.*   [56] *Ibid.*, III. iv. 123.
[57] *Ibid.*, III. ii. 68 *et seq.*; V. i. 385.   [58] *Ibid.*, II. iii. 136.
[59] *Ibid.*, III. iv. 121 *et seq.*   [60] *Ibid.*, III. iv. 137.

77

volio, moreover, has tried to drive Sir Toby from his convenient shelter—convenient for Maria's designs as well as his own comfort—and anyone who comes between a woman and the man she hopes to wed can hardly expect quarter.

With Fabyan and Feste, who have also felt Malvolio's displeasure, Maria is drawn into alliance. Fabyan, as a gentleman in waiting, is her social equal and natural ally against interlopers; and Feste, she undertakes to shield from her noble lady's displeasure on account of his running away.[61] Perhaps she liked him merely for his merry self; or perhaps, when the old Count was alive, he had done her similar good turns. The tone of her proffered help is perhaps a trifle patronizing, and she repeatedly demands, though he is loath to say, where he has been. He makes light of her good offices and gets along without them, and later even twits her on her matrimonial designs.[62] But despite these early discords, the two join in the face of the common enemy, Malvolio, and "gull him into an 'ayward."

Sir Andrew, though also an arch-conspirator against the hapless steward, has more distant relations with Maria. He was a newcomer in the household; he is obviously a fool, and he makes the signal error, at Sir Toby's jocose behest, of attempting to make love to her. Even he is hesitant to woo the lady "in this company." She in return snubs his unwilling and unwelcome courtship; but Sir Toby still holds her to the parley, in huge enjoyment of his practical joke. Perhaps this is Sir Toby's answer, for the moment, to her designs against his own bachelordom. What can one do with a swain who deliberately invites you to flirt with someone else? Maria's decency is outraged: she insults Sir Andrew—though he is too dull to know it—and quits the room. Thus Shakespeare turns the old stage convention of the foolish courtship[63] to his own account in the play; it is only a minor idyll in the plot, but it serves to show the characters of the two knights and the lady, and to illustrate the relations of the three to one another. Sir Andrew

---

[61] *Twelfth Night*, I. v. 3 *passim*.
[62] *Ibid.*, I. v. 26 *et seq.*   [63] Forsythe, *op. cit.*, pp. 106–7.

78

cannot be proposing serious marriage, for not only is he too much of a fool to know what he is saying, but also his avowed purpose in the house is to seek the hand of the Countess. He is using her simply to get practice in the *ars amandi*; and she fears that even an innocent flirtation would spoil her chances with Sir Toby—and, besides, Sir Andrew is not personally attractive. Thus her reputation is armor-proof even against three thousand ducats a year. Later in the play, she and Sir Andrew appear together in several scenes, but she vouchsafes hardly a word to him;[64] and, though in a later scene he echoes Sir Toby's addresses to her, he has not the temerity to "accost" her formally again. She clearly holds him in contempt and does not intend that Sir Toby shall have any cause to doubt her rejection of such a foolish suit.

In the cases of Nerissa and Portia and of Emilia and Desdemona, intimate scenes between maid and mistress rather clearly show their close personal relations; but, perhaps because contemporary custom sufficiently implied this intimacy, Shakespeare shows Maria and the Countess in private dialogue for less than a mere half-dozen lines in the last scene of Act III. Earlier in the play, however, their confidential relationship cannot be doubted: otherwise Maria would hardly have offered her intercession to Feste; she seems, moreover, to know her mistress' mind anent Sir Toby and Sir Andrew and later Viola;[65] the Countess apparently entrusted her with turning away Orsino's messengers; and Olivia's vow of seclusion would indeed leave Maria the chief connection between the mistress of the house and the outside world. Maria then was in a most strategic place, and she made the most of it. Three times she risks her lady's displeasure, and three times the moderate good fortune of her phlegmatic type stands her in good stead: against her mistress' wishes and Malvolio's threats, she supplies the means of revelry in that house of mourning; she forges a letter in Olivia's hand to deceive Malvolio; and, without apparent leave or notice, she weds her mistress' uncle—a nuptial that

[64] Even their mutual dislike of Malvolio brings them together only for an instant (*Twelfth Night*, II. iii. 165 *et seq.*).

[65] *Twelfth Night*, III. iv. 3 *et seq.*

79

certainly should have had the consent, if not the benison, of Olivia as head of the house. All three of these risks were incident to the getting of a husband, and they were great risks to be justified only by so great a cause. Great as they were, however, Olivia never remonstrates. Perhaps Malvolio was kept too busy to lodge his threatened complaints, and the Countess was clearly too much taken up with her own amorous affairs to give attention to her maid's. At all events, the two appear to live in an unbroken, if fragile, harmony; and Olivia learns of her uncle's marriage without a qualm. Perhaps she was glad to shift to Maria's shoulders the thankless task of keeping him in order.

In short, despite her break with Malvolio, Mistress Mary's position in the household seems fairly happy and, for the moment at least, secure; and yet she seeks to change it, for, even if secure, it holds no future. Indeed, she could not dally, for life in those hard-living times had only a "brief springtime."[66] In the Middle Ages women had had two respectable careers, in holy wedlock or in a convent—as the bride of an earthly husband or as the bride of Christ. In the 1530's, the suppression of the monasteries reduced these careers to one. A girl's father was supposed to arrange her marriage[67] and to provide the all-important dowry, but if he were dead as was Olivia's, or in no position to provide a dowry as Maria's apparently was, the lady stood in the parlous case of imminent spinsterhood, a status mean and unregarded.[68] Maria, indeed, without a husband in the offing, was well beyond twelve or fourteen, the usual age of betrothal,[69] and her charms would shortly waste on the desert air unless her native wit could supply her fiscal want. Without parental aid, her wooing must run the unmaidenly risk[70] of general ridicule and opprobrium, and so was limited to a narrow circle. In England, however, such a course

[66] E. Godfrey, *Home Life under the Stuarts* (London, 1903), p. 113.

[67] R. de Maulde la Clavière, *Women of the Renaissance* (New York, 1900), p. 25.

[68] *Ibid.*, p. 37; and T. Master, quoted in Wilkinson, *Conjugal Duty*, Part I (London, 1732), p. 107.

[69] Godfrey, *op. cit.*, p. 128 *et passim*; and A. Niccholes, *Discourse of Marriage* (London, 1615), p. 11.

[70] R. Brathwait, *English Gentlewoman* (London, 1631), p. 41.

was more feasible than on the Continent, for women had much greater freedom.[71] But Elizabethan eligible males, being used to the gay bachelordom that the double standard of ethics encouraged, were generally mercenary in marriage;[72] and indeed the economic pressure of the age, especially on the upper classes, obliged them to be so. Only a very idealistic and very affluent Prince Charming who was very much in love could afford to cast sheep's eyes in honorable fashion at such as Maria—or else a man who, like Sir Toby, had little to lose, serious personal liabilities, and substantial personal reasons for the match.

The marital possibilities of Olivia's household were clearly limited: Feste, even if he were not already married, would be a social falling off for a waiting lady; Fabyan, though of Maria's station, was presumably as penniless as other servingmen; Sir Andrew was intent on having a title for his money, and moreover he was personally unattractive. There remained only the bibulous Sir Toby, who for all his gaucherie was gently born, and for all the shifts to which life had reduced him, was closely enough related to the Countess to have a place, if not exactly a welcome, in her house. With something of a flourish, he had come in from the great outside world, which Maria hardly knew. His fine allusions to Tartary and Persia, together with thoughts of new discoveries in the Indies would of course fire a maid whose common daily pabulum was all too much of brooms and brushes and clothes and horses and fish. He had the aplomb, if not the reality, of traveled worldly wisdom; moreover, he represented knighthood, if not quite knight-errantry; and, above all, he constituted the bona fide potentiality of a flesh-and-blood husband. No less than five of Queen Elizabeth's maids of honor—all supposedly sworn to imitate their mistress' virginity—carried on clandestine love affairs, some of which imprudently ended at the altar;[73] and Maria, in like fashion, did not propose to emulate the shining virtue of a mis-

---

[71] W. Harrison, *op. cit.*, p. 247; Rathgeb's *Faithful Narrative*, in W. B. Rye, *England as Seen by Foreigners* (London, 1865), p. 7; and *Everie Woman in Her Humor* (London, 1609), sig. B 3 v.

[72] C. J. Sisson, *Lost Plays* (Cambridge, 1936), pp. 14 *et seq.*

[73] V. A. Wilson, *Queen Elizabeth's Maids of Honor* (London, 1922), pp. 16 *et seq.*

tress pledged to single blessedness. Luckily for her, mistress and maid simultaneously married. Queens and Countesses could afford to dangle their charms indefinitely before an admiring world; but a girl over twenty without a dowry needed the social éclat, if not the practical protection, of a husband, at least some sort of husband. Sir Toby was Maria's only chance, and Maria made the most of him.

At first, Sir Toby and Maria, like Benedick and Beatrice, are somewhat at cross-purposes. Though she supplies the liquid means that make his revels possible, she fears that his drunken "catterwalling" and "ill houres" will move the Countess to turn him out of the house[74] and so end her chance to catch him; and, furthermore, she would doubtless prefer a not-too-drunken husband.[75] The presence of Sir Andrew is useless, if not a positive danger, for Olivia will certainly not marry him, and meanwhile he only encourages Sir Toby's objectionable vices. In the first scene, Maria plainly tells all this to Sir Toby; but why should he listen to a mere "wench," his niece's "Chambermaid"?[76] He takes his jocular revenge for these unwelcome comments by egging on Sir Andrew to "assail" Maria as a suitor; and later Maria, in turn, has her revenge on him by informing Olivia of Cesario's presence at the gate when Sir Toby, by assuming drunkenness, holds him "in delay."[77] Thus Maria intentionally contributes to the failure of Sir Andrew's suit, and unintentionally to the falling in love and the final marriage of Olivia.

The mutual danger from Malvolio, however, soon brings Maria and Sir Toby close together. The steward upbraids her for giving "meanes for this vnciuill rule";[78] she tells him to go shake his ears, and proposes the plot that so delights Sir Toby and ultimately wins his hand. He had earlier called her "wench" and "Chamber-maid"; now she becomes "a beagle true bred, and one that adores me";[79] she is "Excellent Wench"[80] and "my noble gull catcher,"[81] a "most excellent

[74] *Twelfth Night*, II. iii. 16 and 74 *et seq.*   [75] *Ibid.*, I. iii. 6–11; I. v. 26–28.
[76] *Ibid.*, I. iii. 42 and 51.
[77] *Ibid.*, I. v. 97 *et seq.*   [78] *Ibid.*, II. iii. 118 *et seq.*
[79] *Ibid.*, II. iii. 173–74.   [80] *Ibid.*, II. v. 105.   [81] *Ibid.*, II. v. 176.

diuell of wit"[82] and this "youngest Wren of mine."[83] The repeated possessive pronoun is significant, for Sir Toby has meanwhile plighted a sort of informal troth with the blushing
maiden; indeed, he will even "aske no dowry with her, but
such another iest."[84] This second jest is apparently the gulling of Malvolio in the duel, which Maria assists by telling
when and where Cesario can be encountered. She is shrewd
enough, however, not to play too obvious a part in this fiasco.
She has nothing against Cesario; she may suspect Olivia's feelings toward him, and she well knows that gulling her mistress'
lover—perhaps to his bodily harm—is far more dangerous than
gulling her mistress' steward. Perhaps it is not by chance that
she is so much engaged with tormenting Malvolio that she is
not present at the duel. As things transpire, Sir Toby is doubtless glad that she does not see Sebastian turn the joke against
him and give him a broken head: his knightly glamour on that
occasion did not shine too brightly. In Act V she drops out of
the play, but Fabyan reports that Sir Toby has duly wedded
her "in recompence" for the practical joke against Malvolio.[85]
Thus Maria's arts accomplish their design. According to Overbury, a clever servingman might, with some impudence and
luck, win the heart and hand of his master's daughter; but
Maria, with all the handicaps of womanhood, wins her mistress' uncle and the courtesy title of "Lady" into the bargain;
and so she becomes one of the family and "entails" her posterity on Olivia "for ever."[86] The "lesser fortune" of her
astral type and also her own shrewd foresight have exalted her
estate by swift degrees: from serving-woman to a daughter of
the house, she has risen to be factotum to a great lady and at
last the wife of a knight who is uncle to a countess. She doubtless remains Olivia's personal attendant, but now she is also
a close relative.

Maria is clearly the phlegmatic type under the influence of
Venus; and love (or better marriage) is her major motive,
and brings her the "lesser fortune" that her planet promised

---

[82] *Ibid.*, II. v. 194–95.   [83] *Ibid.*, III. ii. 67.
[84] *Ibid.*, II. v. 172–73.
[85] *Ibid.*, V. i. 384.   [86] Overbury, *op. cit.*, "Serving-man."

her at birth. Her phlegmatic humor, like Sir Toby's, gives her no high ideals and aspirations: like him, she labors only to entrench herself in the solid satisfactions of life—and Sir Toby was very solid, if not always quite a satisfaction. The way she wins him implies that she is cleverer than he, and doubtless she will subtly rule him to their mutual benefit. Her gentle status and her position in Olivia's household were quite compatible in that day, and her relations with her domestic colleagues are quite what one might expect. Of course she resents Malvolio's domineering, and of course joins with the other gentles in putting him down; of course she would angle for Sir Toby, and probably catch him. In both these things she would of course take the unavoidable risk of offending Olivia, and she is clever enough and lucky enough to evade all dire consequences. She rides out the teapot tempest of household transition and intrigue, and finally takes the precious prizes of a husband and a title of respect. Her Shakespearean ancestor is not the outrageous Quickly, but the sprightly Nerissa, who is likewise a lady and likewise gains a proper husband, though with less ado; but beside Maria, Nerissa is a pale figure, with little clarity of motive or device. Shakespeare, indeed, when he conceived *Twelfth Night*, knew much more about the ordering of noble households, and about the men and women who composed them, than when he wrote *The Merchant of Venice*; and this greater knowledge shows in the lifelike realism and sharp individuality of Maria. Her inner psychology and her outward social status deviously or directly permeate her every motive, speech, and action.

Though not a dominating figure in the play, Maria supplies at once motive to the plot and contrast to the other characters. Her impish desire to annoy Sir Toby makes her, in spite of him, announce Cesario and so initiate Olivia's love affair; her desire to win Sir Toby and to suppress Malvolio makes her concoct the plot against the steward and connive at Sir Andrew's duel. Thus Maria's plans and purposes, intentionally or otherwise, more or less lie behind the three main episodes of the plot. Her value as contrast is manifest chiefly in character: as a phlegmatic type, she is a foil both to Sir Andrew and to Sir Toby whom she resembles in humor although not in sex or situation; and Maria, seeking a husband, nicely offsets Olivia, trying to avoid them; and, when Olivia is smitten, the downright way she leads her lover to the altar contrasts with Maria's less direct but quite as efficient methods. Thus, as Mistress Mary, with seeming inconsequence, flits from one jest to another, like the hummingbird from flower to flower, she is, willfully or inadvertently, setting the plot in motion and acting as a foil to the characters about her. In fact, she largely gives the play that adequacy of motivation that raises it from low farce to high comedy. She is at once closely knit into the texture of the piece and so true to her psychological type and to her walk of life, so "framed to the life" that she might indeed "serve for the most common [of] commentaries" on the age.

ᐁMalvolio

AUGUSTINE PHILLIPS had apparently created the roles of Cassius in *Julius Caesar*, Don John in *Much Ado*, and the Duke Frederick in *As You Like It*. He was presumably a master of dignified and saturnine though not always sympathetic parts, and the farewell climax to his Shakespearean career was apparently Malvolio.[1] This has often been the star role of the play, and sometimes has even supplied the title to the comedy.[2] At the performance in 1602, Manningham especially enjoyed it. Bishop King refers to Malvolio as the "sharp, cross-gartered man Whom their [the audience's] loud laugh might nick-name Puritan."[3] Charles I wrote "Malvolio," as if it were the title of the play, on his copy of the second folio in Windsor Castle; and, in 1640, Digges testified to the continued success of the part. Not only does Malvolio supply a highlight of satire to the comedy, but he is also a main figure in the plot: he is one of Olivia's lovers, and he is the gull of Maria, Sir Toby, and Feste. He owes nothing to Shakespeare's sources, and shows little resemblance to any stock character of the stage. His closest Shakespearean forebear is Launcelot Gobbo,[4] who is also an aspiring menial. In short, Malvolio is another consummate addition of Shakespeare to his source, an addition drawn mainly, as were Sir Andrew and Sir Toby and Maria, from Elizabethan life.

The "fantastical Steward"[5] has not lacked the *obiter dicta* of critics. His yellow stockings and the question of his Puritanism have caused some debate; but the main subject of discussion

---

[1] T. W. Baldwin, *The Shakespearean Company* (Princeton, N.J., 1927), Plates II and III.

[2] J. Q. Adams, *Life of Shakespeare* (Boston, 1925), p. 292.

[3] Henry King, *English Poems* (New Haven, 1911), p. 28.

[4] J. W. Draper, "Shakespeare's Rustic Servants," *Shakespeare Jahrbuch*, LXIX, 87 *et seq.*

[5] *Twelfth Night* (ed. Rowe), *Dramatis Personae*.

has been whether or not he deserves the practical jokes that he endures. The older and more usual view seems to be that Malvolio merits his fate. Manningham, who saw the play in 1602 (N.S.), thought the Malvolio plot a "good practise." Dr. Johnson (1765) declared the Steward's soliloquy "truly comick," and felt that pride justified his fall. Hunter (1845), likewise blamed his "proud and tyrannical heart"; Montégut called him "crotchety." Giles imputed his folly to love and "masculine vanity"; but is Malvolio really in love? Ruggles blames his "inordinate vanity"; Furnivall calls him the "self-conceited"; Conrad, the "narrow and prosaic Malvolio"; and Winter says that he is "the image of overweening self-love, of opinionated self-conceit, of narrow-minded, strutting, consequential complacency." The Tudor editors, like Dr. Johnson, consider him "essentially ridiculous." This group of critics does not find in him any violation of poetic justice.

The Romantic point of view, in literary criticism as in life, tended to emphasize all human beings as particularly good or bad: thus it made Iago an inhuman monster[6] and Falstaff, because of his seductive wit, a man of principle, sincere in purpose and truly good at heart.[7] Its democratic bias ruined King Claudius,[8] but turned a sympathetic ear to the vaulting ambitions of Malvolio. Thus, his character became stuff of serious drama rather than of satiric comedy of manners. Charles Lamb and the actor Bensley seem to have set this style. Of course, it throws the part quite out of focus, spoils our enjoyment of Maria's stratagem, precludes poetic justice in the play; and, while it leaves in comic vein the plots of Olivia's marriage and Maria's, it makes the gulling of Malvolio an unresolved tragedy. Kenny (1864), for example, though he admits that "Many people" take Malvolio's misadventures as the "most vigorous and amusing episode" in the piece, nevertheless believes the Steward's punishment "somewhat coarse and excessive," and can see no reason in his conduct to deserve it. Canon Ainger imputes this change in the interpretation of the role to the fact

[6] J. W. Draper, " 'Honest Iago,' " *P.M.L.A.*, XLVI, 724 *et seq.*

[7] *Idem*, "Sir John Falstaff," *R.E.S.*, VIII, 414 *et seq.*

[8] *Idem*, *The "Hamlet" of Shakespeare's Audience* (Durham, N.C., 1938), chapter ix.

that great tragic actors took the part and gave it "a sombre element . . . . to set off the comic interest."

This basic disagreement, somewhat entangled with the less basic questions of Malvolio's Puritanism and of the exact significance of his strange apparel, has produced in some interpreters an uncertainty that creates doubt concerning the motivation and the structural integrity of the play. Sir Henry Irving, if two spectators are both to be trusted, quite changed within ten years his conception of the role from the Romantic dignified Malvolio to a "crafty old fox" whose ridiculous "disdain" received condign punishment.[9] William Archer declared Malvolio "one of the most puzzling of Shakespeare's creations": his misfortunes do not spring from the "spiritual pride" of the Puritan, and he had not "the smallest trace of the zealot"; he is merely a faithful steward trying to put down "ribaldry" in the hall of his mourning mistress—and yet we are intended to laugh at him. Archer finds "vagueness" in Shakespeare's delineation, but hazards the guess that Malvolio is perhaps a "Philistine," and his "radical defect" is "a lack of . . . . sense of humor." More recently, Professor Craig suggests that the theory of humors supplies the key to Malvolio's character, but he attempts no analysis.[10] Mr. Priestley declares that Shakespeare clearly disliked Malvolio, but that modern readers find "pathos" in the part;[11] yet he offers no explanation of this change of attitude between Elizabethan times and ours. The Arden editors state that Malvolio "criticism has become somewhat confused": the high opinion of Olivia and Orsino shows that he "is not merely a solemn prig," he is "conscientious and trustworthy" but "marred by an overweening vanity and a complete lack of humor." His Puritanism is not "theological." (What was Puritanism in that age if not theological?) "He is an example not of its vices but of its follies, a person to be looked upon not with scorn or hate, but with amusement tempered with respect, and even with pity." He has "vanity" but also "underlying worth." Malvolio, in short, is foolish and therefore to be

[9] *Twelfth Night* (ed. Furness var.), pp. 400 and 402.

[10] Hardin Craig, *Shakespeare* (New York, 1931), pp. 309–10.

[11] J. B. Priestley, *English Comic Characters* (London, 1925), pp. 45–46.

88

laughed at, and yet is capable and loyal in his place and therefore to be respected. But this statement does not explain why Shakespeare did the former almost to the exclusion of the latter, whereas the last hundred years have tended to reverse the emphasis. Shakespeare's audience must have shared the playwright's attitude if the play was to succeed—as indeed it did—and, therefore, the explanation should probably be sought in the special social attitudes and social conditions of the Elizabethan age toward men of Malvolio's type.

Puritans attacked the theater, and thus playwrights and playgoers disliked Puritans with obvious good reason. Some scholars would call Malvolio a Puritan and so explain Shakespeare's unsympathetic attitude; but the charge of Puritanism is only the casual fling of a detractor, and calling bad names is rarely done with nicety, and a moment later the term is half-recalled.[12] Malvolio's reiterated belief in his "Fortunes" and his "starres" and like astrological phenomena belies his Puritanism; moreover, he indulges in mild oaths,[13] and he quotes a despised ballad, "Please one, please all." Sir Toby, to be sure, sneers at him as "vertuous,"[14] but his fundamental motive is not godly zeal but a longing for the gauds and vanities of this world. Though "sad and civil," he had, even before the forged letter had urged it, disported himself in cross-garters and yellow stockings. In the fullness of time, moreover, he hoped to recline on a "day-bedde" and toy with "some rich jewell."[15] But the wrath of Sir Toby and the "lighter people" is chiefly aroused, not against his imputed religion or even his sedate demeanor, but against his outrageous ambition to become the husband of a Countess, a most un-Puritanical ambition. Malvolio, furthermore, does not quote Scripture nor moralize at length, even as much as Polonius; he has little in common with Overbury's "Puritan" or with Ben Jonson's Ananias or Tribulation, and his sedate sobriety seems to be merely that of a modern English butler translated to an earlier incarnation. In

---

[12] *Twelfth Night*, II. iii. 136 *et seq.* Puritans and servingmen were not friendly. See W. Basse, *Sword and Buckler* (London, 1602), stanza 45.

[13] *Twelfth Night*, II. iii. 121–22; V. i. 308.

[14] *Ibid.*, II. iii. 113.   [15] *Ibid.*, II. v. 49 *et seq.*

short, he is no Puritan; and, if he were one, the fact does not influence his motives, words, or actions in the play.

Not Malvolio's religion but his social status would seem to hold the key to this change in attitude toward him in the last century; and indeed his position in the household of the Countess reflects a change in the Elizabethan serving classes that was causing both hardship and bitterness: there were too many servants, and not enough wherewithal to feed and clothe them. In the turbulent Middle Ages, when one's house had been perforce a castle, armed retainers on whose loyalty one could rely were well worth their board and keep;[16] and, quite in the tradition of Beowulf's thanes, they feasted in the hall,[17] brawled indoors and out, and scorned all servile duties and the villeins who performed them.[18] With such fine fellows, it was a word and a blow, and the word was commonly an oath.[19] Some were "prowde and euill natured,"[20] and yet were tolerated because they were good fighters or because their fathers were important vassals. As Scott depicts in *Ivanhoe*, humble wayfarers and travelers of note, with less right than Sir Toby and Sir Andrew, were entertained with their retainers;[21] and, over this boisterous crew, drinking and roistering in the hall, ruled the lord of the manor. By degrees, however, the feudal suzerain and his family withdrew to the greater privacy of a soler or a parlor,[22] a sunroom or a conversation place; and a steward, such as Malvolio, would be the logical intermediary between the master of the house and the habitués of the hall.

After the reign of Henry VII, furthermore, the end of private warfare began to bring the nobles by degrees out of their castles into the more convenient but narrower confines of the Tudor house. They no longer required a host of men-at-arms, and had neither room nor money to maintain them.

[16] Basse, *op. cit.*, stanza 14.

[17] G. Markham, *Health to the Gentlemanly Profession of Servingmen* (*ed. princ.*, 1598), in *Inedited Tracts* (ed. Hazlitt, Roxburghe Library), (London, 1868), p. 116.

[18] *Ibid.*, pp. 104 *et seq.*; *Cyuile and Vncyuile Life* (*ed. princ.*, 1579), in *Inedited Tracts*, p. 39; W. Harrison, *Description of England* (London, 1587), Vol. II, chapter v.

[19] T. Becon, *Early Works* (ed. Parker Society), (Cambridge, 1843), p. 361.

[20] *Cyuile and Vncyuile Life*, ed. cit., p. 40.   [21] *Ibid.*, pp. 64 and 92.

[22] J. W. Draper, "Chaucer's 'Wardrobe,'" *Englische Studien*, LX, 238 *et seq.*

Servants perforce became more purely useful,[23] and, especially in town houses, entertainment of strangers gradually ceased to be the rule. The wellborn servingmen were fewer,[24] were more gorgeously attired for display,[25] and in time evolved into the footman of the eighteenth century. The real work of the house was done by "subservingmen," bakers, brewers, "chamberlaines," and the like.[26] The astute Lord Burghley, who realized these changes, advised his son to keep few servants and give them not only board and lodging but also wages regularly paid.[27] Thus the household was evolving from a feudal to a modern economic basis. A stable government provided security for the lord, and the purpose of the household organization became more and more, not mere safety, but his comfort and convenience. Thus, waiting on great men was no longer a matter of doughty deeds, but rather of amusing his leisure or of "slavish" tasks. Servingmen complained, and many were cast off to wander the roads and steal and be hanged, or to live disreputably by their wits.[28] This "incertaintie of service"[29] brought economic insecurity to the entire class[30] and commonly an old age of penury,[31] like Adam's in *As You Like It*. Many a servingman had, in effect, fallen to the status of "a menial servant," to be dismissed offhand by "parol" according to the law of 21 Henry VI, 23;[32] and, because of this, many cheated their masters, as Lord Bacon's steward did, or fell to mean shifts to hold their places.[33] The flood of gold from America,

---

[23] Basse, *op. cit.*, stanzas 56 *et seq.*, stresses the hard work of valet, etc.

[24] *Cyuile and Vncyuile Life*, ed. cit., p. 80; F. Moryson, *Itinerary* (1617), Pt. III, pp. 113–14.

[25] Basse, *op. cit.*, stanzas 19, 27, 31, 44 *et seq.* The standing of servingmen and pages was evidently growing worse. In London, armed retainers were hardly permitted because it was within the 'verge." See W. Darell, *Short Discourse* (ed. Wright), (1578), *Studies in Philology*, XXXI, 115 *et seq.*; Markham, *op. cit.*, p. 123; and [John Fit John], *A Diamond Most Precious* (London, 1577), sig. B ii. Cf. Gobbo's livery in Shakespeare's *Merchant of Venice*, II. ii. 149.

[26] *Cyuile and Vncyuile Life*, ed. cit., p. 39.

[27] *Advice to a Son*, att. to Burghley, reprinted in *The Parental Monitor* (London, 1792), p. 146. [28] Markham, *op. cit.*, p. 142.

[29] [H. Peacham], *Coach and Sedan* (London, 1636), sig. C 3.

[30] *Cyuile and Vncyuile Life*, ed. cit., pp. 91–92.

[31] R. Brathwait, *English Gentleman* (London, 1641), p. 89; Fit John, *op. cit.*, sig. B ii. [32] M. Bacon, *New Abridgment* (Philadelphia, 1811), IV, 557.

[33] Markham, *op. cit.*, pp. 144–46; *Othello*, I. i. 42 *et seq.*

moreover, increased the cost of living[34] and brought hard times to landed families with fixed incomes, while the increasing centralization of all power and opportunity in the royal entourage obliged many of these rural gentry to dismiss their "tall fellowes," rent their "demeanes," and come to London to curry favor at court and to perfect their sons in gentlemanly arts.[35] Here they supplanted their servingmen with a fashionable coach to carry them about in proper dignity.[36] Indeed, the cost of but one yearly visit to the court brought more than one county family to ruin. Shakespeare's *Timon* reflects the fall of a great house through its continued practice of traditional liberality to all comers;[37] and the dismissal of Lear's attendant knights, which Shakespeare invests with such tragic consequence, must have aroused in the audience a sense of sympathetic outrage. Thus, Elizabethans of the serving class, being employed more and more for work rather than for prowess, were losing their hereditary status.[38] Shakespeare would seem to have transferred to Illyria an English household in this transition, with a licensed jester, gently born retainers, dependent relatives, and uninvited guests as in the Middle Ages, and also a Renaissance staff of actual servants headed by the competent and all-too-hopeful Malvolio.

The two knights, Maria, and Fabyan, were gentles all; but, within this charmed circle, Malvolio did not belong. Feste, to be sure, once ironically calls him "M[aster] Malvolio";[39] and once Olivia pityingly terms him a "poore Gentleman,"[40] though she elsewhere calls him a "servant";[41] and he is quite willing to allude to himself as a "Gentleman,"[42] and to reprimand Viola as an equal.[43] On the other hand, he is "a steward . . . . the fellow of servants."[44] Sir Toby and Maria from

<hr/>

34 Markham, *op. cit.*, p. 152.

35 *Cyuile and Vncyuile Life*, ed. cit., pp. 34–35, 62–63.

36 Peacham, *op. cit.*; and Markham, *op. cit.*, p. 151.

37 J. W. Draper, "The Theme of *Timon of Athens*," *M.L.R.*, XXIX, 20 *et seq.*

38 H. W. Farnam, *Shakespeare's Economics* (New Haven, 1931), p. 123.

39 *Twelfth Night*, IV. ii. 86.   40 *Ibid.*, V. i. 296.

41 *Ibid.*, III. iv. 7.   42 *Ibid.*, IV. ii. 84.

43 *Ibid.*, II. ii. *passim*. She once terms him "Gentleman"; *ibid.*, V. i. 293.

44 *Ibid.*, II. v. 146–47.

their social superiority sneer at his "ridiculous boldness,"[45] and address him by the *thou* of condescension, whereas he calls the two knights "My masters."[46] Surely, he is on a higher plane than Saltonstall's "chamberlaine" of an inn;[47] but his origins can hardly have been better than the yeoman who married the "Lady of the Strachy" and to whom he compares himself.[48] Indeed, except for his ambitions, Malvolio is the perfect English servant, always ready at his mistress' call, with "Madam, I will," and "Heere, madam, at your seruice";[49] and, even in his bitter protests at the end, he does not quite forget his courtesy. Olivia values his dutiful attendance, but after all he is only a steward to be referred to as "this fellow."[50]

Malvolio's humble place, in comic contrast to his exalted aspirations, appears best symbolized by the references to costume in the play. The dress of the Elizabethan fine gentleman was variable and conglomerate.[51] Such is Portia's English suitor and Rowlands' "Signieur Fantastike."[52] The lower orders, however, still bound by custom, if not by sumptuary laws, were generally garbed according to their class: the servants at least of more conservative houses in blue coats,[53] and others in accordance with their trades.[54] The servant, however, of a forward-looking gentleman such as Bassanio might hope to be "lapt in Lyverie,"[55] and was envied for his fine clothes.[56] About 1600, Malvolio's yellow stockings and cross-garters seem to have had a plebeian connotation;[57] and thus he aspires to court the Countess in clothes that imply his humble origins. Maria compares his costume to that of a poor country pedagogue;[58] Porter's *Two angry Women* (1599) took cross-

---

[45] *Ibid.*, III. iv. 40–41. [46] *Ibid.*, II. iii. 88.

[47] W. Saltonstall, *Picturæ Loquentes* (London, 1631), sig E 3 v.

[48] *Twelfth Night*, II. v. 40–41. [49] *Ibid.*, I. v. 302 and 310.

[50] *Ibid.*, III. iv. 65–67. [51] W. Harrison, *op. cit.*, Bk. II, chapter v.

[52] S. Rowlands, *Letting of Humours Blood*, *Publications of the Hunterian Club*, XX, Epig. 13.

[53] Brathwait, *op. cit.*, p. 89; Rowlands, *Doctor Merry-man* (1609), *Publ. Hunt. Cl.*, p. 22, and *Knave of Clubs*, *Publ. Hunt. Cl.*, p. 7.

[54] *Julius Caesar*, I. i. *passim*. [55] Markham, *op. cit.*, p. 136.

[56] Basse, *op. cit.*, stanzas 46–47.

[57] Most of the evidence cited by Furness is of too distant a date to have much bearing.

[58] *Twelfth Night*, III. ii. 75–76. Such a costume suggested low class rather than Puritanism (Wright cited in variorum edition, p. 174).

garters as the sign of a servingman;[59] and Overbury associated them with a "gentleman-usher," whom he apparently classed below a footman.[60] Yellow stockings seem to have been the sign manual of a boorish country yeoman.[61] Malvolio then, in the very act of his social apotheosis, is gulled into donning the habiliments, partly of the humble yeomanry whence he seems to have sprung, and partly of the household servitor, the very class from which he is trying to escape. This is an irony even finer than Ben Jonson's treatment of the incongruous coat of arms with which Sogliardo, like Malvolio, attempts to gain gentility.[62] Indeed, the coverings of Malvolio's legs are the very nadir of impropriety. He is seen "practising behauiour";[63] he preposterously declares himself "point-deuise the very man";[64] and, in this incongruous costume, he enters the presence of the Countess herself and assumes, as he supposes, the haughty airs and graces of his betters.

Most Elizabethans regarded the structure of society as divinely ordained[65] and so immutable; and men were therefore supposed to be content with the station in life to which God had appointed them. Writers generally give the upper ranks as follows: "Princes or Potentats, Dukes, Earles [the English earl is a count], Barons, Knightes, Esquires, Gentlemen, Yeomen, Husbandmen . . . ."[66] According to this scheme, Malvolio plans to skip at one bound some four or five gradations, very much as if a petty officer intrigued to become colonel of the regiment! No wonder the steward cons politic authors and studies manners with his shadow, for even

[59] *Twelfth Night* (ed. Furness var.), p. 174.

[60] Overbury, *Characters*, "Foote-man."   [61] *Ibid.*, "Country Gentleman."

[62] A. H. Nacon, *Heralds and Heraldry in Jonson's Plays* (New York, 1907), pp. 89 *et seq.* Jonson's heraldic method of satire is, characteristically, more learned but less dramatically telling than Shakespeare's use of costume.

[63] *Twefth Night*, II. v. 19.

[64] *Ibid.*, II. v. 152–53.

[65] Sir T. Elyot, *Governour*, Book I, Sec. 1; J. Stephens, *Satyrical Essays* (London, 1615), p. 35 *et passim*; H. Peacham, *Compleat Gentleman* (London, 1622).

[66] Markham, *op. cit.*, p. 103. Cf. Sir T. Smith, *De Republica Anglicana* (London, 1565), pp. 41 *et seq.*; W. Harrison, *op. cit.*, chapter v; J. Bodin, *Six Bookes of Commonweale* (tr. Knolles), (London, 1606); A. Hopton, *Concordancy of Years* (London, 1612), pp. 191–92; J. D. Wilson, *Life in Shakespeare's Engand* (Cambridge, 1920), pp. 7–8; W. S. Davis, *Life in Elizabethan Days* (New York, 1930), pp. 19 *et seq.*

the commonest forms of courtesy reflected social class,[67] and bodily carriage, gesture, and titles and pronouns of address varied between every two individuals, depending largely on comparative rank; thus the new "Count Malvolio" must use an utterly new idiom of daily etiquette. This change was overwhelming; nevertheless it was just within the realms of possibility: Malvolio himself cites the precedent of the Lady of Strachy's yeoman; Lord Burghley's father was a mere yeoman of the royal chamber; the Duchess of Suffolk married her Master of the Horse; and a Duchess of Malfi might wed her servant. Indeed, the age was full of "aspiring mindes";[68] Ophelia sang of the false steward who stole his master's daughter, and Hamlet complained that "the toe of the peasant" came near "the heel of the courtier." Indeed, a chamberlain, as the intimate and personal servant of an up-to-date lady,[69] especially a chamberlain who had been used "with a more exalted respect"[70] than her other followers, might feel that he should hope for better things. Thus Malvolio's plans were not only outrageous, but, even worse—possible of fulfillment.

The Elizabethans naturally sympathized with the "cast" retainers and those that suffered from social change. They lamented the decline of liberality, the[71] "incertaintie of service," and the growing severity of masters who would use any excuse to relieve themselves of one more hungry mouth.[72] England had indeed become the "Purgatory of Servants";[73] Falstaff's Robin pathetically depicts the wretched case of page and man-at-arms,[74] and Feste might well beware of Olivia's displeasure for his unpermitted absence, when merely the "breaking of a Bulrush"[75] might cast one out on the highway. A "great

[67] R. Kelso, *The English Gentleman in the Sixteenth Century* (Urbana, Illinois, 1929), p. 87.

[68] Markham, *op. cit.*, p. 103.

[69] N. Breton, *Forte of Fancie* (*ed. princ.*, 1582), *Works*, ed. Grosart, I, 15.

[70] *Twelfth Night*, II. v. 25 *et seq.*; III. iv. 65–67.

[71] Markham, *op. cit.*, pp. 127 *et seq.*

[72] Basse, *op. cit.*, stanza 10; Brathwait, *op. cit.*, pp. 88–89; T. Becon, *Prayers* (ed. Parker Society), (Cambridge, 1844), pp. 30–31, 134.

[73] Moryson, *op. cit.* (ed. Furnivall, New Shakespeare Society), p. 271.

[74] J. W. Draper, "Falstaff's Robin and Other Pages," *Studies in Philology*, XXXVI, 476 *et seq.*   [75] Markham, *op. cit.*, p. 133.

swarm" of masterless men had no choice but to turn thieves and beggars, for they had served no apprenticeship for any trade. These vagabonds were the terror of the countryside and a constant problem to the government.[76] In short, not only was change per se unwelcome, but Malvolio, as the symbol of a change that was generally deplored and was associated with obvious social evils and painful maladjustments—Malvolio, flaunting his impudent designs before his social betters and glorying in the dominion that he hopes shortly to assume—would naturally present to the Elizabethans a most odious figure and thus become a Saint Sebastian for every shaft of satire. The Elizabethans were troubled with the problem of a superabundance of retainers who were falling in status below the very servant class—a situation unknown to recent times. Thus the keen enmities of an Elizabethan household in which the wellborn retainers are fighting for their livelihoods are lost upon those modern critics who ignore the social background of the play. Malvolio, like Shylock,[77] was detested because the audience saw in him a social type that it despised and an unsolved social problem that it feared. This antipathy of the Elizabethans toward Malvolio, an antipathy both of the auditors in the pit and of the characters on the stage, clearly arose, not from his Puritanism—if, indeed, he be a Puritan—but from his social effrontery: it sinned against God's ordinance; and it endangered a society already rocked to its foundations by the fall of age-old feudalism. Indeed, Malvolio's very clothes attest him a particularly blatant upstart, and he clearly planned to curtail the lavish bounty that, before the founding of Virginia, was the only means of livelihood for many younger sons of county families. No wonder the young lawyers of the Middle Temple relished his downfall. A successful play is a collaboration of dramatist and audience; and, in judging a piece, critics must not ignore the audience's part in the performance, its likes and dislikes, its pent-up feelings that the plot may express and so release. Without a knowledge of the current attitude toward such as Malvolio, the motivation of

[76] A. V. Judges, *The Elizabethan Underworld* (New York, 1930), "Introduction."
[77] J. W. Draper, "The Psychology of Shylock," *Bull. Hist. Med.*, VIII, 643 *et seq.*

Twelfth Night is obscured, the action unconvincing, and the play mere farce.

Indeed, the plot of a true comedy must grow out of the traits of the chief characters; and Shakespeare, to illustrate his theme of a presumptuous and pushing menial, had to conceive a servant who contemned his lot and whose mental bent must therefore be ill fitted to his walk of life. As Lamb remarked, the "pride" that actuates his hopes and the "gravity" that is its outward semblance must be "inherent and native to the man." Since each social degree was more or less linked with a given humor, planet, and mental tendency, Malvolio's humor should be portrayed as one that would make him aspire, as one that belonged, not to servants but to masters—indeed to very nobles. Such a dynamic force must lie behind so exalted an ambition; and Malvolio's predominant humor must be the key to it. To complete an understanding, therefore, of Malvolio's part, an investigation of his humor and psychology is needful.

A perfect balance of blood, phlegm, bile, and black bile was supposed to bring mental poise and perfect health; but this fortunate condition was rare, and Malvolio is clearly not enjoying it. His noble mistress introduces him to the audience as "sicke of selfe-loue" and having "a distemper'd appetite"; and the comment of others, including his own, seems to put him in a special class apart. He declares himself of a different "element" from Olivia's other followers;[78] he is sure that his mistress would prefer a man of his "complection";[79] he refers again and again to his "starres,"[80] to his "Fortune,"[81] to the "Fates" that guide him;[82] and he attributes his success to "Ioue."[83] Sir Toby, moreover, conjures "the spirit of humors" to get him to read aloud Maria's fraudulent love letter;[84] this missive is designed to affect his "Liuer,"[85] the organ subject to such tender passions,[86] and the whole practical joke is intended to "Physicke" his malady.[87] Shakespeare could hardly reiterate

---

[78] *Twelfth Night*, III. iv. 127. [79] *Ibid.*, II. v. 28. [80] *Ibid.*, II. v. 159.
[81] *Ibid.*, II. v. 25 *passim*. [82] *Ibid.*, II. v. 134, 137.
[83] *Ibid.*, II. v. 161; III. iv. 78, 85. [84] *Ibid.*, II. v. 84–85.
[85] *Ibid.*, II. v. 94. [86] Chapter vi. [87] *Twelfth Night*, II. iii. 166.

these recognized terms of popular science without meaning or dramatic purpose, and one may properly inquire what this "element" and these "starres" might be, and what overmastering humor needed Maria's "Physicke." Like so many other characters drawn by Shakespeare and Ben Jonson at the time, Malvolio seems to be conceived as impelled and dominated by a humor, but the evidence as to just which humor at first seems conflicting and obscure.

The humor most appropriate to "lackies" as a class was phlegm;[88] it was thought to be cold and moist and to make men dull and slow,[89] "faint hearted .... mild of nature,"[90] and given to "bellycheere."[91] Malvolio, the busy and capable steward, is not idle or dull; his treatment of Sir Toby and of the Duke's emissary does not show him "faint hearted"; and he certainly has no part nor lot in the free "bellycheere" of the midnight revelry. Some of the phlegmatic type, like Sir Toby, were under the astral influence of Venus, and these Dariot describes as "lovers of delights," "yong women," and those "giuen to idlenes and pleasures";[92] but Malvolio is no Sir Toby. On the other hand, some, like Sir Andrew, were under the duller and more inconstant influence of the moon; and such were "vacabonds .... messengers, shipmen, Queenes, Ladies .... fishers .... fooles, delighting in journeis and variety of life . . . . they which are in continual motion, as legats, lackies. . . . ."[93] Except for being perhaps a fool and a "lackey," Malvolio fits into no part of this description. The group also includes "commanding, common people" and those who made a "studie of historie," and this touches him somewhat nearer; but his prowess to command fits far better under another humor, and he studies "politic authors" for the very purpose of escaping his status as a steward.

---

[88] C. Dariot, *Iudgement of the Starres* (tr. F. Wither), (London, 1598), sig. E 1. On the characteristics of the humors, see J. W. Draper, *The Humors and Shakespeare's Characters* (Durham, N.C., 1945).

[89] T. Elyot, *Castel of Helth* (London, 1541), leaf 2 v. *passim*; *Batman vppon Bartholome* (London, 1582), leaves 31 v and 32 r.

[90] T. W.[alkington],*Optick Glasse of Humors* [? 1631], pp. 118 *et seq.*

[91] L. Lemnius, *Touchstone of Complexions* (tr. Newton), (London, 1576), leaf 111 v. Cf. leaves 23 v and 81 r.

[92] Dariot, *op. cit.*, sig. D 4 r.   [93] *Ibid.*, sig. E 1.

Malvolio, in short, if one class him as a lackey, should be phlegmatic; but he shows the characteristics neither of Sir Andrew nor of Sir Toby, and one must therefore seek his humor beyond the pale of his vocation. Indeed, if his humor and vocation had agreed, he would have had no ambition to change it, and so would have supplied neither plot nor comedy to the play.

The planet, Mercury, was also thought to govern "servants."[94] This temper was inconstant and unstable;[95] and, chameleon-like, it showed the traits of one humor or another as the astrological influences about it changed.[96] Maria declared that Malvolio was not "anything constantly but a time-pleaser";[97] and, indeed, the whims of my lord or lady forced on a servant many shifts and changes.[98] But these were the accidents of Malvolio's station rather than the native bent of his character, and his ambitious pursuit of Olivia certainly does not waver.[99] Feste slyly suggests that "Mercury"[100] should "indue" Malvolio with a facility in lying[101]—mendacity was, to be sure, part of the device and craft[102] of the mercurial temper; but Feste's very exhortation implies that Malvolio is lacking in the art, and, indeed, he is never shown as telling an untruth. Malvolio, moreover, is not "doubtful"—given to fear,[103] and he has none of the "cloudy imaginations, fancies, fictions and forced dreams" of the mercurial man.[104] He is, in short, no wavering Macbeth;[105] he is fixed in purpose, blunt rather than devious, bold rather than fearful, and matter of fact rather than visionary. Even when he daydreams, it is of such practical commonplaces as a day bed and a velvet gown, not of imagined daggers and gory thanes. Neither is he a

---

[94] Dariot, op. cit., sig. D 4 v.

[95] Ibid., sig. D 4 v; T. Adams, Diseases of the Soule (London, 1616), pp. 7 et seq.; The Booke of Arcandam (tr. Warde, London, 1592), sig. L 7.

[96] Dariot, op. cit., sig. D. 1 r.   [97] Twelfth Night, II. iii. 142–43.

[98] This applied even to servingmen. See Overbury, op. cit., "A Serving-Man," and J. Earle, Microcosmographie, "A Serving Man."

[99] Cf. Adams, op. cit., p. 10.

[100] Most editors take this as referring to the pagan god of thieves.

[101] Twelfth Night, I. v. 95.

[102] Dariot, op. cit., sigs. D 4 v and E 1 r; T. Hyll, Schoole of Skill (London, 1599), leaf 50 v.

[103] Dariot, op cit., sig. D 4 v.   [104] Adams, op. cit., p. 9.

[105] J. W. Draper, "Macbeth, 'Infirme of Purpose,'" Bull. Hist. Med., X, 16 et seq.

nimble Feste, calculating his words and deeds to a nicety for the differing gusto of many masters. Malvolio, in short, has neither of the complexions proper to a servant.

The melancholy humor was sometimes associated with "base trades" and menials;[106] Phillips, who seems to have played Malvolio, also played the melancholy Cassius and Don John;[107] but Malvolio does not appear to have a preponderance of this humor. It was ill-omened and dangerous to all concerned, and sometimes led the sufferer even to madness.[108] It was the most discussed and the most diverse in its effects: it belonged to conspirators like Cassius,[109] to frustrated idealists like Hamlet,[110] and to Bishop Hall's "Ambitious" man, who, when foiled, turns to revenge and fury.[111] It was "malevolent" and "terrible in all [astrological] aspects";[112] it might be dour and somber,[113] or it might achieve a bitter wit from deep exasperation.[114] It could affect the imagination with dreadful shapes;[115] and it was like to cause a "lamentable and shameful end."[116] Malvolio is too much a comic character to belong in this category; and, until the very end of the play, he does not consider himself foiled and so has no thought of revenge. The similarity of his name to that of Marston's Malevole[117] has suggested that both belong to the "malcontent type," which was taken to be melancholy; but Malvolio's name seems to have been borrowed from *Gl' Ingannati*, and it would seem to point, not to his cast of mind, but merely to his ill wishes toward the merrymakers. He is obviously sober and disinclined to smile until urged to by the letter;[118] but well-trained servitors are not supposed to display emotion, especially in a

[106] Dariot, *op. cit.*, sig. D 2 r.   [107] Baldwin, *op. cit.*, Plates II and III.
[108] T. Bright, *Treatise of Melancholy* (London, 1586 and 1613).
[109] Walkington, *op. cit.* (ed. 1639), p. 129.
[110] J. W. Draper, "Hamlet," *ed. cit.*, pp. 175 *et seq.* ·
[111] J. Hall, *Characterisms of Vices* (London, 1608), "Malcontent."
[112] Dariot, *op. cit.*, sig. D 2 r.
[113] Lemnius, *op. cit.*, leaf 23 v; and R. Burton, *Anatomy of Melancholy*, Part I, Sec. ii, Memb. 5, Sub. 4.
[114] Bright, *op. cit.* (ed. 1613), p. 158; and W. Vaughan, *Directions for Health* (London, 1633), p. 128.
[115] T. Nashe, *Works* (ed. McKerrow), I, 353 *et seq.*; Elyot, *op. cit.*, leaf 3 r.
[116] Lemnius, *op. cit.*, leaf 23 v.   [117] See E. E. Stoll, *Mod. Phil.*, III, 281 *et seq.*
[118] *Twelfth Night*, II. v. 164; III. iv. 6 and 12.

house of mourning. Malvolio, furthermore, definitely announces to Olivia that he is not "black" in his "mind"—that is, he believes himself encouraged in his suit, and so does not suffer from the melancholy of the unrequited lover.[119]

Neither Malvolio's general characteristics, his time of life, nor his immediate circumstances, suggest a melancholic temper. Dariot summarized at length the attributes of the type:

He signifieth ould men, fathers, grandfathers and such like, husband-men, beggars, Iewes, Moores, diggers for metals or stones, potters, Curriers, sink-cleaners, etc. all such base trades, obstinate in opinion, laborious, of deepe cogitation couetous, enuious, solitarie, mournfull, few woords, rauenous, decieuers, superstitious, treasorers, deepe memorie, experience, and knowledge of many things, professions, buildings, tillage, inheritances, it causeth imprisonments, and secret enemies.[120]

Of this long list of items, only two apply to Malvolio: he is in a way covetous, and he does experience a temporary imprisonment. In short, he is not by nature melancholy. Sometimes, however, the humor arose from special reasons at the time, and thus it afflicted the religious fanatic and the unrequited lover. If Malvolio were a Puritan, he should be melancholy, but he shows no signs of the disease; if Malvolio were an unrequited lover, he should be melancholy, but his love up to the last act looks forward to requital. Dotage, moreover, brought on melancholy, as in the case of Lear;[121] and Irving is said to have played the part as "old"; but Malvolio, the efficient steward and the hopeful lover, though not a youth, is certainly not senile. The humor was associated with lunacy, but Malvolio's is only a "merry madness."[122] Maria's letter has put him "in such a dreame, that when the image of it leaues him, he must run mad";[123] and Fabyan fears that the plotters will "make him mad indeede";[124] but, as both these passages imply, this is only jocular false imprisonment for a purely

[119] Ibid., III. iv. 29–30; and M. C. Linthicum, Costume in Shakespeare (Oxford, 1936), p. 50.

[120] Dariot, op. cit., sig. D 2.

[121] J. W. Draper, "The Old Age of King Lear," J.E.G.P., XXXIX, 527 et seq.

[122] Twelfth Night, III. iv. 18.

[123] Ibid., II. v. 182–83. [124] Ibid., III. iv. 136.

supposititious lunacy.[125] This is no melancholy madness. And finally, if the others really intend, as they declare, to cure his malady, their treatment is quite wrong for melancholy, which should be treated by exercise and diet,[126] or by diversions, games, and music,[127] and by "Moderate myrthe and banqueting."[128]

The two humors that were most commonly associated with nobles and high dignitaries were the sanguine and the choleric, and it remains to examine Malvolio's relationship to each of these. The sanguine temper was thought to be "the paragon of complexions."[129] It was appropriate to "Noblemen";[130] and such persons were handsome, "affable in speech," "liberally minded," of "constant loving affection," but "too prone to Venery,"[131] and so liable to "riot, watonnesse, drunkenes, wastfulnes, prodigality, filthy and detestable loues, horrible lustes . . . ."[132] None of these traits is evident in Malvolio. He is, to be sure, "faithful"[133] in his service to Olivia both as steward and as lover; and he mentions "Joue," but this probably refers to the pagan god rather than to the sanguine planet which was usually called Jupiter. He is hopeful of becoming a nobleman, but is certainly not fortunate in having his hopes fulfilled. Whether he even loves Olivia very deeply is a question, for his attachment to her seems to arise more from a politic interest than from passion. In short, Malvolio is no sanguine Romeo.[134]

Only choler remains. It was almost as unlucky and dangerous as melancholy, and it also might end in madness.[135] Its more extreme form was under the astral influence of Mars,

---

[125] False imprisonment of imputed lunatics was a current abuse. See Bucknill, *Psychology of Shakespeare* (London, 1859), p. 249.

[126] Bright, *op. cit.*, pp. 30 and 302.

[127] S. Guazzo, *Civile Conversation* (London, 1925), I, 18 *et seq.*

[128] Lemnius, *op. cit.*, leaf 154 v.　　[129] Walkington, *op. cit.*, p. 111.

[130] Dariot, *op. cit.*, sig. D 2 v.　　[131] Walkington, *op. cit.*, pp. 115 *et passim.*

[132] Lemnius, *op. cit.*, leaf 23 v; T. Cogan, *Haven of Health* (London, 1589), sig. Hh 2 v.

[133] Dariot, *op. cit.*, sig. D 2 v.

[134] J. W. Draper, "Shakespeare's 'Star-Crossed Lovers,'" *R.E.S.*, XV, 16 *et seq.*

[135] Lemnius (ed. 1581), leaf 23 v; Dariot, *op. cit.*, sig. D 3 r; N. Coeffeteau, *Table of Humane Passions* (London, 1621), pp. 599 *et seq.*; Batman, *op. cit.*, leaf 32 v.

appropriate to soldiers; but a more genial sort was under the influence of the sun, and this was attributed to rulers and to courtiers. Malvolio's "humor of state" and affected elegance of diction suggests this second, less heroic type; and his bitter complaint at the "hideous darknesse"[136] of his prison may represent the natural reaction of the sun's man to deprivation of his planet's light. Galen and his followers associated an acid wit with the choleric type;[137] and Malvolio is introduced as turning a sharp epigram and criticizing his mistress' taste in foolery and playing on words in the approved Elizabethan style.[138] Dariot describes the choleric man as "valiant, secret, honest";[139] and Malvolio, at his mistress' supposed behest, beards Sir Toby and insults Cesario, keeps the secret of the love letter even while in durance, and seems to render honest and competent service as a steward. The solar type of choler, moreover, made one "industrious, prouident . . . . quiet, thoughtful . . . . sincere";[140] and Malvolio is abstemious and reserved and hesitates to trust his "imagination."[141] He does not favor Sir Toby's festive cheer, doubtless because the choleric type, like Cassio,[142] easily succumbed to its bad influence, and so had to be restrained in food and drink.[143]

But above all, Malvolio's moving passion betrays his choleric nature: he displays a personal pride that brings about his efficiency as a steward, but makes him arrogant even toward his superiors, and encourages him in the preposterous notion that he might wed the Countess. He is "over-weening" even before the forged letter urges him to be "proud."[144] He imprisons the captain who befriended Viola;[145] and, at the end, he roundly accuses even his noble mistress: "Madam, you have done me wrong, Notorious wrong."[146] He cultivates this "hu-

[136] *Twelfth Night*, IV. ii. 33.

[137] J. Huarte, *Examen de Ingenios* (tr. Carew), (London, 1604), p. 73; Arcandam, *op. cit.*, sig. M 2 r; T. Wright, *Passions of the Minde* (London, 1601), pp. 212–13.

[138] *Twelfth Night*, I. v. 73 *et seq.*   [139] Dariot, *op. cit.*, sig D 3 v.

[140] *Ibid.*, sig. D 3 v.   [141] *Twelfth Night*, II. v. 153–54.

[142] J. W. Draper, "Choleric Cassio," *Bulletin of the History of Medicine*, VII, 583 *et seq.*

[143] Walkington, *op. cit.*, pp. 104 and 108; Coeffeteau, *op. cit.*, p. 612; Vaughan, *op. cit.*, p. 135.

[144] *Twelfth Night*, II. v. 31.   [145] *Ibid.*, V. i. 291–92.   [146] *Ibid.*, V. i. 346–47.

mor of state," this same choleric humor proper to courtiers and to kings.[147] He declares that he "will bee proud";[148] he longs "To be Count Maluolio";[149] he luxuriates in the pomps and appurtenances of greatness—a "branched velvet gowne," a "day-bedde," and "some rich Iewell."[150] Fabyan exclaims, "How he iets vnder his aduanc'd plumes,"[151] comparing him to a peacock. The Elizabethans associated pride with choler;[152] and, in *Coriolanus*, Shakespeare developed just this theme.[153] They believed that choleric people should avoid each other for fear of a clash;[154] and Malvolio's native choler certainly clashes with the assumed choler of Sir Toby. Ridicule and contempt of others[155] and misfortune at their hands[156] were thought to aggravate choler; and so it is with Malvolio.[157] As in *Coriolanus*, this leads to the "revenge"[158] that he threatens in the final scene; or, if the case were truly tragic, like Lear's, it might lead to the lunacy that Maria and Fabyan suggest as a possible outcome of their plot.[159] Indeed, choler, expressed in pride, seems to guide the course that Malvolio steers throughout the comedy.

Linked closely to this emulous pride, and a natural outgrowth from it, is Malvolio's ambition[160] to marry Olivia and so become a count. The role of lover was particularly fitting for the courtly children of the sun; and they were also by nature "ambitious" and "desirous of honours."[161] Malvolio proposed to rise, like the House of Hapsburg, by the felicitous

[147] Dariot, *op. cit.*, sig D 3 v. [148] *Twelfth Night*, II. v. 150–51.
[149] *Ibid.*, II. v. 36. [150] *Ibid.*, II. v. 48 *et seq.*
[151] *Twelfth Night*, II. v. 33.
[152] J. Downame, *Spiritual Physicke* (London, 1600), leaves 25–26 and 59–60.
[153] J. W. Draper, "Coriolanus," *Bulletin West Virginia Philological Society*, 1939, III, 22 *et seq.*
[154] Downame, *op. cit.*, leaf 69 v; Coeffeteau, *op. cit.*, p. 623.
[155] *Ibid.*, pp. 559–60.
[156] *Ibid.*, p. 580. [157] *Twelfth Night*, II. v. 182–83; III. iv. 136.
[158] Coeffeteau, *op. cit.*, pp. 615–16.
[159] *Twelfth Night*, II. v. 183; III. iv. *passim.*
[160] Ambition was thought "most dangerous." See T. R[ogers], *Philosophical Discourse, Entituled, The Anatomie of the minde* (London, 1576), leaf 10; R. C[leaver], *Goodly Form* (London, 1598), p. 68; Wright, *op. cit.*, p. 308.
[161] Dariot, *op. cit.*, sig. D 3 v; Coeffeteau, *op. cit.*, p. 567; Huarte, *op. cit.*, pp. 220–21; Adams, *op. cit.*, pp. 39–40; P. de la Primaudaye, *French Academy* (London, 1576), pp. 313–14.

means of marriage. How else attain the "Princely dignities, and riches" that rightfully belonged to this astral type?[162] To Malvolio's choleric mind such high aspirations would not seem untoward: they were but the preordained fulfillment of his "starres" and "Fortunes" and "Fates." Surely, he can readily learn to express this "humor of state"[163]—which indeed he had better cultivate if Olivia is an independent ruler!—and he proceeds to put it into practice in true choleric fashion, with a "frown."[164] Truly, as the Countess at the first declares, he is "sicke of selfe-loue";[165] and this sickness is not melancholy but choler. This is the malady that Maria proposes to "Physicke" with her practical joke, and a serious malady it was both to the sufferer and to those about him. In actual fact, however, her remedy is misapplied, for ridicule only augmented the complaint,[166] and Malvolio leaves the stage determined to be "reueng'd on the whole pack of you." Luckily, his choler was not of the more dangerous martial sort or one might expect a tragedy on the heels of the comic denoument.

Intelligent people who knew and accepted the science of the age, i.e., astrology and alchemy and the theory of the humors, must have noted scores of human anomalies about them: rulers, like Lear, who were not choleric; merchants, like Antonio, who were not mercurial; courtiers, like Don John, who were not sanguine; and a playwright, with his eye upon theatrical effect, must have seen in these misfits and psychosocial incongruities striking opportunity for comic and tragic effects. Just such a misfit is Malvolio, the choleric steward, whose choler makes him aspire, and aspire especially through marriage. His disparity of humor is the perfect complement to Sir Toby's and Sir Andrew's: as knights, they should be choleric, but by the fact of birth are actually phlegmatic; Malvolio, as a servant, should be phlegmatic, but by birth is choleric. Indeed, this minor plot is a sort of every man out of his humor; and, as the piece followed shortly after Jonson's, it might be taken (had

[162] Dariot, op. cit., sig. D 3 v.   [163] Twelfth Night, II. v. 60.
[164] Ibid., II. v. 65.   [165] Twelfth Night, I. v. 88–89.
[166] Coeffeteau, op. cit., pp. 559–69, 589. The usual cure was diet in food and drink. See ibid., p. 612; Walkington, op. cit., pp. 104, 108; Cogan, op. cit., p. 211.

not Shakespeare used humors so amply in earlier plays) as an example of Jonsonian influence. In any case, this disparity of personality with social station produces the incongruity that is the essence of the comic, and makes that unstable equilibrium that sets plot in motion, the plot of high comedy based in character.

The foregoing paragraphs have sketched the background, neglected by former critics, of Malvolio's outer life in his social relationships and of his inner life as a psychological entity: the former shows the enormity of his ambitions and explains the enmity of his domestic colleagues; the latter shows why he might cherish such daring hopes. Thus, in the play, motive and action and reaction on others are all consistently and convincingly integrated—integrated as the twentieth century, with its different social problems, different ideals and different theories of psychology, could hardly understand them. It remains to sketch Malvolio's earlier life and his education, as far as Shakespeare glimpses them in the play, and to trace his course in the plot in relation to the other characters.

Malvolio surely did not come of gentle stock, or he would have been a servingman like Fabyan. He compares himself, moreover, to the yeoman who espoused the Lady of the Strachy; and, at some period before the play began, he had doubtless worn the yellow stockings that properly belonged to the humbler rural classes.[167] His language, furthermore, lacks even such courtly allusions and high astounding terms as Sir Toby could command, and makes reference merely to garters and stockings, to nightingales and jackdaws,[168] to a peapod, an apple,[169] a dram, and a scruple,[170] to an alehouse, tinkers and cobblers,[171] to a zany—the professional butt for a jester's wit[172]—to a broadside ballad,[173] and to the sign before a sheriff's door.[174] These are indeed the homely furniture of a plebeian mind. He doubtless came of the rural yeomanry, not of the Puritan *bourgeoisie* as some critics have thought, or of the gentle classes that produced Sir Toby and Maria. His

[167] *Cyuile and Vncyuile Life*, p. 40.   [168] *Twelfth Night*, III. iv. 39.
[169] *Ibid.*, I. v. 157–58.   [170] *Ibid.*, III. iv. 82.   [171] *Ibid.*, II. iii. 90–92.
[172] *Ibid.*, I. v. 87.   [173] *Ibid.*, III. iv. 26.   [174] *Ibid.*, I. v. 148.

efforts at more elegant and learned allusion emphasize his limitations. He can read, but Maria's forgery easily deceives him; religion is represented only by "hell"[175] and an oath "By the Lord";[176] he trusts in "Fortune,"[177] and vaunts an elementary knowledge of astrology; though he has heard of Pythagoras' theory of the transmigration of souls,[178] he accepts the clown's mock learning as coming from the parson. He attempts two rather obvious puns on "mankinde" and on "manner,"[179] which his mistress tastefully ignores. His knowledge of Roman mythology seems to be limited to "Joue" to whom he refers three times;[180] and he knows that the Countess has a seal with a picture of Roman Lucrece.[181] Indeed, his conception of the great and elegant and noble has little of its intellectual attributes—he hopes to pick up these from perusing "polliticke Authours," as a tired businessman might attend ten lectures on world culture; and, like the tired businessman, he concentrates on culture's obvious attributes and solid satisfactions, the things that he has seen in noble houses and in lordly hands—a chair of "state," a "branch'd Veluet gowne," a "day-bedde," the luxury of a watch, and a "rich Iewell."[182] These things dominate Malvolio's idea of courtly finesse and of the cares of statecraft, and his gentility is of the sort to be purchased from a fashionable tailor. In fact, Archer may be right in calling him a Philistine.

This lack of *savoir-faire*, a lack most offensive to Elizabethan taste, was doubtless characteristic of the pushing new-made gentles whom the age so much decried; and Shakespeare presents Malvolio with a stupendous tactlessness that contravened all Renaissance etiquette and must have been at comic discord with his elegant pretensions. He has the temerity to criticize his mistress' taste in wit;[183] and he begins a letter to her "By the Lord Madam"[184]—no way to address a Countess! He cannot rise to the occasion of Cesario's importunate demand for entrance.[185] He is not keen enough to sense, as Maria and

[175] *Ibid.*, IV. ii. 38, 49.   [176] *Ibid.*, V. i. 308.
[177] *Ibid.*, II. v. 25, 70, 148.   [178] *Twelfth Night*, IV. ii. 54–55.
[179] *Ibid.*, I. v. 151 and 153.   [180] *Ibid.*, II. v. 161; III. iv. 78 and 85.
[181] *Ibid.*, II. v. 92.   [182] *Ibid.*, II. v. 46.   [183] *Ibid.*, I. v. 81 *et seq.*
[184] *Ibid.*, V. i. 308.   [185] *Twelfth Night* (ed. Furness var.), pp. 23–24.

Feste do, that his mistress loves the handsome youth, and he returns the ring with impudent and needless gaucherie. He is rude enough himself to impute rudeness to Cesario and accuse him of throwing the ring at Olivia.[186] Truly, his veneer of courtesy wears very thin. A Renaissance gentleman to the manner born, like Browning's much-married Duke, prided himself never to stoop in matters of courtesy. Malvolio's passing crudities imply an education, not in the court or even in the school, but in the scullery, where the visible pomp and circumstance of high position might be known, but not its finer obligations or its culture. He had clearly risen in the household from the ranks; he had been a "subservingman," and now aspired to become a very superservingman.

The first half of the comedy thus presents Malvolio's choleric malady, already chronic, and shows in his marital project the symptoms of a critical condition; the second half shows how those about him, either with witting malice like Maria and Sir Toby, or with an unwitting regard, like Olivia, undertake to "Physicke" this malady, or at least curb its extremes, first by treating the sufferer as a lunatic and finally by leaving him without the revenge that his choleric nature craved. Malvolio is confined in darkness and baited by Feste disguised as the local curate; but at last Feste, *persona propria*, brings him the pen and paper that he begs, and carries his letter of remonstrance to Olivia. This letter is read; he is restored to liberty and to his former duties, and Orsino wants him entreated "to a peace." But Olivia is in no mood to countenance the revenge he threatens; for, like all the others, she would be shocked at his impudence. Whether his choler was really purged by Maria's heroic therapy is doubtful; but, at least, the patient had full warning to restrain it in the future, and comedy as an art is justified once more as the scourge of folly and the castigation of the time. Sir Andrew, as the fool simpleton, really harms no one, and so loses only some money that he can well afford; Sir Toby only plays the fool; but Malvolio is the fool rampant intruding on the ancient rights of others;

[186] *Twelfth Night*, II. ii. 7 et seq.

and so he merits punishment more humiliating than Sir Andrew's—an utter loss of "face" among those with whom he must spend the remainder of his days. True to his rude spirit, he is not wise enough to take his punishment with prudent dignity and let it be forgotten, but instead he threatens a revenge he cannot take. This empty threat is perhaps the final clue to his personality, inflated with ambition and choleric pride that finally falls to empty bluster. Malvolio failed utterly in the part of noble lover—Olivia did not even guess his purposes—and he would have failed quite as disastrously in the role of "Count Malvolio."

By meticulous service during his master's lifetime, Malvolio had worked himself up to the commanding place of major-domo; and Maria, through policy or malice, had flattered him into thinking that even the daughter of the house might favor his advances. He was now steward, overlord of cooks and brewers, with a chain of office.[187] At the old Count's death, he naturally took charge, and even more after Olivia's brother died, for Olivia was inexperienced, was a woman, and was in the seclusion of deep mourning. Certainly, Sir Toby had neither the energy nor the liking nor the ability to manage a great household. Malvolio, moreover, was in no mood to take his orders. Thus the choleric steward assumed command, extended his oversight to servingmen such as Fabyan,[188] threatened Maria with ill favor,[189] and practiced even for the castigation of Sir Toby.[190] In the first act, indeed, Malvolio has the assurance to reprove his noble mistress' taste in wit; and, before the play began, his authority was already stepping beyond the household when he dared to order the Captain imprisoned;[191] like the Frankish mayors of the palace, he was rising from a domestic to a public power. Even the gentles began to feel his pre-emptory sway. He is the parvenu par excellence, and the exponent of such a democracy as would raise himself to rule over the ruling class; and no ruling class can tolerate such doings. Both the exalting of Malvolio and his fall, like

187 *Ibid.*, II. iii. 128.
188 *Ibid.*, II. v. 8–9.
189 *Ibid.*, II. iii. 119 *et seq.*
190 *Ibid.*, II. v. 55 *et seq.*
191 *Ibid.*, V. i. 290–91.

Lucifer's, through pride, were as inevitable as high tragedy, the characters and the conditions being what they were. Had he progressed far enough to have gained real control over the state, and had he been of more heroic temper, his fall would have had a tragic magnitude like Julius Caesar's, for, like Caesar's, it would have dragged the whole social order down into chaos. But Shakespeare, though verging toward tragic themes, was still writing comedy, and he drew Malvolio's humor as the less dangerous of the choleric types, under the blander influence of the sun. His marriage with Olivia, if one can imagine his actually bringing it to pass, could not have been successful: the two were in no way suited; and marrying for ambition, especially "for gentility," was thought foredoomed to failure;[192] but, fortunately for all concerned, Maria and Sir Toby saw to it that failure came earlier than this.

Of late years scholars have been seeking living models for the lifelike figures that Chaucer and Shakespeare drew; and Malvolio's prototype has been variously recognized. As early as 1884, Fleay suggested the playwright John Marston chiefly on account of the propriety—somewhat dubious—of the anagram M O A I; but Marston and Malvolio have little else in common. More recently, Sir Isreal Gollancz took as Malvolio's prototype "Sir Ambrose Willoughby, Queen Elizabeth's Chief Sewer and Squire of the Presence,"[193] who had quarreled publicly with Southampton and Raleigh for playing cards in the Presence Chamber after the Queen had retired. But Elizabeth supported Willoughby, and Shakespeare would hardly have taken sides publicly against the Queen. Sir E. K. Chambers proposes Sir William Knollys, Comptroller of the Royal Household, who is supposed to have kept the Maids of Honor in order and to have had a secret affair with one of them,[194] but Chambers' documentation has been questioned;[195] and again one doubts whether Shakespeare and his company, who were continually dependent on the Royal Household for co-

192 A. Niccholes, *Discourse of Marriage* (London, 1615), pp. 14, 19.
193 I. Gollancz, *A Book of Homage to Shakespeare* (Oxford, 1916), pp. 177–78.
194 E. K. Chambers, *Shakespeare, a Survey* (London, 1925), pp. 177 et seq.
195 A. Thaler, "The Original Malvolio?" *Shak. Asso. Bull.*, VII, 57 et seq.

operation, would have staged a public attack on one of its chief functionaries. Professor Thaler suggests Sir William Ffarington, Esq., steward until 1594 to Lord Derby, who was patron of Shakespeare's company. Like Malvolio, he seems to have been sad and sober and acquisitive; but, as one of the landed gentry and son of a knight, he would hardly seem to the Elizabethans, with their keen sense of class distinctions, a fit prototype for the parvenu Malvolio. Taken together, all these critics seem to prove too much; Shakespeare must have come in contact with many stewards, and why should he model Malvolio on only one? Most stewards, as part of their routine, had to keep the household in order, and so were disliked by its more exuberant members. Probably to the Elizabethans the outstanding fact about Malvolio was not his suppression of revelry but his low birth for such a high position in so great a household; and, if he have but one original, this probably is the clue by which to find it. The Romantic movement interpreted Shakespeare's plays according to its heart's desire as gorgeous fantasies; and now realism insists that they are mere photographs of living models. The present writer deprecates these extremes unless the proof be incontestable; he believes that Shakespeare, like all great artists, used both actual life and his imagination, the one in general as his raw materials, the other as an artistic, shaping force.

The interpretation of Shakespeare's plays is a somewhat humble business, like the cleaning and restoration of the canvas of some old master; and, in both cases, the greatness of the originals enforces humility on whoever works on them. Humble though the interpreter may be, his activity is nevertheless needful to restore the lights and shades and fine tints of the original, for words dim quite as colors do, and only painstaking care and study can bring back the fleeting harmonies in shades of meaning and implied suggestion—those fine nuances that separate mere clever caricature from a great portrait. Malvolio is indeed a master portrait; but the world has moved so far away from him that generations of accumulated change have begrimed the colors, erased detail, and obliterated the background.

The modern reader, with his modern democracy and his modern liking for efficient management at any cost, finds Malvolio a rather commonplace, perhaps even a pathetic, type. The Industrial Revolution has made us used to social change and its hardships and its social interlopers: we do not condemn ambition that reaches out beyond its class, nor see in Malvolio's the symbol of social misery and disorganization. We neither suffer from, nor see, the hardships that these household changes shown in the play effected in the Elizabethan world; and so, as in the case of Shylock,[196] the bitterness of the dramatist and of the other characters finds no answering chord in us. This is the tragedy of great art, that a thing of beauty cannot be a joy forever, unless one can recapture the essential background of the age that brought it forth. Not only do we fail to see Malvolio's social implications, but we also miss his choleric nature and the implications of this choler; for, not merely social structure but intellectual beliefs and scientific theories are passing, temporal things. Thus we have either spoiled the comedy of the play by making Malvolio a sympathetic character, or tried to explain his disagreeable qualities on the mere basis of his being disagreeable, without realizing that his actions arise from a psychology that clashed with his lowly station and from a social change that made both his social class and his ambitions pernicious and odious.

[196] See J. W. Draper, "Usury in *The Merchant of Venice,*" *Modern Philology,* XXXIII, 37 *et seq.*

~ The Duke Orsino

HE Countess, by all the proprieties, should have married the Duke and so made him the Orlando-Romeo of the comedy. Until Act V, he cannot believe that she really means to refuse him, and thus his action in the play is a prolonged and bootless importunity, until he finally cures his passion by a second choice. Indeed, according to the old chivalric code, she should modestly delay as long as possible, and Orsino would naturally impute her denials to this convention. In Riche's *Apolonius*, the only one of Shakespeare's sources that develops the Duke, this episode is only one of several, but Shakespeare has prolonged it throughout four acts. In Riche, Orsino appears as "a verie yong man," but already "a worthie duke," who, fresh from the Turkish wars, tarries at Cyprus, meets the noble Silla, but is still too choleric from his recent fighting to requite her love. He goes on home to Constantinople, becomes enamored of a wealthy widow, the Lady Julina, woos her with all the proper signs of lovers' melancholy, but is repulsed. Silla runs away from home, enters his service as a page, and finally wins his love. This Byzantine romance presents Orsino as the usual hero, flawless in character and person, and all too amenable to the convenience of the author and to the exigencies of the melodramatic plot. Shakespeare takes him over, abbreviates his role, and humanizes him as far as possible.

Despite this reduction in Orsino's part, he remains a major character. His ducal rank alone would give him importance in Elizabethan eyes; and the presence in the winter of 1600–1601 at Elizabeth's court of that famous gentleman Virginio Orsino, Duke of Bracciano,[1] suggests that Shakespeare's Duke

[1] G. Sarrazin, *Shakespeare Jahrbuch*, XXXII, 168. See also "Letters Written by John Chamberlain," *Camden Society Publications* (1861), pp. 99–100. His embassy from Florence seems to have been purely a good-will visit of no particular political importance. My colleague, Professor J. P. Brawner, and Professor G. V. N. G. Orsini of the University of Florence (a descendant of the Duke), have been unable to find in the Florentine archives any material that suggests a connection between this embassy and the play.

was named in honor of an actual nobleman known to Londoners of the day. The love-melancholy, moreover, from which he suffers, would also have made him a sympathetic figure. Unfortunately, however, the twentieth century does not care for dukes, takes no stock in love-melancholy, and prefers success to failure even in love affairs; *ergo*, Orsino has passed under a cloud, and is usually presented on the modern stage, like the King in *Hamlet*,[2] as a rather wooden type. Indeed, the star system, so common in the theater, tends in any play to reduce all but the two chief roles to this lame and impotent conclusion. But to the Elizabethans, so important was the part that it was played, possibly by Shakespeare himself,[3] or more probably by the great Burbage.[4] Orsino appears in four scenes and speaks over two hundred lines; and the other characters reiterate his sovereign qualities. He is, moreover, crucial in the plot: he is Viola's protector in her hour of need and weds her at long last; he woos Olivia, delights in Feste, and dominates, by virtue of his rank, the final distribution of pardons and rewards. Nevertheless, time has so withered him and custom changed, that his colors must be renewed in order that their harmonies may be restored.

Critics have lent him but casual remark and that to little purpose. Schlegel refers in passing to "the music-enraptured Duke." Gervinus thinks that "something in the very nature of the Duke must have provoked Olivia's proud disdain," and so finds in him a "refined conceit"—doubtless because he proposed (like every husband of the day) to dominate his wife. Ruggles thinks him unrestrained; Kenny complains that his passion "is neither very deep nor very dramatic," and so seems to blame both the character and the dramatist who created him. The Arden editors declare Orsino "weak," though "highly cultivated": he is "a spoiled child who has set his heart on a particular toy," Olivia is the toy, and his love for her is not

[2] J. W. Draper, *The "Hamlet" of Shakespeare's Audience* (Durham, N.C., 1938), chapter ix.

[3] Suggested by Canon Ainger in 1884. See *Twelfth Night* (ed. Furness var.), pp. 389–90.

[4] T. W. Baldwin, *Organization and Personnel of the Shakespearean Company* (Princeton, 1927), Plate III.

real. (Why then does he so clearly show the symptoms of love-melancholy?) The Tudor editors do not find him "sympathetic," but think that Olivia's praises show that "we do not see him at his best." Gray likewise is not sympathetic, and thinks the play "has no hero."[5] Critics, in short, either dislike Orsino outright or damn him with faint excuses. He has been neglected in his status as a duke and in his more private capacity as a lover; the former dominates his social life, the latter, his psychology. An understanding of both the exterior and the inner man is essential for an understanding of his part.

Orsino's political status raises several questions. The Captain first mentions him as a "noble Duke"; on occasion, Viola and Valentine give him this title; and, in the folio, his speeches are commonly labeled "Duke" or "Du." On the other hand, Sir Toby, Sebastian, Antonio, and even Viola at times refer to him as "Count";[6] he is called "my Lord" rather than "Your Grace"; and one of his officers in official conversation actually calls him "Orsino" to his face,[7] a blunder deserving heavy chastisement but apparently overlooked on the occasion. Of course, he might well have been both Count and Duke, though in that case propriety required that he be called by the higher title; or perhaps the inconsistency arose in a revision of the play, or perhaps from Shakespeare's original carelessness. In like fashion, the "Emperor" in *Two Gentlemen of Verona* appears also as a "Duke," and the players King and Queen in *Hamlet* appear also as "Duke" and "Dutchesse." In any case, Orsino belongs high in the feudal hierarchy.

Whether Duke or Count, Orsino has the political sovereignty of a contemporary Italian or German noble rather than the dependence on the king to which the English aristocracy had fallen. In the first scene, he appears as a sovereign ruler surrounded by courtiers rather than as the courtier to a king. In the second scene, Viola is told that he "governes here," meaning Illyria or at least the seacoast part of it where Viola and the Captain have just been wrecked. Orsino has

[5] H. D. Gray, "Evolution of Shakespeare's Heroine," *J.E.G.P.*, XII, 122 *et seq.*
[6] *Twelfth Night*, I. iii. 102; I. iv. 10; II. i. 40; III. i. 38; III. iii. 30.
[7] *Ibid.*, V. i. 60.

"gallies," and apparently makes war on his own account.[8] He personally acts as judge of Antonio; and, though he usually speaks in his private capacity, he once uses the royal "we."[9] Shakespeare seems, therefore, to have thought of Illyria as a semi-independent fief of the Holy Roman Empire, like the contemporary Italian duchies, and so gave Orsino sovereign rights like those of the Dukes in *As You Like It* and *Measure for Measure*. The political side of his life, however, appears but little in the play, for comedy hardly requires the national scope of tragic themes.[10] The reasons of state that impelled Orsino to seek Olivia's hand are never mentioned—indeed, he professes no interest in her "quantitie of dirtie lands"[11]—and his entourage consists of charming courtiers rather than practical soldiers and statesmen.

Great as Orsino is as Duke of Illyria, however, the Countess Olivia seems to be quite independent of him, and in no sense his vassal. Viola's declaration that she brings "no ouerture of warre, no taxation of homage"[12] does not necessarily imply that Olivia had ever owed homage to Orsino. The fact that both live in the same "Towne"[13] proves nothing, for many semi-independent Italian nobles had palaces in the larger cities; and Orsino's threat in the end to kill Olivia out of hand certainly does not imply that he had any legal power over her. Indeed, if he had been her feudal suzerain, he would doubtless, as her guardian, have claimed the right to dispose of her hand in marriage as he saw fit, and so need not have troubled with a long and unsuccessful wooing; and, to clinch the matter, Olivia declares that her husband is "As great as" the Duke;[14] and this could hardly be if Orsino were her overlord. Orsino, therefore, though a more exalted noble than Olivia[15] and the holder of a title that took precedence of hers, was not her immediate

---

[8] *Twelfth Night*, III. iii. 30.   [9] *Ibid.*, V. i. 404.

[10] A. Huneke, "Shakespeares Englische Könige," *Shakespeare Jahrbuch* (1930); and J. W. Draper, "Political Themes in Shakespeare's Later Plays," *J.E.G.P.*, XXXV, 61 *et seq.* W. Clemen, "Shakespeare und das Königtum," *Shakespeare Jahrbuch* (1932), pp. 56–79. Cf. L. B. Campbell, *Shakespeare's Histories* (San Marino, Calif., 1947).

[11] *Twelfth Night*, II. iv. 87.   [12] *Ibid.*, I. v. 208–9.

[13] *Ibid.*, V. i. 85. Cf. III. iii. 27 and 47.

[14] *Ibid.*, V. i. 158–59.   [15] *Twelfth Night*, I. iii. 102–3.

Schiauone,ò vero Dalma-
tino.

AN ILLYRIAN GENTLEMAN
From Vecellio's *Habiti*, 1608

superior; and the political relationship of the two is that of sovereign states, one presumably larger and more powerful than the other, but each separate and distinct. Orsino could readily have been depicted as seeking the match for the good political purpose of augmenting his domains—and Elizabethans considered prudential marriages quite justified[16]—but, if so, the comedy would have taken on a far more serious cast. Thus Orsino is depicted as moved only by the love that so consumes him.

Nevertheless, Orsino is a reigning Duke, and this fact has its influence on his character, his psychology, and his ultimate good fortune. The Renaissance justified the absolute monarchies of the age on the basis of the Bible and the Classics.[17] Thus rulers, being more or less divinely authorized, should generally be virtuous and admirable, especially so because "a veniall sinne" in another was "a great crime" in a king.[18] Drama, moreover, was supposed to be "instructive";[19] and so a wicked, or even a weak, man in high place must make the play tragedy, as it does in *Hamlet*,[20] *Macbeth*,[21] and *Lear*.[22] Orsino, of necessity, must be all that was good and virtuous in a ruler: even the usurping Duke in *As You Like It* has to repent, though somewhat unconvincingly, before a happy ending is assured. Comedy does not consort with evil in high places.

The hero of Riche's novel had "verie greate" wealth, and had showed "prowesse" against the Turks so that "all the world was filled with the fame of this noble Duke." Shakespeare likewise endows Orsino with high reputation and great estate, but does not particularly stress his martial deeds. The Captain

[16] H. P. Pettigrew, "Bassanio, the Elizabethan Lover," *Philological Quarterly*, XVI, 296 *et seq.*

[17] J. W. Allen, *Political Thought in the Sixteenth Century* (New York, 1928), pp. 126 *et seq.*; J. N. Figgis, *The Divine Right of Kings* (Cambridge, 1922), pp. 89 *et seq.* See also J. W. Draper, *Shakespeare Jahrbuch* (1938), p. 129.

[18] King James, *Workes* (London, 1619), p. 148.

[19] A. H. Gilbert, "Seneca and the Criticism of Elizabethan Tragedy," *Philological Quarterly*, XIII, 370 *et seq.*

[20] J. W. Draper, *"Hamlet,"* ed. cit., chap. ix.

[21] J. W. Draper, "Macbeth, 'Infirme of Purpose,' " *Bulletin of Medical History*, X, 16 *et seq.*

[22] J. W. Draper, "The Old Age of King Lear," *J.E.G.P.*, XXXIX, 527 *et seq.*

tells Viola that he is "A noble Duke in nature, as in name,"[23] and even the obdurate Olivia declares:

> Yet I suppose him vertuous, know him noble,
> Of great estate, of fresh and stainlesse youth,
> In voyces well divulg'd, free, learn'd, valiant,
> And in dimension, and the shape of nature,
> A gracious person . . . .[24]

In short, he is, like Chaucer's Knight, a nonpareil of noblemen, and a complete foil to Sir Andrew and Sir Toby. Perhaps Shakespeare in these eulogies was complimenting the actual Duke for whom Orsino seems to have been named; perhaps he was merely following his source; but, in either case he was delineating Orsino not as a choleric type just returned from the wars as in Riche, but as sanguine, the humor proper to courtiers and nobles.[25] Blood was considered the best of all the bodily fluids;[26] and the planet Jupiter, which ruled the sanguine type, brought to those it influenced "the greatest fortune. . . . ."[27] Such men were "moderate, mery, pleasant"; they were "iust, true, benevolent, liberall, faithfull, milde, godly, shamefast, magnanimous . . . . honorable, faithfull and happie";[28] they were "affable in speech" and "liberally minded."[29] Olivia's description states or implies that Orsino is all these things. He is especially possessed of that magnanimity that Spenser celebrated in the *Faerie Queene* as the crowning glory of a prince's character, and that Dariot associated with sanguine men. Walkington's description of the type as "liberally minded" seems to imply it; Hill declared them good natured;[30] and Elyot said that they were "Angrie shortly."[31] Orsino, indeed, is the very exponent of conciliation: he forgives the snubs of Olivia, though hurt pride is a painful wound; his only revenge on Viola is marrying her; indeed, he accepts the

[23] *Twelfth Night*, I. ii. 27.   [24] *Ibid.*, I. v. 256 *et seq.*
[25] C. Dariot, *Iudgement of the Starres* (London, 1598), sig. D 2 v.
[26] *Batman upon Bartholome* (London, 1582), leaf 30 r; L. Lemnius, *Touchstone of Complexions* (London, 1581), leaves 86 v and 87 v.
[27] Dariot, *op. cit.*, sig. D 2 v.   [28] *Ibid.*, sig. D 2 v.
[29] T. W[alkington], *Optick Glasse*, London (1631?), p. 116.
[30] T. Hyll [Hill], *Schoole of Skill* (London, 1599), leaf 7 v.
[31] Sir T. Elyot, *Castell of Helth* (London, 1541), leaf 2 r. Cf. leaf 8 r.

Countess' offer of a double wedding at her house, and he condescends even to wish Malvolio entreated "to a peace." In short, Orsino's noble rank and far-famed excellencies are in accord with each other and also with his naturally sanguine humor and the associated astral influence of Jupiter.

His physique and age, moreover, agree with this complexion. Olivia in her initial eulogy declares that "in dimension and the shape of nature," he is "A gracious person"; and his part clearly calls for the commanding charm and elegance of address that Shakespeare and Burbage as actors doubtless gave it: sanguine men were supposed to be handsome,[32] and Dariot describes them as of "faire stature."[33] Orsino's age, furthermore, would seem to imply this humor. In Riche, he was "verie yong," in fact, had not previously known love; and Olivia seems to echo this in attributing to him "fresh and stainless youth." On the other hand, he is no boy: he has a nephew, Titus, presumably the son of an elder sister, who is old enough to have fought in a sea battle;[34] and he is apparently older than Viola.[35] Elizabethan writers link the sanguine temper with various periods between adolescence and old age: Cuffe associates it with the "Prime" of life beginning about twenty-five;[36] and Lemnius likens it to spring, and thinks it "proper to lustye flourishinge age."[37] Orsino, therefore, would seem to be sanguine, not only because of his birth and station but also because of his period of life; and, if one may place the action of the comedy in the month of May,[38] then the springtime of the year also consorts with his jovial complexion.[39]

In Shakespeare's comedy, Orsino appears primarily as a lover, and sanguine men were thought to be especially susceptible to love.[40] The liver was "the shop of Bloud," the heart

---

[32] Walkington, *op. cit.*, p. 115; *The Most Excellent Booke of Arcandam* (London, 1592), sig. M 2 r.

[33] Dariot, *op. cit.*, sig. D 2 v.

[34] *Twelfth Night*, V. i. 63. [35] *Ibid.*, II. iv. 33 *et seq.*

[36] H. Cuffe, *Differences of the Ages of Mans Life* (London, 1607), pp. 118–19.

[37] Lemnius, *op. cit.* (ed. 1576), leaf 86 v.

[38] See Appendix A. [39] Elyot, *op. cit.*, leaf 71 v.

[40] R. Burton, *Anatomy of Melancholy*, Part III, Sec. 2, Mem. 2, p. 1; J. Ferrand, Ἐρωτομανία (Oxford, 1640), p. 64; N. Coeffeteau, *Table of Humane Passions* (London, 1621), sigs. D and E.

121

its "fountaine,"[41] and sanguine men were especially given to diseases of these two organs.[42] Cogan declared that this "complection is most giuen to Venus,"[43] and Lemnius took as its chief defect its susceptibility to "horrible lustes."[44] But honest love between two persons of the sanguine type, according to Ferrand, was likely to prove "happy and full of delight."[45] In short, Orsino is by innate humor a Romeo or an Orlando. He differs, however, from the former in that Romeo has already experienced unrequited love, and emerges from it in his triumphant courtship of Juliet; he differs from the latter in that Orlando never knows the melancholy pains of having loved and lost. Strange that the critics should so readily forgive Romeo for his desertion of the cruel Rosaline, but hold against Orsino his like desertion of the cruel Olivia. Indeed, Orsino's part is an expansion of Romeo's plight before he found his Juliet, or a picture of Orlando's sufferings if Rosalind and Fortune had not favored his tender passion. In short, the Duke has succumbed to love-melancholy, a malady "most evident among such as are young and lusty, in the flower of their years, nobly descended, high fed, such as live idly and at ease."[46] Possibly Orsino's father and Olivia some time before their deaths had planned for such a match, though in that case the children would doubtless have been formally betrothed, and Orsino's problem of courtship would have been simpler. Perhaps, without parental guidance, he himself fell violently in love; and, just as Riche's Apolonius, because current occasion gave him another humor, ignored the love of Silla, so Shakespeare's Olivia, melancholy at the death of father and brother, refused to listen to Orsino. But how did he fall in love when the two hardly knew one another by sight!

Thus Orsino, as a noble, is sanguine, and as a man of sanguine humor, is in love; but, despite the good fortune of his planet, this love is not returned, and so his innate temper

---

[41] Lemnius, *op. cit.*, leaf 89 v.

[42] Dariot, *op. cit.*, sig. D 2 v.

[43] T. Cogan, *Haven of Health* (London, 1589), sig. Hh 2 v.

[44] Lemnius, *op. cit.* (ed. 1576), leaf 23 v.

[45] Ferrand, *op. cit.* (ed. 1645), p. 93.   [46] Burton, *op. cit.*, III, 2, 1, 2.

gives way to melancholy, a dangerous disease. Like Polonius when a youth, he

> Fell into a sadness, then into a fast,
> Thence to a watch, thence into a weakness . . . .

Indeed, Orsino suffers from such extremity of love that it "could be but recompenc'd, though you [Olivia] were crown'd The non-pareil of beautie."[47] Of course, by all the proprieties, she should have married him; but, like most Elizabethan men, he thought of the weaker sex as inferior to his own, even in their love.[48] And so the lady, who apparently valued her political and personal independence, repeatedly declares that she "cannot loue him,"[49] and Viola has no choice but to return him this reply. Nevertheless, he "cannot so be ansewr'd,"[50] and he pursues his bootless quest. Indeed, the lady's "graces"[51] and the rich emotion that she displays at her brother's death[52] make her all the more attractive. He cannot court in the conventional way through her father or a male relative; he cannot see her himself without risking the contumely of a direct rebuff. And so he resorts to Valentine and then to Viola as go-betweens, and, by evading them, Olivia continues in the role of "soueraigne crueltie" for over a month before the play begins,[53] and then for four full acts, lets her lover pine in misery until his messenger proposes to build "a willow Cabine"[54] at her gate, and sing songs of "contemned loue."[55] Indeed, Orsino was the very man to fall in love, and Olivia was the very woman to refuse him.

This love-melancholy that dominates Orsino throughout almost the whole play appears in the tempo of his speech, which is variable and sometimes even jerky. The general average of his verse is 1 to 1½+, a proportion that would probably be faster if his prose could be taken into account, for prose was

---

[47] *Twelfth Night*, I. v. 250–51.
[48] *Ibid.*, II. iv. 99 *et seq.* Cf. Ferrand, *op. cit.*, p. 213, citing Aristotle.
[49] *Twelfth Night*, I. v. 255, 260, 281.   [50] *Ibid.*, II. iv. 92–93.
[51] *Ibid.*, I. v. 239.   [52] *Ibid.*, I. i. 38 *et seq.*   [53] *Ibid.*, I. ii. 32 *et seq.*
[54] Cf. Burton, *op. cit.*, Part III, Sec. 2, Mem. 5, p. 5.
[55] *Twelfth Night*, I. v. 269. On the willow as a symbol of unrequited love, see J. W. Draper, *The Funeral Elegy* (New York, 1929), Appendix A.

doubtless rendered on the stage in tripping, colloquial style. This average is not notable; and, in his four scenes, he maintains it fairly evenly: in Act I, scene i, his tempo runs 1 to 2+; in I. iv, it is 1 to 1+; in II. iv, it is 1 to 2; and, in V. i, it is again 1 to 1+. Possibly its slower pace suggests the gradual cure of his love-sickness for Olivia—in preparation for the change to Viola in the last scene. Orsino's melancholy, however, did not express itself so much in fast or slow tempo per se, as in a variable, rubato rhythm, apparent less in the mere enumeration of items of evidence than in the juxtaposition of extreme and opposite indications. In his very first speech, for example, he uses "o'er" and "'Tis," suggesting speed, and then "it was" in slow time, and then "spirit" slurred quickly into one syllable, and, shortly after, "affections" slurred into three syllables and then "perfecti ons" spaced out in four. His first speech in the fourth scene yields in less than seven lines six items of evidence, three clearly slow mingled with three others equally fast, so that a smooth delivery seems hardly possible. In Act II, scene iv, likewise, when he discusses the pangs of true love, he interlards clear evidences of fast and of slow speech. This jerkiness continues into Act V, until the Duke realizes that Viola is a girl and determines to marry her. His speech suddenly becomes both slower and more even, or legato. These lines show nine definite items for fast and only four, much less definite, for slow delivery. In short, when Orsino's malady is cured, he drops his nervous trick of speech; his inner conflict is resolved, with a resurgence of his normal sanguine self.

Some critics have imputed a lack of depth, if not absolute insincerity, to Shakespeare's "music-enraptured Duke."[56] Gray stigmatizes his passion as "sentimental,"[57] and Sir E. K. Chambers calls him a "thistle-down amorist."[58] Indeed, as Burton admits, the dejected look of lovers, might be simulated.[59] But

[56] *Twelfth Night* (ed. Furness var.), pp. 378 and 382.

[57] H. D. Gray, *op. cit.*, p. 125.

[58] Edmund Chambers, *Shakespeare, a Survey* (New York, 1926), p. 174.

[59] Burton, *op. cit.*, Part III, Sec. 2, Mem. 2, p. 4. Cf. T. Wright, *Passions of the Minde* (London, 1604), p. 204.

the Duke, on his part, protests that he does not court the Countess because of her "quantitie of dirtie lands";[60] and so, unless we suppose the virtuous Orsino to be something of a liar, his statement shows that at least he thought he loved the lady for herself—even though he finally accepted the inevitable in Act V. Certainly, he had been persistent for a long time despite her reiterated refusals. Just what is the depth and the nature of this love, and what is its importance in the comedy?

In Greek, Arabic, Medieval, and Renaissance medicine, lovesickness was a well-recognized disease,[61] a condition of the system in which a superfluity of black bile produced "melancholy" in the patient; and this condition might cause insanity or death. That Shakespeare should portray Orsino as melancholy from love is not surprising: he had so depicted Romeo;[62] and Burton expressly interprets the courtship of Benedick and Beatrice in *Much Ado About Nothing* in terms of this disease.[63] Orsino's melancholy, furthermore, follows the medical authorities of the day in its origin, symptoms, and development and also in its effects on the psychology and the way of life of the sufferer.

As one should expect, Orsino's malady entered his system through his eyes;[64] the Greek Theocritus[65] and the Medieval Dante[66] had so experienced it, and Castiglione so describes its advent.[67] Contemporary medical authorities such as Boaistuau,[68] Burton,[69] and Ferrand[70] take the eyes as the source of infection; and Olivia herself, later in the play, contracts the malady in this manner.[71] The text suggests the disease's progress: the organs most affected are "Liuer, Braine and Hart";[72] Orsino's passion is written in the first chapter of his "hart," and true

[60] *Twelfth Night*, II. iv. 87.
[61] See J. L. Lowes, "The Loveres Maladye of Hereos," *Mod. Phil.*, XI, 491 *et seq.*
[62] See J. Cole, "Romeo and Rosaline," *Neophilologus*, XXIV, 285 *et seq.*
[63] Burton, *op. cit.*, Part III, Sec. 2, Mem. 2, p. 4.
[64] *Twelfth Night*, I. i. 23–24.
[65] Theocritus, *Idyllium ii*, "Pharmaceutria."   [66] Dante, *Vita Nuova*, Sec. ii.
[67] B. Castiglione, *Courtier* (ed. Rouse and Henderson), p. 247.
[68] P. Boaistuau, *Theatrum Mundi*, tr. Alday (London, 1581), 192–93.
[69] Burton, *op. cit.*, III, 2, 2, 2; III, 2, 3; and III, 2, 5, 2.
[70] Ferrand, *op. cit.*, pp. 11–12, 41–42, 124. Cf. N. Breton, *Melancholike Humours* (London, 1600), No. 21.
[71] *Twelfth Night*, II. ii. 21 *et seq.*   [72] *Ibid.*, I. v. 224.

love apparently must show itself in the "Liuer."[73] This is all good contemporary medicine. Of course, a superfluity of black bile would at once affect the liver and in time other organs.[74] Ferrand, following Ficino, describes the whole process:

Love, having first enterd at the Eyes, which are the Faithful spies and intelligencers of the soule, steales gently through those sluces, and so passing insensibly through the veines to the Liver, it there presently [at once] imprinteth an ardent desire of the Object, which is either really lovely, or at least appears to be so. Now this desire, once enflemed . . . . presently layeth siege to the Heart: of which having once fully possesst itself, as being the strongest fort of all, it assaults so violently the Reason, and all the noble forces of the Braine, that they are suddenly forced to yeeld themselves to its subjection.[75]

Ferrand terms the erotic the third type of melancholy, seated in the "Liuer, Spleen, Mesentery, Guts, the veine of the Matrix and other adjoining parts";[76] and he argues that the heart rather than the brain is the chief organ of love.[77] Laurentius finds that the malady starts in the eyes and proceeds in order to the liver, heart, and brain.[78] Boaistuau states that it begins in the heart of the adorer, proceeds to his eyes, and so to the eyes of the adored, thence to her heart and so to her whole body; he even declares that he has seen patients, "theire poore heart all burned, their Liuer and Lights all vaded and confumed, their Braines envomaged."[79] In short, the physical course of Orsino's sickness follows the pattern ascribed to the actual disease of love-melancholy, and this implies the depth and sincerity of his passion, and seems to confute Gray, Chambers, and the Arden editors.

The effect of black bile on the brain gave the disease a psychological aspect, and here likewise Orsino's symptoms ac-

[73] *Twelfth Night*, I. i. 42–44.

[74] Lemnius, *op. cit.*, leaf 89 v; and Burton, *op. cit.*, Part III, Sec. 2, Mem. 2, p. 1, and Part III, Sec. 2, Mem. 3. The Greeks seem to have believed that black bile belonged rather in the spleen; but Elizabethans associated the spleen more with choler. E.g., *Julius Caesar*, IV. iii. 39 *et seq.*

[75] Ferrand, *op. cit.*, pp. 67–68.   [76] *Ibid.*, pp. 25–26.

[77] *Ibid.*, chaps. ix and xiv.

[78] A. Laurentius, *Discourse of the Preservation of the Sight* (tr. Surphlet), (London, 1599), p. 118.

[79] Boaystuau [Boaistuau] *op. cit.* (ed. 1574), pp. 202–3.

126

cord with contemporary science. In Riche's story, the Duke woos the Lady Julina with "faire woords, sorrowfull sighes, and piteous countenances"; and Shakespeare develops this suggestion. Love was thought to be an exquisite anguish. The very rapidity of Orsino's first speeches suggests his passion, especially since, as a Duke, he should speak with dignified deliberation. He compares his feeling to "fell and cruell hounds,"[80] he refers to it as his "passion" and his "woes";[81] his "adorations" are composed of "fertill teares" and "groanes" and "sighs of fire";[82] and yet these are "sweet pangs."[83] Olivia, moreover, in love with the disguised Viola, suffers no less a "passion."[84] Nicholas Breton, to be sure, refers to the "pleasure" of love-melancholy;[85] but most writers dwell rather, as Orsino does, on its pains. Burton terms it a "grievous wound," a "consuming fire," an "intolerable pain";[86] he lists its torments,[87] and declares them greater than the tortures of the Inquisition.[88] Ferrand ascribes to it "diverse and violent perturbations";[89] Boaistuau and Bullein consider it the "most grieuous" of all human experiences;[90] and Laurentius calls it "the greatest miserie."[91] For all his fine speeches, however, Orsino's suffering seems rather a weary boredom than a sharp agony; and Burton remarks how slowly time passes for a lover in the absence of his lady.[92]

Such a passion, if protracted, could not but change the lover's way of life, manners, and character. Melancholy men were thought to be shy and taciturn.[93] They were "of deepe cogitation . . . . solitarie, mournfull" and given to "few woords."[94] They "have no pleasure to bee any where but in solitarie places."[95] In extreme cases, they are such that what

80 *Twelfth Night*, I. i. 26.   81 *Twelfth Night*, I. iv. 26 and 28.
82 *Ibid.*, I. v. 253–54.   83 *Ibid.*, II. iv. 19.
84 *Ibid.*, II. iii. 130–31.   85 N. Breton, *Fantastics* (London, 1626).
86 Burton, *op. cit.*, Part III, Sec. 2, Mem. 3.
87 *Ibid.*, Part III, Sec. 2, Mem. 1, p. 2.
88 *Ibid.*, Part III, Sec. 2, Mem. 3.   89 Ferrand, *op. cit.*, p. 7 *et seq.*
90 Boaystuau, *op. cit.* (ed. 1574), pp. 201–2; Bullein, *Bulwarke of Defence* (London, 1579), leaves 25 v and 30 v.
91 Laurentius, *op. cit.*, p. 119.   92 Burton, *op. cit.*, Part III, Sec. 2, Mem. 3.
93 Lemnius, *op. cit.*, leaf 146 v.   94 Dariot, *op. cit.*, sig. D 2.
95 Laurentius, *op. cit.*, pp. 81 and 82.

"nature made sociable . . . . a crazed disposition has altered."[96] Orsino declares that he is "best When least in companie";[97] and, perhaps partly for that reason, he woos by proxy. According to Burton, lovers seek to be alone,[98] and "neglect all ordinary business";[99] and Orsino never appears as attending to affairs of state. Olivia calls him "valiant"; but, in the play, love-melancholy has reduced him to a shy diffidence.

Indeed, Orsino, like the "poor Inamorato" of Ferrand, can think "of nothing but his dearely beloved Mistresse";[100] his judgment and imagination have become "depraved,"[101] and so he grows "churlish . . . . and ill to please"[102]—all the more credit to Viola for winning her way to his good graces! Though naturally, "A gracious person," the intensity of his passion leads him to unmannerly rudeness, and he tells his messenger to "Be clamorous, and leape all ciuill bounds"[103] to bring his sad case to Olivia's deaf ears; and quite so, according to the best authority, the lover was supposed to go to any length to move his mistress.[104] Like Orsino, he might even cast all decorum aside and "forget all honesty."[105] Indeed, the Duke, by losing his ducal sanguine humor, has lost the graciousness that ought to grace his station and his wooing.

Love-melancholy makes Orsino not only shy and rude but also unstable and whimsical. Generally, the sanguine type was considered "faithfull"[106] and "constant,"[107] and Valentine tells Viola that Orsino is not "inconstant";[108] and Orsino certainly does pursue his love with a constant persistence. Melancholy, however, was thought to impart a changeable and fickle disposition: Burton quotes Lucian on the contradictory passions of lovers;[109] Ferrand declares love "humorsome and Inconstant";[110] and Coeffeteau[111] and Boaistuau[112] agree. This is the

[96] T. Overbury, *Characters*, "Melancholy Man."   [97] *Twelfth Night*, I. iv. 39–40.
[98] Burton, *op. cit.*, Part III, Secs. 2–3.   [99] *Ibid.*, Part III, Sec. 2, Mem. 3.
[100] Ferrand, *op. cit.*, p. 68; and Coeffeteau, *op. cit.*, pp. 170 *et seq.*
[101] Ferrand, *op. cit.*, p. 31.   [102] Lemnius, *op. cit.* (ed. 1576), leaf 146 r.
[103] *Twelfth Night*, I. iv. 23–24.   [104] Burton, *op. cit.*, Part III, Sec. 2, Mem. 3.
[105] *Ibid.*, Part III, Sec. 2, Mems. 3 and 4.   [106] Dariot, *op. cit.*, sig. D 2 v.
[107] Walkington, *op. cit.*, p. 117. Cf. Coeffeteau, *op. cit.*, p. 238.
[108] *Twelfth Night*, I. iv. 8.   [109] Burton, *op. cit.*, Part III, Sec. 2, Mem. 3.
[110] Ferrand, *op. cit.*, p. 320.
[111] Coeffeteau, *op cit.*, pp. 173–74.   [112] Boaystuau, *op. cit.* (ed. 1574), p. 204.

abnormal Orsino that the comedy presents; and well may Feste commend him to "the melancholly God" in the same passage that he describes his mind as "a very Opall."[113] The Duke himself admits that he is like "all true Louers . . . . Vnstaid and skittish."[114] When he first appears at the very beginning of the play, this symptom of his disease is at once evident: he calls for music, then suddenly for silence; he wants his love to "sicken and so dye," and yet in a moment he is asking for "newes" of Olivia. He himself blames these shifting moods on the "spirit of Loue." Thus, even when the curtain rises, Orsino is far gone in "heroical [erotic] melancholy." Its physical effects already influence his liver and other organs, and its psychological effects have quite changed his sanguine geniality: his passion is truly a suffering; he avoids company; he grows unmannerly; and he has lost stability of character and purpose.

Of course, the patient must seek relief. In the first scene, one of Orsino's courtiers suggests that he go hunting, for hunting was supposed to have a therapeutic value;[115] but Orsino replies merely by punning on the word "hart," for he is too much in love to hunt. He does, however, try to relieve his troubles by telling them to Cesario; and Burton notes that the lover may assuage his pain by confessing his love "to some judicious friend."[116] He turns to music, not to frivolous tunes but to an "old and Antike song," which, he thinks, will "releeue my passion much";[117] but, unfortunately, as he himself well knows, music is the "food of Loue,"[118] and so the palliative in the end was liable to augment the malady. Castiglione,[119] Wright,[120] Ferrand,[121] and Burton,[122] all mention the power of music as "a great enticement" to love. Perhaps it is this "straine" of music that renews his eagerness for tidings of

[113] *Twelfth Night*, II. iv. 78 *et seq.*   [114] *Ibid.*, II. iv. 20–21.

[115] See Laurentius, *op. cit.*, p. 123; and Ferrand, *op. cit.*, p. 328.

[116] Burton, *op. cit.*, Part III, Sec. 2, Mem. 5, p. 2.

[117] *Twelfth Night*, II. iv. 3 *et seq.*

[118] *Ibid.*, I. i. 4. Cf. *Antony and Cleopatra*, II. v. 1. Some critics think that music was supposed to feed on love, but Furness corrects this: music feeds (i.e., increases) love.

[119] Castiglione, *op. cit.*, pp. 75–76.   [120] Wright, *op. cit.*, pp. 163 and 165.

[121] Ferrand, *op. cit.*, pp. 46 and 251. But "Doricke Musicke" (i.e., martial) was thought to cure love. See *ibid.*, pp. 314 and 329.

[122] Burton, *op. cit.*, Part III, Sec. 2, Mem. 2, p. 4.

Olivia when he had just expressed the wish that his "appetite" might "sicken and so dye." Orsino has experienced sighs and tears,[123] and they were credited with giving some modicum of ease.[124] But all these things were mere alleviations. The final cure appears at the conclusion of the play. In the scenes immediately preceding, other events have crowded the Duke's love affair off the stage; but apparently, during this interim, he sees nothing of his lady, and perhaps this continued absence helps to effect his cure.[125] In the final scene, Orsino and Olivia meet; she rejects him to his face; and he turns for consolation to his favorite servitor, Cesario, who has suddenly turned out to be a girl. Perhaps this is the inconstancy of love-melancholy asserting itself.[126] Thus at the end of the play, he tries the cure that Romeo used at the beginning—the substitution of another love. This method of treatment accords with the advice of Burton[127] and Ferrand,[128] and apparently it is successful. In short, the whole course of Orsino's infatuation, from its beginning in his eyes, through its months of suffering, to its conclusion when he weds Viola, runs true to the best authorities and must have seemed to the Elizabethans very realistic.

Several critics, nevertheless, imply that Orsino's love savored of fashionable affectation, that he was merely acting out the polite conventions of Medieval courtly love or of the so-called Platonic love that was so popular in the Renaissance. These systems, of course, had much in common with contemporary medical theory, but some distinguishing criteria exist. The noble Duke is obviously not indulging in the purely ideal ecstasies of Platonic love: he is no nympholept; his aim is clearly marriage; and, when Olivia, face to face at last refuses him, he takes Viola to wife. The courtly love of the Middle Ages is almost equally remote: Viola is not Orsino's social superior, nor is she the wife of another; nor do Orsino's sufferings approximate the violence of those described by Fowler as

[123] *Twelfth Night*, I. v. 253–54.

[124] Coeffeteau, *op. cit.*, pp. 170 *et seq.*; and Burton, *op. cit.*, Part III, Sec. 2, Mem. 3.

[125] Ferrand, *op. cit.*, p. 218. On the length of this interim, see Appendix A.

[126] Some authorities associated inconstancy also with the sanguine type. (Lemnius, *op. cit.*, leaf 101 v; and Coeffeteau, *op. cit.*, p. 238.)

[127] Ferrand, *op. cit.*, p. 257.   [128] Burton, *op. cit.*, Part III, Sec. 2, Mem. 5, p. 2.

belonging to courtly love.[129] Either of these conventions would have regarded his turning to Viola as a cardinal sin, and cardinal sins consort neither with the character of a noble Duke nor with the conclusion of a comedy. No, no. Orsino is genuinely ill with a mild case of a serious disease, and his cure in the end is essential to the comic conclusion of the play. He is not a "thistle-down amorist," as Sir E. K. Chambers would suppose, but, like the Prince in Ford's *Lover's Melancholy*, he is sincerely and seriously in love; and Viola doubtless makes him a better wife than the self-willed Olivia would have.

The narrative form in which Riche cast his *Apolonius* allowed time for the hero to recover at leisure; but Shakespeare was forced by the confines of drama to greater speed and compression. Orsino's illness becomes a sort of frame to the play, and helps to give it the predominant tone of high-life elegance that belongs to comedy of manners. Indeed, his very disease was a prerogative of the gently born and of a life of leisure: the "coystrill" Malvolio and the parvenu Sir Andrew are free of this fine malady; it affects only Orsino, and Olivia, and possibly Viola, setting them off, along with their gorgeous clothes and exquisite manners and blank-verse speeches, from those of lesser station. Thus the Elizabethans recognized a sort of social class in medicine, quite as physicians find today the prevalence of certain diseases in certain social groups. Indeed, from this angle, *Twelfth Night* is a genial satire on the vulgar love of Malvolio and Sir Andrew in contrast to the refined passion of Orsino, Olivia, and Viola-Sebastian. Truly, as Burton says, "Such acts and scenes hath this tragicomedy of love."[130]

In Shakespeare's *Twelfth Night*, Orsino appears rather as man than as a duke and rather as a lover than as a man, for his love has warped him from his normal self. He is a great nobleman, and as such is by nature sanguine; but his passion for the stony-hearted Olivia has overwhelmed him and turned the

[129] E. B. Fowler, *Spenser and the System of Courtly Love* (Louisville, Ky., 1934), pp. 1–2 and chap. iv. Cf. L. E. Pearson, *Elizabethan Love Conceptions* (Berkeley, Calif., 1933).

[130] Burton, *op. cit.*, Part III, Sec. 2, Mem. 4.

vital heat and moisture that belonged to the humor blood into a cold and dry black bile of weariness and exhaustion, the humor of illness, debility, and old age. He has jumped from one end of the Galenic gamut to the other; and, astrologically likewise, he has lapsed from the highest fortune to the lowest. This is indeed a sad situation for a young and virtuous prince, and surely only the carping critic will object to the consolation and cure that he seeks in Viola. Indeed, according to all the canons of propriety, Olivia, after a proper mourning and a proper pause to express her maidenly coyness, should have jumped at the chance; and Orsino was socially chagrined and publicly snubbed when she did not; but his princely magnanimity asserts itself, and he forgives and forgets, and joins in a double wedding as outward sign that he bears no grudge. Whether Romeo would have been as accommodating if Paris had won Juliet, or Bassanio if the Prince of Aragon had won Portia, belongs in the sphere of learned hypothesis along with the question of what song the sirens sang; but the present writer is sure that these two pre-eminent lovers could not have shown a more considerate affabilty than the sick and suffering Orsino. Truly, he deserves an honorable place among those who loved and lost, and promptly made the best of a bad bargain that, one guesses, turned out to be a good one after all.

ɶ The Lady Viola

HAKESPEARE's Viola appears in the second scene, a young lady without a past, without visible means of support (though she has "gold" to give the worthy Captain),[1] and indeed without most of those trappings of current realism so apparent in Sir Toby and Maria. Like a fairy princess, she appears from nowhere in particular; her ship, of unrecorded port and destination, has been wrecked; and no one ever tells the purpose of this voyage that she so readily abandons.[2] The truculent waves merely toss her on the Illyrian shore, and the comedy begins. Her own first comments are entirely devoted to her brother's fate and to her own immediate plans; and even that little of her past that inference fragmentarily supplies has elements of question. Clearly, she is of gentle birth: on her first appearance, the Captain, who should know more than we do of her antecedents, calls her "Ladie" and "Madam," whereas she addresses him by the *thee* and *thou* of condescension; both Maria and Sir Toby accept her, disguised as Cesario, as a "gentleman"; the Duke calls her twin brother "right noble";[3] and indeed, she could not have been so successful a "Seruing-man," an exacting occupation,[4] and could not have impressed the Countess with her "fiue-fold blazon" of heraldic ancestry,[5] had she not possessed the arts and elegancies that were the prerogatives of rank. In that case, however, she should be married, or at least betrothed. Her father, to be sure, had died when she was but thirteen;[6] but, unless he was remiss, he should have had her future safely settled long ere that;[7] and yet she is apparently un-

[1] *Twelfth Night*, I. ii. 20.   [2] See Appendix B.

[3] *Ibid.*, II. i. 19; V. i. 246; V. i. 279.

[4] *Ibid.*, III. ii. 8; [G. Markham], *Gentlemanly Profession of Servingmen* (London, 1598).

[5] *Twelfth Night*, I. v. 294.   [6] *Ibid.*, V. i. 246 *et seq.*

[7] C. L. Powell, *English Domestic Relations, 1487–1653* (New York, 1917), pp. 13 *et passim.*

attached, voyaging about for no known purpose with, as it seems, only her youthful brother as a chaperon. In short, Viola does not evolve into the play, as Sir Toby does, from a clear and convincing past, but miraculously rises, like Venus, directly from the sea.

Her actions, upon safely reaching shore and stepping into the plot, are even more inexplicable. Why does she decide to conceal her "estate" and serve the local Duke, instead of going straight home to her presumably anxious relatives, or continuing on the errand of her voyage? Why does she linger in Illyria, a country described by Antonio to Sebastian as "Rough and vnhospitable"? And finally why, without fit pomp and circumstance, does she woo and wed Orsino (unmaidenly procedure!) in disguise, unknown to her people and unprotected by a formal betrothal and a proper financial settlement? Her father, indeed, had been famous, and was apparently known to the Duke,[8] who doubtless would have entertained her in fit fashion had she told her name; but instead, she becomes a mere pseudonymous servingman, a most unhopeful status, improbable of future fame and fortune[9] excepting in romance. Indeed, this fair young lady quite dispenses with the current mores of her sex and station; and, to the Elizabethans, her background must have seemed a most conspicuous vacuum, for they were socially minded and thought in terms, not of the untrammeled individual, but of regulated families and classes. This situation of twin brother and sister at loose ends in a strange town perhaps should be explained as the consequence of some usurper's seizing on their patrimony and thus driving them forth as partners in exile: Viola's reference to her fallen fortunes[10] lends credence to this view; and yet she says that her estate is "well," and she has "gold" to give away. In short, her past reverses are something shadowy and obscure, and she herself shows no more sorrow for them than does a princess in a story. Having

<hr />

[8] *Twelfth Night*, II. i. 16–18; V. i. 279.

[9] J. W. Draper, "Falstaff's Robin and Other Pages," *Studies in Philology*, XXXVI, 476 *et seq.*

[10] *Twelfth Night*, I. v. 278.

134

closed these former chapters of her life, she steps forth into the future with an unquenched expectation, as if she had never known disappointment and misfortune: in short, Viola's past, whatever it may have been, makes little impress on either her later actions or her mental bent. She *is*, and however she *became*, we do not know. She *does*, but the outcome of her *doing* depends but little on the laws of normal life.

Sometimes Shakespeare's sources, by revealing the dramatist's changes and thus his purpose in a given character or action, offer a clue to matters not directly revealed; and, as many of these old stories were popular, the audience, unless the text of the play definitely interfered, was likely to fill in from the original motives and actions that the dramatist omitted. In Riche's tale, Viola's past is told at some length, and her actions, limned in the vivid colors of Byzantine romance, grow from this past like an opal rooted in its matrix. Silla, the prototype of Viola in Riche, is daughter to Pontus, King of Cyprus. Duke Apolonius, on his way home from the Turkish wars, is tempest-tossed to Cyprus, is entertained there by Pontus and the "peerlesse" Silla, and unwittingly inspires the latter's love. He goes on home to Constantinople, whither she embarks to follow him with the faithful Pedro, who passes as her brother. The Captain of the ship is so smitten with her charms as to neglect his nautical duties, and so comes the shipwreck with which Shakespeare's comedy begins. Pedro is drowned; but Silla floats to shore on the Captain's chest, from which she takes apparel to disguise herself as a man. She calls herself Silvio after her twin brother in Cyprus, and so goes to Constantinople, enters the service of the Duke Apolonius, and becomes, as in Shakespeare, the *galeotto* between him and his love, the Lady Julina. Like Francesca da Rimini, this lady at once becomes enamored of the fair messenger, Silla-Silvio, whose "torments" of love and jealousy are amply described. The real Silvio meanwhile comes to Constantinople in search of his twin sister, with whom the other characters confuse him as in *A Comedy of Errors*. Thus the Lady Julina by mistake marries him, as Olivia marries Sebastian in *Twelfth*

Night. The Duke at first believes his go-between treacherous; but at last all is explained, and the two pairs of lovers live happily for ever after. Had Shakespeare taken this diffuse and rambling story as it stood, *Twelfth Night* would have been as inconsequential as *Pericles*; but he omitted the Cyprian episode, began with the shipwreck in the middle of the story, and let it obscure the past, explain the separation of Viola and Sebastian, and so open the comedy.

Usually, Shakespeare changes his source to give his characters and action greater realism, but here he not only omits the earlier part of Riche's narrative that explains Viola's arrival at her lover's court, but also makes other changes, such as her never having met the Duke, which show that he did not intend the audience to infer as his pre-play the material in the early part of Riche's narrative. Shakespeare adds the duel in Act III; but the plots of Sir Toby's marriage and of Malvolio's gulling crowd Viola out of Act IV; and Act V dismisses her betrothal to the Duke in less than ten lines, and makes no allowance for her kith and kin even to be present at the wedding. In short, he treats both her and Riche's story very cavalierly; and, for the early part that he omits, he gives but little explanation. In fact, despite the added duel, Viola is less important than in Riche's romance, and her actions are less clearly motivated: by chance, she is shipwrecked; by chance, she wins the Duke's instant high favor, and so is sent to woo Olivia for him; by chance, Olivia falls in love with her; and this leads to the duel from which by chance she escapes; and, as a consummation of all these chances, the Duke at last turns to her for marital consolation. What a tissue of fortunate coincidence, surpassing even the happy vagaries of the original Byzantine romance! The chances of the shipwreck and winning the Duke's favor seem to have been forced on Shakespeare as a substitute for the early episodes in Riche that he omitted; and the duel scene with its accidental outcome he doubtless added, partly because of its inherent comedy and partly to resolve the Viola-Sebastian love affair and connect Viola with the Sir Toby plots; and the merry solution, with marriages all around, was essential to comedy. The result is a success story that outdoes Horatio Alger, and that requires a heroine whose address and charm can play fairy godmother to her future and win her a fortune and a husband. What a contrast to the realistic Maria, who only by much scheming won a title and a spouse!

Thus Viola's eccentric orbit can be explained only in part by Shakespeare's source and only in part by contemporary realism. How far she is the creature of Elizabethan stage convention remains to be explored. Her entire role, except for the beginning and the end, is played in the disguise of a man, a common device fostered by boy actors' taking women's parts. Disguise leads naturally to all the laughable intrigue incident to mistaken identity; Shakespeare in his earlier comedies used it to the full,[11] and in *Love's Labour's* and *As You Like It* combined it with romance. Social conditions did not permit ladies of rank to wander unprotected; under such circumstances, they would therefore disguise themselves as well-born youths; and, since such youths were generally pages or servingmen—the Renaissance equivalent of a squire—this was their social status. Such were Julia, Jessica, Celia, and Rosalind. The trouble with mistaken identity on the stage is that it hardly carries conviction; and, though Viola says that she is imitating her twin brother in "fashion, colour, ornament," and though the Duke testifies to the perfect likeness of the two, yet this convention, which so dominates her role, is sufficiently unconvincing, no matter what the dramatist might do, to tune her whole part to romance rather than to reality. Indeed, Shakespeare does not even trouble to explain where she got copies of Sebastian's clothes; for the two must be dressed alike, or Sir Toby and Olivia would have noticed the difference in the duel and the marriage scenes, and the Duke and Antonio could hardly have confused the two. Truly, it must have seemed impossible to give Viola's inexplicable past, improbable disguise, and phenomenal success any sort of workaday Elizabethan realism; and so Shakespeare perforce gave her

[11] J. W. Draper, "Mistaken Identity in Shakespeare's Comedies," *Revue Anglo-Américaine*, XI, 289 *et seq.*

the allurement of romance, and let our delight in her charms persuade us to accept that mixture of a lie that doth ever add pleasure. Her role is, indeed, a tissue of common stage devices. Dr. Forsythe, in showing the ample borrowings of the late Caroline dramatist, James Shirley, composed in effect an index of conventional situations in Elizabethan drama, listed and numbered with references to the plays where they are found; and Viola's role owes something to at least eight of the situations that he lists. In effect, she offers her love to Orsino before he makes advances (No. 1); she takes part in his courtship by proxy (No. 3); as a love-agent, she is the rival of the woman for whose love she sues (No. 5); in the disguise of a man, she makes love to another woman (No. 8); she has combats of wit with Orsino and Olivia (No. 19); the ambiguity of her speech repeatedly leads others, especially Orsino, to mistaken impressions (No. 27); she is disguised as a man throughout most of the play (No. 32); and often this disguise allies her to the stock figure of the clever page (No. 48). In fact, stage convention contributes more to the situations—and so to the character—of Viola than to any other figure in the play. The conventions in which Sir Toby is involved belong not only to the stage but to Elizabethan life, and so reinforce his realism; but Viola's have no tang of the earth earthy or the workaday world. Thus she is more stagy and less true to life; but, since she was not Elizabethan in the first place, she has had less to lose by the passing of the Elizabethan age, and this may account for her popularity with actresses in recent times. Her part, like the stock types of Victorian melodrama, is composed of dependable acting conventions that (to the sacrifice of reality) are sure to be effective on the boards.

The early critics indeed accept Viola with little or no comment. The "appreciative" Romantics of the nineteenth century have luxuriated over the wide expanses of her role that Shakespeare left to random conjecture; and so, both as a star part on the stage and also in the critical heavens, she has climbed to the very zenith, and is generally accounted one of Shakespeare's loveliest creations and the heroine of the play.

138

Criticism, in short, has invested her with an emotional attraction that forbids too close an examination into the probability of her actions. In 1811, Schlegel declared that her love, though fallen into "arbitrarily," nevertheless "touches the tenderest chords of feeling"; and Hazlitt found in her "the great and sweet charm" of the play. Her wooing of Orsino troubled them no more than Desdemona's wooing of Othello,[12] though in real life such feminism would have shocked them, as it would have an Elizabethan. The Victorian Hallam, to be sure, chides her as indelicate; but Mrs. Jameson defends her "deep, silent, patient love" and the "genuine sweetness and delicacy of her character." Ruggles, Sir Edward Russell, and Canon Ainger find her altogether praiseworthy; and Oeshelhäuser and Winter call her the chief character in the play. Knight declares that Shakespeare's text allows for either of two conceptions of her character: "There is the sentimental view . . . . [set forth by Schlegel and the rest]; and there is the more realistic view, which makes her assumption of masculine attire something of a madcap freak" to win the Duke Orsino. This latter view, which he prefers, will not, as he develops it, concur with the actual text, for it requires that she dress as a page only after she has come to Orsino's court and fallen in love with him. More recently, the Arden editors and Professor Hardin Craig[13] compare her as a heroine to Rosalind. Thus Viola, though Shakespeare so reduced her part that she has fewer lines than Sir Toby and is much less central to the plot than Olivia, has risen, because she charmed the Romantic nineteenth century, to a supremacy where all unite to praise her virtues and excuse her faults and flaws. Of course, the very fact that she is less true to Elizabethan life has made her lose less vividness in the whirligig of time. She is not so much a portrait as a decorative piece, and time cannot wither nor custom stale the grace of purely decorative forms.

Viola's character, being compounded of Riche's Silla, of dramatic-romantic convention, and here and there of the realities of Elizabethan life, is a tangled skein for the critic to un-

[12] J. W. Draper, "Desdemona," *Revue de Littérature Comparée*, XIII, 337 *et seq.*
[13] Hardin Craig, *Shakespeare* (New York, 1931), p. 309.

ravel, and demands a thorough examination of such evidence as her speech and her actions offer. Her age and appearance, her character and ladylike accomplishments, her humor and the effect of her love for the Duke on her psychology, must all be inferred, as far as possible, from the text; and her external relationships with those about her—with her brother, her master, his lady, and the lesser people—must be traced. Whereever possible, the pertinent backgrounds of Elizabethan society and of Elizabethan psychology must be applied to these data so that one may finally ascertain both the nature and the importance of her role.

The exigencies of Elizabethan etiquette required a certain variety of styles of address in speaking to various classes of persons. In this complex matter, Viola is not unschooled; and yet her speech is generally plain and to the point and lacking in the pungent allusion of Sir Toby and of Feste. She can answer Sir Andrew in French;[14] either she, or possibly Orsino, has prepared a "Poeticall" speech to woo Olivia;[15] she plans to speak to Orsino "in many sorts of Musicke,"[16] and so becomes his favorite servingman in a mere three days.[17] She can play at wit on occasion with the Countess and with Feste: for the former, she combines it with courtly compliment, and for the latter, with a crisp, tart style; and thence she can turn rapidly to moralizing and to elegant parley with the two knights.[18] Sir Andrew admires her choice diction and hopes to array himself in its borrowed plumes. She can develop the favorite theme of contemporary sonneteers when she urges Olivia to marry and so not "leade these graces to the graue";[19] and she can catch the hyperbole of the sonnet style when she describes Orsino's groans of "thunder" and "sighes of fire."[20] Indeed, she might well appreciate Feste's clever adaptation of his address to the taste of different auditors,[21] for she does so herself. In short, Viola, when she pleases, is a master of the fine art—almost a

[14] *Twelfth Night.* III. i. 73.
[15] *Ibid.,* I. v. 172 *et passim.* Cf. R. Burton, *Anatomy,* Part III, Sec. 2, Mem. 3.
[16] *Twelfth Night,* I. ii. 60 et seq.   [17] *Ibid.,* I. iv. 3 *et seq.*
[18] *Ibid.,* III. i. *et passim.*   [19] *Ibid.,* I. v. 239.
[20] *Twelfth Night,* I. v. 254.   [21] *Ibid.,* III. i. 60 *et seq.*

lost art today—of conversation nicely fitted to the hearer and to the occasion.[22] This, in itself, would suggest her rearing in a court and also her possession of a natural mother wit.

She has, moreover, acquired some of the elegancies of current rhetoric, and her wit can be as dry as the remainder biscuit. She can deliver herself of a double meaning too sly even for the nimble-witted Feste.[23] To tip the points of her discourse, she can use sharp parallel structure combined with antithesis and ellipsis.[24] But, most of all, she can, like Polonius, command the popular sententious style of pat and precious epigram, which the Elizabethans deemed the outward form and pressure of gravity and wisdom. She observes that "nature with a beauteous wall Doth oft close in pollution";[25] she says, "Disguise, I see thou art a wickednesse";[26] she remarks how easily "womens waxen hearts" are seduced by handsome falsity;[27] and she declares it "a vulgar proofe That verie oft we pitty enemies."[28] Such a didactic style was recommended by the writers of the time,[29] and seems to have been an essential stock in trade for the higher type of public servant who hoped to found his career on weighty service to the state as well as on the lighter amusement of his lord. Indeed, as Viola rose more and more into this higher class, beyond the mere vapid courtier, she speaks in a constantly plainer, crisper style, without the embellishments and graces by which the ordinary servingman entertained his master. She had achieved the dignity of the Duke's envoy amorous extraordinary; she was becoming an official rather than a mere courtier.

Except in these first prepared speeches to the Countess, Viola on the whole speaks plainly and to the point. In the first scene in which she appears, she questions the Captain tersely; when she first sees Olivia face to face, she comments on the view, "Excellently done, if God did it all,"[30] and she later

[22] J. W. Draper, "Shakespeare and the *Conversazione*," *Italica*, XXIII, 7 *et seq.*
[23] *Twelfth Night*, III. i. 47.   [24] *Ibid.*, I. v. 208 *et seq*; II. ii. 35 *et seq.*
[25] *Ibid.*, I. ii. 51–52.   [26] *Ibid.*, II. ii. 29.
[27] *Ibid.*, II. ii. 31–32.   [28] *Ibid.*, III. i. 127–28.
[29] J. W. Draper, *The "Hamlet" of Shakespeare's Audience* (Durham, N.C.., 1938), pp. 40–41.
[30] *Twelfth Night*, I. v. 233.

blames Olivia in brusque terms as "too proud." Of course, she responds in kind to Malvolio's studied rudeness, and declares, "She tooke the ring of me, Ile none of it."[31] Neither love[32] nor fear[33] inspires her to many words, though Elizabethan drama usually records these emotions *in extenso*. Perhaps this direct simplicity, in contrast to the convolved felicities of others, which time has somewhat tarnished, accounts in part for Viola's more lasting popularity. At all events, it makes her speech a sharp stylistic foil to the earthy tang of Sir Toby, to the spicy rhetoric of Feste and to the lyrical luxuriance of the Duke. In short, she is a downright, plain-spoken fairy princess with few superfluous verbal flourishes; and this helps to make her convincing.

Shakespeare often uses a character's allusions to express his past life and the nature of his mind. This is amply evident in Feste and in the two knights, and somewhat in Orsino and Olivia; but Viola's allusions, perhaps because she was something above natural with a problematical past, are comparatively few and neither striking nor very revelatory. She refers to the olive branch of peace,[34] to Elysium,[35] to the sun as "that Orbed Continent . . . . that seuers day from night,"[36] to a type of falcon called the "Haggard,"[37] to patience as a statue,[38] to an echo,[39] to music,[40] to "a worme i'th budde."[41] All these are so commonplace and obvious that they mean little; and hardly better are the references to the green sickness of young women[42] and to the willow as a symbol of unrequited love.[43] Viola's late unhappy voyage has apparently given her an occasional nautical turn of phrase, and she knows that sailors swab decks[44] and that the London watermen cried "Westward hoe" to tell the direction they were going.[45] On the other hand—strangely enough for one who has lived in

---

[31] *Twelfth Night*, II. ii. 14. [32] *Ibid.*, II. iv. 31 *et seq.*
[33] *Ibid.*, III. iv. 226 *et passim.* [34] *Ibid.*, I. v. 209. [35] *Ibid.*, I. ii. 6.
[36] *Ibid.*, V. i. 287. [37] *Ibid.*, III. i. 64. [38] *Ibid.*, II. iv. 122.
[39] *Ibid.*, II. iv. 24. [40] *Ibid.*, I. ii. 63. [41] *Ibid.*, II. iv. 119.
[42] *Ibid.*, II. iv. 121.
[43] *Ibid.*, I. v. 267. See J. W. Draper, *The Funeral Elegy* (New York, 1929); Appendix A; and R. Greene, *Grootsworth of Witte*, ed. Harrison (London, 1923), p. 26.
[44] *Twelfth Night*, I. v. 203; III. i. 78. [45] *Ibid.*, III. i. 139.

courts—she does not seem to know the meaning of a "knight dubb'd with vnhatch'd Rapier, and on carpet consideration."[46] Indeed, these are flat, stale, and unprofitable gleanings from a role of some three hundred and fifty lines; and, as far as the wit of the dialogue is concerned, the part of Viola seems to be that of foil for others rather than primary in the play. Of course, some such parts are necessary to bring the brilliance of the rest out into relief; and Shakespeare gave this function to Viola perhaps because her enigmatic past and her coincidental and romantic course through the plot made it wise to show at least her conversation in the light of common day, and so save her from the utter unreality of a thoroughgoing fairy princess.

Even more vivid on the stage than speech is the personal appearance of the characters. Both Orsino and Olivia clearly find the youth Cesario attractive; she is "a faire young man";[47] even Malvolio describes her as "verie well-fauour'd." Sebastian declares her "of many accounted beautiful,"[48] and Olivia likewise terms her "beautifull."[49] Such praise is vague, but its reiteration is convincing; and this vagueness doubtless arose from the fact that the boy actors who took women's parts quickly outgrew them, and so, at successive revivals, such parts would shortly have to be cast for a different boy who might have a style of beauty different from his predecessor's. Viola is clearly young: she was only thirteen when her father died apparently not many years before; she is a "good youth," not of "graue" aspect, beardless, and with an unbroken, boyish voice; and Orsino is seemingly older than she.[50] On the other hand, her twin brother Sebastian is old enough to be a swordsman and a finished gentleman; but life was brief and the responsibilities of manhood came early in those times. In short, the twins can hardly be younger than fifteen and hardly more than two or three years older; and either Sebastian must be somewhat feminine in looks, or Viola must have a more striking masculine type of beauty than the nineteenth century has generally allowed her.

[46] *Ibid.*, III. iv. 234 *et seq.*
[47] *Ibid.*, I. v. 101 and 169.   [48] *Ibid.*, II. i. 25.
[49] *Ibid.*, III. i. 149.   [50] *Ibid.*, II. iv. 33 *et seq.*

According to Sebastian, Viola has "a minde that enuy could not but call faire";[51] and "minde" would seem to refer somewhat vaguely both to her intelligence and her character. She is shrewd at judging the Captain and so trusting him with the secret of her intentions; she shrewdly insinuates herself within three days into the good graces of the Duke; she shrewdly sees through Feste's motives and way of life; and, all too shrewdly, she wins the good opinion of the unapproachable Countess. She grasps at once the tangled love affairs of Orsino and Olivia and herself, and neatly states the case.[52] Nowhere does she show herself more quick-witted than in the short scene when Malvolio forces on her the ring that she is supposed to have given Olivia. The Countess is determined to induce, or to oblige, the handsome go-between to return to her, and to that end has invented this ring episode. At the end of an earlier scene, she had therefore summoned Malvolio, sent him after Cesario-Viola, told him to return the ring and to ask the youth to come back "tomorrow" to hear her reasons for refusing the Duke's hand. Malvolio hurries after, soon catches up with Viola, and asks her whether she was not recently with the Countess. All unmindful of the enamored Countess' true motive, he brusquely tries to return the ring, and gives his mistress' message. The passage has fine values of comic irony. During this speech of some seven lines, Viola's expression should show her growing enlightenment of the true state of affairs—an enlightenment later definitely expressed in her soliloquy when Malvolio departs. In answer to Malvolio, she does not deny the ownership of the ring, but plays up both to Olivia's artifice and to Malvolio's crabbed humor: "She took the Ring of me, Ile none of it." Malvolio throws it on the ground, tells her that she may stoop for it if she cares to, and goes off. Thus Viola by indirection finds direction out: she learns that Olivia loves her but wishes to keep this love a secret even from her trusted steward; and Viola's sharp perception saves her from betraying the Countess' stratagem.

In character, Viola is all that one could wish. Although she

[51] *Twelfth Night*, II. i. 28.   [52] *Ibid.*, II. ii. 35 *et seq.*

144

is "no fighter,"[53] yet up to the very point of battle can she convincingly play the part of a man. She shows fortitude and self-reliance in misfortune; and, indeed, she meets a series of them: shipwreck, Orsino's love for Olivia, Olivia's love for herself, the duel, and finally Orsino's bitter speech to her when he thinks that she has stolen the Countess from him. She has a sweet reasonableness, and can sympathize objectively even with the love pangs of her rival;[54] and this magnanimity extends to a hatred of ingratitude;[55] and she herself shows a very real gratitude toward Antonio by trying to intercede for him.[56] In short, Viola, for all her feminine charm that is so essential to the plot and that so attracts the other characters, is shrewd— a necessary quality in winning one's own way—and has an objective magnanimity that is not usually thought a characteristic of her sex.

This feminine charm suggests that Viola should be dominated by phlegm, which belonged with the passive virtues that the Elizabethans so admired in women; and her slow tempo certainly implies this humor. The average speed on the contemporary stage was, as Hamlet says, tripping. The construction and size of the theaters allowed for rapid speech; *Romeo and Juliet*, according to its Prologue, took two hours to perform, and stenographers had trouble in stealing the texts of the plays in the theaters. Indeed, the system used by the present writer in counting the evidences for fast speech and slow suggests that most actors spoke at a rate of one for slow to two or even three for fast delivery. Viola, however, in her verse lines throughout the play shows almost fifty percent more evidence for slow than for rapid speech; and she employs such forms as "deni al," "contemnèd," and "orbèd," and repeatedly fails to slur "I am," "I will," and the like. One of her slowest passages, moreover, is her soliloquy in Act I, scene ii —a ratio of 3 to 1—when she is most freely expressing her inner mood. Of the eight scenes in which she speaks in verse, only one, Act III, scene iv, supplies more evidence for fast than for slow speech; and her ratio there stands 17 to 18, or

53 *Ibid.*, III. iv. 241.   54 *Ibid.*, II. ii. 28.
55 *Ibid.*, III. iv. 354.   56 *Ibid.*, V. i. 66 *et seq.*

about 1 to 1. The impending duel with Sir Andrew and the strange demands of Antonio have forced her to a faster speech as she seems to assume a more choleric mood. Her tempo, in short, suggests that Viola was the ideal Elizabethan woman of phlegmatic humor.

Other evidence, however, does not suggest a phlegmatic Viola; and this inconsistency supports the theory that she is not realistic but a figure of romance. The plot does not show her in a mere passive role like Hero or Ophelia. By tact and wit, as well as by the fortune of her stars, she crowns her sturdy independence with success. This independence and success against hopeless odds perhaps account for her recent popularity as much as do her romantic situation and her charm; but they certainly do not accord with her having a phlegmatic temper. Her youth and susceptibility to love suggest the sanguine type; for blood belonged to the springtime of life, the "lustye flourishinge age."[57] She must, moreover, have the good looks[58] and "faire stature"[59] of this humor; and she is "moderate, mery, pleasant [witty and agreeable], fayre . . . ."[60] Orsino tells her that her "constellation is right apt" for wooing[61] Olivia for him; and the sanguine type under the planet Jupiter was most dexterous in amorous intrigue, as witness also Romeo[62] and Orlando.[63] The humor, furthermore, could be intellectual and "graue," and is twice termed by Dariot "faithfull." Viola shows gravity in her aphoristic style, and a difficult fidelity at once to Orsino's trust and to her love for him. This humor was appropriate to "Noblemen, Bishops, prelates, Iudges, Lawyers, honest men, iust, true, benevolent, liberall, faithfull, mild, godly, shamfast, magnanimous . . . ."[64] and Viola has the magnanimity and fortitude of high station. This was the luckiest of all the humors—quite proper to fairy princesses—and, like Orlando, Viola achieves the greatest fortune in the outcome of

[57] L. Lemnius, *Touchstone of Complexions* (London, 1576), leaf 86 v.
[58] T. W[alkington], *Optick Glasse of Humors* (London, 1631), p. 115.
[59] C. Dariot, *Iudgement of the Starres* (London, 1598), sig. D 2 v.
[60] *Book of Arcandam*, tr. Warde (London, 1592), sig. M 2 r.
[61] *Twelfth Night*, I. iv. 38–39.   [62] See J. W. Draper, R.E.S., XV, 29.
[63] See J. W. Draper, "Shakespeare's Orlando Inamorato," *M.L.Q.*, II, 179 *et seq.*
[64] Dariot, *op. cit.*, sig. D 2 v.

the story. The sanguine type, moreover, such as Romeo, Orlando, and Hamlet,[65] was prone to fall in love, a tendency also noted in the medical opinion of Cogan,[66] Coeffeteau,[67] and Burton.[68] Indeed, love was the Achilles' heel of this "paragon of complexions";[69] but Viola, like Orlando, turns her chief danger into her final triumph, and in the end establishes her future and her fortunes on a brilliant marriage.

Unlike Orlando, however, she seems to suffer along the way from quite understandable doubts and even from the danger of love-melancholy; and, for all her being a fairy princess, the course of her true love somewhat follows the accepted mundane pattern. The recognized motives of beauty and profit[70] seem to have impelled her, and apparently she used music[71] as "a great enticement."[72] Burton says that the lover would be a page or lackey to the beloved;[73] and Viola occupies this status with Orsino. As the eyes were the organ most immediately affected,[74] love at first sight was supposed to be the rule; and this explains how she became so deeply enamored within three days.[75] For a time her love seemed unrequited, and Orsino even obliges her (unhappy pass!) to act as his implorator with Olivia. Bitterest irony of all, he even promises her, if she succeeds, that she shall "liue as freely as thy Lord, To call his fortunes thine"[76]—a promise of all he has except the love she craves. Such a situation would be a sore trial, even in fairyland; and, although Viola does not directly appear as suffering, like Orsino, the pangs of love-melancholy,[77] yet under the guise

[65] J. W. Draper, *Hamlet*, ed. cit., pp. 173 *et seq.*; pp. 201–2.

[66] T. Cogan, *Haven of Health* (London, 1589), sig. Hh 2 v.

[67] N. Coeffeteau, *Table of Humane Passions* (London, 1621), p. 551.

[68] R. Burton, *Anatomy of Melancholy*, III, 2, 2, 2, 1.

[69] Walkington, *op. cit.*, p. 111.

[70] T. Wright, *Passions of the Minde* (London, 1601), p. 199; Burton, *op. cit.*, III, 1, 2, 1.

[71] *Twelfth Night*, I. ii. 62.   [72] Burton, *op. cit.*, III, 2, 2, 4.

[73] *Ibid.*, III. 2, 3.

[74] J. Ferrand, 'Ερωτομανία (Oxford, 1640), pp. 41–42 (*ed. princ.*, Paris, 1624); Burton, *op. cit.*, III, 2, 2, 2.

[75] *Twelfth Night*, I. iv. 45–46.   [76] *Ibid.*, I. iv. 42–43.

[77] P. Boaystuau, *Theatrum Mundi* (London, 1574), pp. 201–2; A. Laurentius, *Discourse of the Preservation of the Sight* (London, 1599); Ferrand, *op. cit.*, 7; Burton, *op. cit.*, III, 2, 3.

of telling Orsino of a mythical sister, she describes, if not her present state, at least her fears for the future:

> . . . . she neuer told her loue,
> But let concealment like a worme i'th budde
> Feede on her damask cheeke: she pin'd in thought,
> And with a greene and yellow mellancholly,
> She sat like Patience on a Monument,
> Smiling at greefe. Was not this loue indeede?[78]

Green sickness was the term generally applied to the love-melancholy of young women who might even pine away.[79] It was "sometimes joyned with a gentle Fever" and also with "heart-beating, swelling of the face, want of appetite, griefe, sighing, causeles teares, insatiable hunger, extreame thirst, swonings, oppressions, suffocations, continuall watchings, Headach, Melancholy, Epilepsy, Ragings . . . . and diverse other desperate Symptomes."[80] One may be surprised that Viola does not show more of these sad effects, and she says that she is "almost sicke" for a husband;[81] but perhaps her status as fairy princess mitigates her pains, and at least she does fear their prologue to the omen coming on. The sanguine Viola, in short, is threatened with melancholy.

As one might expect in the sanguine type, affection and loyalty, two of the most pleasing human traits, dominate Viola's major relationships, her feelings toward her brother and toward the Duke. Even toward her rival, Olivia, whose independence she could hardly understand, she is magnanimous. She appreciates Feste, and fences with his wit, and of Sir Toby and Sir Andrew asks only to be let alone. In return, she inspires loyalty in the Captain and affection in her brother and in the Duke. In fact, Viola lives on so lofty a plane that there is little of sordid everyday humanity about her, and she might well escape the effects of neglected love. She is, moreover, noble, young, and beautiful, accomplished in speech and manner, shrewd and nimble-witted: in truth, not only her fortune but her mind

---

[78] *Twelfth Night*, II. iv. 118 *et seq.*
[79] Burton, *op. cit.*, Part III, Sec. 2, Mems. 3 and 4.
[80] Ferrand, *op. cit.*, p. 11. [81] *Twelfth Night*, III. i. 47.

and character also are too good to be quite true, and she is a creature rather of romance than the commonplace earth earthy.

The dramatic requirements of the plot, when reduced from Riche to the proper length for comedy, cut Viola off from her past, and leave her only the unconvincing stage conventions of an unmotivated disguise improbably successful, and of an equally improbable love affair with the Duke crowned with a hurried and unforeseen betrothal. The plot required the former, and the comic conclusion the latter; and so the playwright had no choice. He humanized Viola where he could, and where he could not convince us to accept her as reasonable, at least he persuaded us to delight in her as charming.[82] He gave her, therefore, a ready wit, wide accomplishments, and a sanguine personality that also motivated her apparently hopeless love; and thus she appears in the alluring guise of virtue in distress; and we forget, as Shakespeare wished us to forget, her obscure past, and accept by wishful thinking her unexplained present and her sudden and improbable good fortune.

A drama is somewhat like a picture, with some things brought into the relief of foreground and some left in the chiaroscuro of the distance, and just as Rembrandt throws on the faces of his portraits a light that comes from an unknown source and rarely penetrates into the depths behind, so Shakespeare sometimes shades the alpha and omega of his dramas into a doubtful obscurity that may even impinge on the start and finish of the play. Thus Viola's initial shipwreck and instant rise to Orsino's favor and her final betrothal to the Duke form a romantic frame to set off the realistic picture of Malvolio and Sir Toby and the calculating Olivia, and offer something of a foil to the main action. The audience hurries into the theater from its commonplace affairs, sees a lovesick duke and a romantic shipwreck, passes on to a stage presentation of everyday life, and then back into romance in the last act; and doubtless the realism of the central scenes was all the more vivid for this contrasting framework, which at once served

---

[82] Cf. his treatment of Desdemona. See J. W. Draper, *R.L.C.*, XIII, 337 *et seq.*

them as a foil, and separated them from too close comparison with the street life outside the theater doors.

The Romantic critics are perhaps right in celebrating Viola as the nonpareil of virtue and loveliness; but are they right in making her the central figure of the play, or even its heroine? If she be the heroine, then Orsino is presumably the hero; and, though he is a Duke and therefore entitled to a sort of dramatic precedence, do either the number of his lines or his importance in the plot give him this place? Is he a Romeo, the cynosure of the spectator's eyes throughout the piece? Even in the nineteenth century, when Viola was most exalted, great actors have not usually preferred his role to that of Sir Toby or Malvolio. If he were the hero, the solution of the other plots should somewhat depend on him; but Maria's winning of Sir Toby, the reunion of Viola and Sebastian, and even Olivia's final giving of her hand are not governed by the Duke and his affairs. Viola herself, moreover, is not in this key position; Olivia rather than she decides the fate and future of the other characters, of Sir Andrew, of Sebastian, of Malvolio, even of the Duke; and indeed Viola's own course through the comedy is governed not so much by her single efforts as by lucky chance or (if one prefers) by the fortune of the stars. Moreover, if she were the heroine of the play, why does Shakespeare omit so many of her doings told in Riche, and give her dialogue so modest a modicum of wit and of poetry in a comedy replete with both? In fact, she seems, like Maria in her plainness, to be rather a mere foil to the others who are intended to stick fiery off. The last scene, moreover, disposes of her future in a few rapid lines, and Malvolio's release and anger get its final climax. Indeed, Viola seems to be a romantic contrast to the dominant realism of the play—low-life realism in the case of Sir Toby's schemes and Maria's aspirations, and high-life realism in the case of the self-willed and astute Olivia; but Viola is a silver strand of romance, glinting here and there to set off this kersey web of everyday buffs and browns and mourning black, a necessary part of Shakespeare's complex pattern, but hardly a part predominant.

150

Viola in the beginning sets foot on the firm shores of Illyria and proceeds to treat it like fairyland; and Illyria, for all its Sir Andrew and Sir Toby and their "Cakes and Ale," responds in kind, and, as if it were a fairy godmother, grants her the three wishes of her brother's life, her own security, and the husband of her choice. How different from Maria's shrewd maneuvering that finally gains her the bare recompense of Sir Toby! But Maria is only common clay. Viola does not need to toil or spin; the world is her oyster; and, for all her quick wit, her matter-of-fact talk, and her fear of melancholy, she is really a fairy princess for whom it opens at a word. She may have no past, but her roseate future is as assured as fairyland itself. What sort of changeling wife she made Orsino is not quite beyond conjecture: having brought him by her charm and her good luck to the happy pass of marriage-out-of-hand, she may well trust this sanguine good luck and charm—promised doubtless by the stars at her nativity—to keep him in the joyous faith of his masculine superiority, whilst she deftly leads him by the nose. Orsino is a bit too realistic for a fairy prince; but at least they both are sanguine, and so, according to high medical authority, should enjoy together the serenest marital felicity. Thus unquestionably, Orsino's wedded bliss, like Sir Toby's, is assured; and Viola has security and a fortune and a husband; and both he and she, as in all good fairy tales, doubtless live happily forever after.

❦My Lord Sebastian and the Rest

I F VIOLA is a fairy princess, then her twin brother Sebastian should be a fairy prince, with no more past and no more realism of action and dialogue than she. All this, however, is not obvious, for he is sketched in pastel shades, and thus, on his own account, is hardly noticeable. Like Fortinbras in *Hamlet*, who is likewise essential only to the conclusion of the piece, he is early spoken of by others, and here and there appears *personâ propriâ* so that his part in the ending will not seem too unconvincing a surprise. He is among those present in only five scenes; and his hundred and twenty-odd lines contain no purple patches. Indeed, Shakespeare does not even present on the stage either his formal betrothal or his marriage. Just as Viola's part, moreover, was reduced in the play from its proportions in Riche's story, so Sebastian's was even more curtailed: shortly after Silla (Viola) had run away from home to seek her lover, her brother Silvio (Sebastian) returned from the wars to Cyprus, heard of her disappearance, determined to find her, and by good chance followed her to Constantinople, where, as in Shakespeare, the Lady Julina (Olivia) mistakes him for his disguised sister and marries him. In short, Shakespeare treats Sebastian as a minor character. Modern critics have been equally casual: in 1864, Kenny remarked that his "hurried and strange marriage" was "manifestly melodramatic"; and, more recently, the Arden editors point out that he is "so young that his smooth face can be mistaken for his sister's, but he is a man in manners . . . ." Indeed, Sebastian is thought of only as Viola's brother and Olivia's husband; but surely these relations are sufficiently important to require a full survey of his role. One may, moreover, properly inquire how far he is, like his sister, a product of fairyland, and how far and in what respects a normal Elizabethan youth, what effort did Shakespeare make to justify his

152

sudden marriage, would the audience have accepted it as reasonable, and might it after all have turned out well?

Sebastian, like Viola, is given to plain speech, perhaps because his lines are so taken up with important exposition and his character has but slight comic possibilities. He can use the polite circumlocutions of contemporary elegance, but he is more generally direct and to the point, and, even under the stimulus of Feste's repartee, shows no great skill at persiflage. Also like Viola, he uses little allusion, and that of slight significance. Like Malvolio (and many Elizabethans), he believes in astrology; but, whereas Malvolio is too sure of his good luck, and so is disappointed, Sebastian says that his stars "shine darkly," and yet he climbs to a future beyond his highest dreams. He mentions "Fortune," Lethe, the tortures of the rack, and a "bias" that diverted a bowl from its straight course: all this merely implies that he was acquainted with the commonplace notions, social facts, and sports of the age. He has enough courtly experience to know that a court jester expects a tip; but he shows neither depth nor individuality of knowledge or experience. His dialogue has no wit or emotional climaxes, and usually serves as a mere foil for the talk of Olivia or Feste or even of the humble Antonio; for, if he had been too outspoken with the Countess, she would soon have discovered her mistake. To an actor, his role must be especially ungrateful. In appearance, he is handsome and attractive, for he resembles the fair Viola, and Antonio and Olivia take to him at first sight. His clothes are apparently the usual habiliments of wellborn youth on travel bent. This consorts with the plainness of his speech, his direct character, and the essential fact that Viola in her disguise apparently has no trouble to match his dress, detail for detail. He is introduced as "Most provident in perill," a virile and foresighted youth. His part in the plot requires one who was at once agreeable and retiring in speech and appearance; and Shakespeare, by not individualizing him too much, but giving him, like Conrad's Lord Jim, ability in the abstract, has made him a possible subject for the mistaken identity of the last two acts. He is prudent, direct, and manly, as a hero should be; but he is also pleasing and reserved and unobtrusive, as Olivia required of a husband.

In the comedy, Sebastian appears—in Viola's comment—early; but he enters the plot very late, and contributes nothing to it until the resolution. He is essential to the comic outcome of Olivia's plans, but otherwise he fulfills no function. By putting together bits of Viola's and his and Antonio's dialogue, one can, however, follow his earlier course. He had accompanied Viola on her voyage, presumably from Messaline,[1] and shared in the shipwreck. As the vessel struck he had bound himself to a mast to float to shore. At the beginning of Act II, he appears in person, rescued by Antonio "from the breach of the sea" and cared for at the latter's home. The two had not met before and had not been long in company, for Antonio does not even know his true name; and, for reasons not vouchsafed to us, Sebastian has called himself Roderigo. Now he reveals himself and his family, but declares that he must not stay longer or accept Antonio's guidance to his unrevealed destination, for this might involve the latter in misfortune. The play never tells either the destination or the impending misfortune. Antonio, however, will brook no denial; and, despite the fact that Orsino's city is a hostile town where he will be imprisoned if recognized, the two fare forth (for no clear reason) in the same direction that Viola had previously taken. Why they should both remain in this dangerous locality while Sebastian merely does sight-seeing is not explained. Antonio must indeed "adore" him to take so great a risk for so little reason. The two, like Viola, are clearly mere figments of romance, and close question is impertinent. The middle of Act III shows them in the town, the one on pleasure bent, the other on concealment; and the generous Antonio presses his purse on his friend, who seems to be in narrow circumstances but who might see in the market "some toy" that strikes his fancy. Antonio outdoes even Hamlet's Horatio as a *fidus Achates*! They plan a reunion at a tavern in the malodorous "Suburbes," and so part. According to Professor Baldwin, Se-

[1] See Appendix B, p. 262.

bastian's romantic and impetuous role was played by William Sly, who also did Fenton and Laertes—an appropriate casting by the manager!

Hitherto, Sebastian's course has been more aimless and inexplicable than that of Viola; now the convention of mistaken identity overwhelms his part; and, although the events are hardly more convincing, their point in the plot is at least clear and unquestionable, for they lead him to Olivia and to the altar, where all good comedies should end. Indeed, Olivia could hardly be satisfied, and the piece be a true comedy, if Sebastian had not experienced these changes and chances that make him at last her husband. This is his somewhat belated but nevertheless important function in the play. Antonio first prepares the way for Olivia's mistake of the twins by taking Viola for her brother; then Feste takes the brother for Viola, and thus summons Sebastian to attend the lovesick Countess. Sebastian gives the fool short shrift, and then at once runs into the two knights and Fabyan, who wish to continue the duel with Viola interrupted in the preceding scene. Sir Andrew attacks Sebastian, who responds with a will and a swordsmanship that astonish Sir Toby and oblige him to save his friend. Feste runs off to warn Olivia that her beloved Cesario is fighting two opponents. Sir Toby lays hands on Sebastian to stop the fight, and to his surprise finds that he has merely involved himself in it. Then Olivia hurries in, calls the truce that Sir Toby could not, rates her uncle soundly, and triumphantly carries off the prize (that is Sebastian), a somewhat puzzled victim to the matrimonial altar. All this is stark coincidence; and perhaps the most surprising part of it is Sebastian's willing acquiesence; for indeed he does not seem to be overwhelmed by love at first sight. Matrimony was a serious matter of family alliance, and the domestic conduct books of the time warn against "too rash and hastie" a choice;[2] but Sebastian hardly had a choice at all. Perhaps, however, he agreed with the advice of Niccholes: "If thy estate bee weake and poore marry farre off and quickly;

2 R. C[leaver], *Godly Form of Household Governement* (London, 1598), p. 149; and W. Whately, *A Care-Cloth* (London, 1624).

155

if otherwise firme and rich, at home and with deliberation."[3] Elizabethan youths, like Bassanio,[4] were obliged by economic pressure to marry money; and a wife's fortune was at the disposal of her lord.[5] Thus he makes no protest when Olivia invites him into the "Chantry" for a formal betrothal with the blessing of the Church; and many Elizabethan Bassanios would probably have done the same. Such spousals *de præsenti* constituted in effect a legal marriage;[6] and Sebastian swears "truth" to her. In Act V, Viola repudiates the match. Then Sebastian comes in and apologizes to his "sweet one" for having hurt her kinsman; the mistaken identity is discovered, and a joyous recognition scene between the twins ensues. The Duke assures the Countess that Sebastian's blood is "right noble"; and, after the business of Malvolio's letter is dispatched, Olivia suggests an immediate double wedding at her house and her expense. Thus terminates the thin and somewhat erratic strand that Sebastian's career weaves in the tapestry of the plot.

In a really satisfactory comedy, the concluding weddings should be not only reasonably probable, but also, so far as one can foresee, reasonably happy. Olivia seems to have agreed with the Wife of Bath that dominance was the thing that women most desire; she had tried to arrange her marital affairs accordingly, and one hopes that Sebastian was duly instructed in Robert Cleaver's admonition:

But yet when it hapeneth, that a man marrieth a woman of so high a birth, hee ought (not forgetting $\overset{t}{y}$ he is her husband) more to honour and esteeme of her, then of his equall and of one of nearer parentage: and not onely to account her his companion in loue, and in his life, but (in diuers actions of publike apparance) hold her his superior.

Indeed, in the last hundred and fifty lines, Sebastian sinks into a politic silence, an earnest perhaps of future years; and, if his faithfulness to Antonio expresses his true character, he made

---

[3] A. Niccholes, *Discourse of Marriage* (London, 1615), p. 48.

[4] H. P. Pettigrew, "Bassanio, the Elizabethan Lover," *Phil. Quart.*, XVI, 296.

[5] W. Vaughan, *Golden Groue* (London, 1608), sig O 4 r; and Holdsworth, *History of English Law* (Boston, 1923), III, 525.

[6] C. L. Powell, *English Domestic Relations, 1487–1653* (New York, 1917), p. 3 *et passim*; and J. W. Draper, "Signior Brabantio," *English Studies*, XXII, 193 *et seq.*

Olivia just the sort of husband that she craved. So perhaps the end of this marriage justified its dubious dramatic means.

Sebastian's early references to his "starres" and his "fate" suggest that Shakespeare conceived him as having a definite astrological background, and so a definite humor. In this speech, he describes his fate as malignant, and so implies that his planet is Saturn and his humor melancholy; but his twin birth with the sanguine Viola requires that they both came into the world under the same constellation and the same planet, and so would have the same astral complexion and the same humor. Sebastian's extraordinary luck, moreover, shows that he cannot be under the malefic influence of Saturn; and doubtless his despondent speech arises from his fallen fortunes and his recent shipwreck. The fidelity, furthermore, that he shows Antonio and promises Olivia suggests the sanguine temper. On the other hand, his purposeless inactivity when he comes to Orsino's city suggests the phlegmatic humor, though he is no Sir Toby or Sir Andrew; and his readiness to fight the knights, even to fight both of them at once, implies choler rather than phlegm. Perhaps, like Macbeth,[7] he is mercurial, taking his humor from those around him; but he shows none of the weak vacillation of this temper. As the hero of Olivia's love affairs, and so in a sense of the comedy, he should belong to one of the fortunate and pleasing types; and he seems to represent that harmony and happy balance of the humors and complexions that was thought to be perfect health. This was the psychomedical expression of the Aristotelian mean, the perfect man with nothing in excess. Thus he might seem melancholy from his shipwreck, phlegmatic at loose ends in the city, choleric in impromptu swordplay, and charmingly sanguine to his Pythias and to his lady. This is a proper type for the Romantic hero. He is Shakespeare's *deus ex machina* who toward the close descends upon the plot, and by his mere presence assures its comic end; and a *deus ex machina* need not be exceedingly convincing or extremely true to life.

Sebastian's friend, Antonio, seems to have been played by

---

[7] J. W. Draper, "Macbeth, 'Infirme of Purpose,'" *Bull. Hist. Med.*, X, 16 *et seq.*

Cundall, later an editor of the First Folio. The role appears in the Dramatis Personae added to the play in the eighteenth century by Rowe as "a Sea-Captain" and in Shakespeare's text as a "Notable Pyrate"; but he may well be neither. If a pirate, he is certainly the most genial and obliging that ever scuttled ship, and most trusting with his purse to his new friend Sebastian; and to have been in a sea fight "That took the *Phœnix*" does not prove him even a sailor, for marines were unknown, and sailors and soldiers were interchanged on land and sea. Indeed, the fact that he led the boarding party in the fight with the *Tiger* suggests rather that he was a soldier. At all events, he is certainly living on land when the play opens, and has nothing nautical about him. Piracy and privateering and internecine wars between families and little city-states blunted the line between piracy and war; and thus perhaps the critic may be allowed to doubt Orsino's term of opprobrium, even though it issued from the lips of a very duke.

The fact that Antonio's house is on the seacoast might imply to the cynical that he is by avocation a wrecker; but his treatment of Sebastian contradicts this libel. He appears in four scenes, has almost as many lines as Sebastian, and inspires the commentators to almost as short shrift. Kenny remarks that his arrest is "melodramatic"; Montégut finds unconvincing his sudden friendship for the man he saves from the sea; and the Arden editors characterize him as a "warm-hearted, hot-headed sailor . . . . loyal, daring to recklessness." He seems to exist in the play for two purposes, as a rescuer and a friend to whom Sebastian can unfold himself and so inform the audience, and as someone who can mistake Viola for her brother and so introduce the intrigue of mistaken identity. He is not very life-like in the several regards noted by the critics; and the Arden editors have given him the traits that come nearest to support his doubtful role. At best, he is more romantic than convincing; but, after the improbabilities of Viola and Sebastian, one must expect some consequent dislocations of verisimilitude in the surrounding minor roles. This is part of the price one pays for the glamour of romance.

158

What Antonio is to Sebastian, the Captain who rescues her is to Viola. He appears in only this initial scene, and speaks but thirty lines; but Shakespeare is thought to have played this role, and it is important both in the exposition of the play and in getting her to Orsino's court. This seems to be all that is left in Shakespeare of the Captain who, in Riche, took Silla from Cyprus and fell in love with her so much that he wrecked his vessel. But in *Twelfth Night* the Captain does not fall in love, or, if so, he is perfect master of his emotions, for he treats the unprotected Viola with scrupulous chivalry—most scrupulous in view of her situation, age, and beauty. The shipwreck had apparently been so sudden that the Captain had managed to save only Viola and a few others in a boat, while the unfortunate Sebastian was cast into the sea with nothing but the chance help of a floating mast to reach the shore. When Viola's boat lands, she and the Captain discuss Sebastian's fate and Viola's plans. He is a native of Illyria and can tell her all about its Duke and the Countess Olivia and her family. In fact, he had left the place only a "month" before to start on this ill-fated voyage. The few lines that he speaks, strangely enough, draw their allusions, not from the sea, but from the court and classics. He knows the story of "*Orion* on the Dolphines backe," and he has some knowledge of the eunuchs and mutes that surrounded Oriental royalty. Apparently, he is not only traveled but also educated—in fact, a cut above his class as "Captain." Viola remarks on his "faire behauior" before she entrusts herself to his guidance, and apparently he is all that he seems. He takes her to his home where she is fitted out in attire like Sebastian's so that she can go to court: in short, he is her Antonio, and by providing the proper garments makes possible the mistaken identity of the later scenes. One only hopes that Viola rewarded him in due course as richly as she promised, and did not forget him, as the audience does, by the end of the fifth act. But fairy princesses are presumed to have superior memories.

The minor characters in a play generally develop from the demands of plot or setting; and, just as the plot of *Twelfth*

Night required an Antonio to save Sebastian and get him to the city, and a Captain to do like service for Viola, so the setting of the play, in order to achieve the realism incident to comedy of manners, required servitors and attendants, menial and gently born, to run the errands of the great and to lend the proper awe and majesty of dress and manner. The menials, such as the servant who announces Viola's return at the summons of Olivia,[8] can readily be dismissed; he speaks his message of three lines and is forever silent. But the "servingmen" such as Fabyan, who occupied by birth a higher social status, require consideration.

In the Middle Ages, wellborn boys became pages and later squires to their fathers' overlords; but the falling off of knight-errantry in quieter times and the economic decay of feudalism left them in a social cul-de-sac without a future profession, an unhappy state of affairs depicted in Falstaff's Robin.[9] The law of primogeniture provided for the eldest son, but "Service" became the only "inheritance" of the younger;[10] and, since his lady was a countess, Fabyan is presumably a "Knights seconde sonne."[11] These "tall fellowes," who had previously been necessary men-at-arms, now became mere stage properties of greatness, to "attend vpon our Table, and follow vs in the streetes."[12] The growing poverty of the nobles, so vividly portrayed in Shakespeare's *Timon*,[13] forced upon many lords the question, why feed "such idle folke" who have nothing to do for seven days a week? Harrison is disturbed at the "great swarms of idle servingmen," who are "profitable to none" and all too easily became highwaymen.[14] Indeed, the decline of servingmen had reached a nadir and had run to "ruine and decay"[15] until England was regarded as the "Purgatory of Servants";[16]

[8] *Twelfth Night*, III. iv. 60–62.

[9] J. W. Draper, "Falstaff's Robin," *Studies in Philology*, XXXVI, 476 *et seq.*

[10] G. Markham, *Gentlemanly Profession of Servingman* (ed. *princ.*, 1598), in *Inedited Tracts*, ed. Hazlitt (London, 1868), p. 110.

[11] *Ibid.*, p. 107.

[12] *Cyuile and Vncyuile Life* (ed. *princ.*, 1579), in *Inedited Tracts*, ed. cit., p. 35.

[13] J. W. Draper, "The Theme of 'Timon of Athens,'" *M.L.R.*, XXIX, 20 *et seq.*

[14] W. Harrison, *Descriptions of England* (ed. 1587), Bk. II, chaps. v and xi.

[15] Markham, *op. cit.*, pp. 104–5.

[16] F. Moryson, *Itinerary* (ed. *princ.*, 1617), ed. Furnivall, p. 271.

and, for fear of lapsing into the degraded status of a menial "dayly and hourely imployed,"[17] a servingman had to pander in any way he could to his master's tastes.[18] Perhaps the best that he might hope for appears in Overbury's description; and probably Fabyan's life under the late Count was something of this sort:

He tells without asking who owns him by the superscription of his livery. His life is for ease and leisure, much about gentleman-like. His wealth enough to suffice nature, and sufficient to make him happy, if he were sure of it; for he hath little and wants nothing, he values himself higher or lower, as his master is. He hates or loves the men, as his master doth the master. He is commonly proud of his master's horses: he sleeps when he is sleepy, is of his religion, only the clock of his stockings is set to go an hour after his. He seldom breaks his own clothes [because they are his master's cast-off garments]. He never drinks but double, for he must be pledged [not having the price of a drink himself]; nor commonly without some short sentence nothing to the purpose: and seldom abstains till he comes to a thirst. His discretion is to be careful for his master's credit [reputation], and his sufficiency to marshal dishes at a table, and to carve well. His neatness consists much in his hair and his outward linen. His courting language, visible bawdy jests; and against his matter fail, he is always ready furnished with a song. His inheritance is the chamber-maid, but often purchaseth his master's daughter, by reason of opportunity, or for want of a better; he always cuckolds himself, and never marries but his own widow. His master being appeased, he becomes a retainer, and entails himself and his posterity upon his heir-males for ever.

Fabyan seems to have been rather more respectable, and Maria certainly had aspiration higher than he; but otherwise the description may well be apposite. Now, however, the Count is dead, and Fabyan becomes a sort of bodyguard to his young daughter, comparable to Queen Elizabeth's yeomen captained by Sir Walter Raleigh. His status is like that described in Brathwait:

A Gentleman Usher is his Ladies Creature; One who stands much upon his dimention and posture. A tall man he is of his *Legges*, and no

---

[17] Markham, *op. cit.*, p. 157.   [18] Earle, *Microcosmographie*, No. 1, ix.

less it behoves him to be tall of his *Hands*; being engaged in such desperate encounters for the Wall . . . .[19]

He carries his Lady's favorite dog, and grows more and more familiar, until she either rebukes him or takes him as her paramour. "He must make no love to the *Maid*, lest it beget a jealous suspect in the Mistresse." He takes her driving to church and to the theater, and then spends the night drunk in the cellar. As he has nothing of his own, he must keep her favor or else die a beggar. "The fortune of a younger brother call'd him to this *place*." His best hope is to become his Lady's lover, or, if he can, her husband; but his ill life ages him soon. Brathwait allows that a few good ushers exist,[20] and apparently Fabyan was one of these; but the insecurity of his position must have made him especially irate at Malvolio for having brought him "out o' fauour with my Lady, about a Beare-baiting."[21]

Fabyan is the last of the tormentors of Malvolio to make his appearance. Late in the second act he enters with the two knights, delighting in their plot against the steward, and he declares that he would sooner be "boyl'd to death with Melancholly" than lose "a Scruple of this sport." When Malvolio comes strutting down the garden walk, Fabyan comments on his pompous bearing, and then chiefly concerns himself with keeping Sir Andrew quiet through Malvolio's soliloquy and with gloating over the ludicrous effect of Maria's stratagem. All this did not require an extra character, and for the time one wonders why Shakespeare introduced him. In the later scenes leading up to the duel, however, Fabyan is essential. He helps Sir Toby persuade Sir Andrew to continue his lukewarm siege of Olivia's heart, and with his tongue in his cheek tells Sir Andrew that her recent favors to Viola are "a great argument of loue in her toward you." He urges the knight to some clear expression of his ardent passion, and so opens the way to the duel. Later he laughs with Sir Toby over Sir Andrew's challenge, and, like the gentleman he is, assists in arranging the

[19] R. Brathwait, *Ar't asleepe Husband?* (London, 1640), p. 161.
[20] *Ibid.*, p. 166. Cf. T. Scott, *Foure Paradoxes of Arte* (London, 1610), *passim.*
[21] *Twelfth Night*, II. v. 8–9.

162

duel. He helps to terrify Viola by his description of her opposite's prowess. He warns Sir Toby of the coming officers. In short, he is a necessary handy man in the scene. Early in Act IV, when Sebastian bests the two knights, Fabyan seems to be present, but prudently takes no part in speech or action, and so escapes without either a broken head or his mistress' displeasure. In Act V, he reads Malvolio's letter, explains the "device" against the steward, and tells the news of Maria's and Sir Toby's marriage.

Fabyan appears in four or five scenes and has about as many lines as Sebastian; but his part in the action is less crucial, and indeed, at times he is little more than background. The low-life scenes in the play rise in a crescendo. In Act I, scene iii appear Sir Toby and Maria and later Sir Andrew; in I. v, Maria and Feste and later Olivia and Malvolio, and so the scene changes to high life; in II. iii, Sir Toby and Sir Andrew, then Feste and finally Maria and Malvolio; in II. v, Fabyan is finally added to the others, making the sixth of the genre figures in the play. In short, he enters late, at first does little, and is never much more than a stage convenience, and, therefore, despite Shakespeare's fine characterization of his part, the critics have neglected him. Hunter remarks that his name was probably suggested by Fabia in *Gl' Ingannati*; and Rowe, followed by nearly every subsequent editor, describes him in the Dramatis Personae as "Servant to Olivia." In a moment of exasperation, to be sure, she does call him "sirrah";[22] but he is clearly a well-born servingman, and this description is therefore most misleading. He never stains his hands with menial tasks; he consorts with the gently born; and, indeed, "no man of base calling" could presume to arrange a duel, even for Sir Andrew.[23]

The prose Fabyan speaks is revelatory of the man, his life and training and interests: and, as he is more realistic, his talk is much more highly colored than that of Viola or Sebastian. On a formal occasion, he can be dignified and plain in speech;[24]

[22] *Ibid.*, v. i. 317.
[23] *Book of Honor and Armes* (London, 1590), Bk. III, chap. i; Bk. IV, chap. i, usually attributed to Sir W. Segar, but more probably by Richard Jones (R. Kelso, *M.L.N.*, XXXIX, 33).
[24] *Twelfth Night*, III. iv. 259 *et seq.*

but, when he is himself, his accent and allusion are racy of the soil from which the landed families sprang. From his rural youth come such references as the strutting "Turkey Cocke,"[25] the "dormouse valour" of Sir Andrew,[26] the festivities of May Day,[27] the allusion to fox hunting as a dishonorable sport,[28] and such a term of venery as "faults."[29] Partly from folklore and partly from contemporary science come the reference to a "Woodcocke" as having no brains,[30] to Fortune,[31] to the liver as the seat of love,[32] to the popular use of urine for divination,[33] and (ironically) to melancholy as a cold, dry humor.[34] The sermons of the parish vicar have assured him that "the Fiend is rough";[35] and perhaps sad experience has taught him that it is best to keep on the right side of the law.[36] His references to the minting of coin[37] and to the stage[38] are more likely to have been gleaned from his later years in town. Doubtless, here also he has picked up, like Sir Toby, his two or three cant travel references: the ungrateful cold of the "North,"[39] the "ysickle on a Dutchman's beard,"[40] and the fabulous wealth of the Persian "Sophy."[41] This picturesque portrayal even of a very minor figure shows the boundless wealth and realism of Shakespeare's art. Fabyan is a scion of a good county family sent up to the Illyrian counterpart of London to act as page and later servingman to the Count, his father's feudal overlord. Changes in the social and political system made this career abortive; and here he has remained, a servingman, lucky to have food and clothing in return for his purely ornamental value, and struggling to maintain himself against pushing menials like Malvolio; and his every speech and action reflect his origin and present way of life.

Curio and Valentine belong essentially to the same class

[25] *Twelfth Night*, II. v. 32.
[26] *Ibid.*, III. ii. 20.   [27] *Ibid.*, III. iv. 145.
[28] See J. W. Fortescue in *Shakespeare's England* (Oxford, 1917), II, 346.
[29] *Twelfth Night*, II. v. 117 *et seq.*
[30] *Ibid.*, II. v. 83. Cf. *Shakespeare's England* (ed cit.), II, 370.
[31] *Twelfth Night*, II. v. 129.   [32] *Ibid.*, II. v. 94; III. ii. 21.
[33] *Ibid.*, III. iv. 106.   [34] *Ibid.*, II. v. 5.   [35] *Ibid.*, III. iv. 114–15.
[36] *Ibid.*, III. iv. 155 and 164.   [37] *Ibid.*, III. ii. 23.
[38] *Ibid.*, III. iv. 130–31.   [39] *Ibid.*, III. ii. 26–27.
[40] *Ibid.*, III. ii. 27.   [41] *Ibid.*, II. v. 168–69.

as Fabyan, but they appear in full dress and formal manners, as befits the court of the local Duke. Their speaking parts are early in the play, but perhaps they show themselves later as attendants on Orsino. In the first scene, Curio tries to persuade his lord to treat his love-melancholy by the recognized cure of hunting. Later in the play, when Orsino wants music, Curio tells him that the singer Feste is away; and then he identifies Feste as the jester of Olivia's father. At Orsino's request he goes out and shortly after brings Feste in. He probably appears elsewhere accompanying the Duke, but he has nothing to do or say. Valentine comes in during the first scene. He has been to Olivia's house and brings back word that she has gone into two years' mourning, will neither see him nor consider betrothal to Orsino. This brings Orsino's wooing, which had been going on for more than a month, to a definite stalemate, and makes him turn to a new ambassador with less "graue" and conventional methods. Thus Viola takes over Valentine's thankless post. The older servingman is luckily not jealous, and kindly tells "Cesario" that she is like to be "much aduanc'd," that Orsino is by nature constant in his favors; and with these felicitations, he seems to drop out of the play as if his task as unsuccessful intermediary had quite exhausted him. His magnanimity to Viola, without apparent motive, makes him seem a bit too good for this wicked world, for very few of us rejoice to be supplanted by others more successful. At all events, like the Fool in *Lear*, he disappears in the hurly-burly of the comedy, and the audience, having hardly noted his presence, has for his absence neither surprise nor question. This ends the chronicle of the servingmen in *Twelfth Night*, a class of highborn servitors who were the very eyes and hands of their noble patrons and who, though they no longer fought, were often the practical expression of that awe and majesty that rulers must possess.

The later scenes of the comedy present three new characters, each of whom fills a small but necessary niche—a priest and two "officers." The priest betroths Olivia and Sebastian, and then testifies to the fact before the assembly. Most of the clerics of Shakespeare's plays are but meagerly depicted, and appear only for marriages or burials as in *Much Ado About Nothing* and *Hamlet*. Friar Lawrence, to be sure, in *Romeo and Juliet* has a real part in the plot, and is also individualized for his own sake with a long soliloquy; but Shakespeare merely inherited his importance from the original story in Brooke. Ecclesiastical questions were matters of dangerous controversy, and the Elizabethan Settlement in the Church of England was a nicely balanced compromise rather than a clear-cut expression of consistent policy. Therefore the government was somewhat precariously poised between contending religious views; and it behooved a prudent dramatist to avoid giving offense. Of course, as the government, after the accession of James I, assumed a more definite policy, the Puritans, who had never been friends with the players, became a common object of attack; but earlier plays are likely to touch on such questions lightly, and indeed one can rarely guess whether a Shakespearean cleric is High Church or Low, so severely were these parts conventionalized. Thus the representative of the cloth who betrothed Sebastian and Olivia is a pale and purely official figure and lacks not only individual character but also discernible churchmanship. In Illyria, furthermore, he would presumably be a Roman Catholic, and this would raise even further complications in a realistic portrayal.

The two "officers" who arrest Antonio in Act III and bring him before the Duke in Act V are rather puzzling. The "first officer," who does most of the talking and seems to be in command, may be a soldier, for he apparently fought Antonio in one or more naval engagements, and he is of high enough place, or blunt enough in speech, to address the Duke informally as "Orsino." The second, who makes the actual arrest, seems more competent and intelligent than a mere Dogberry;[42] and he keeps urging the reluctant Antonio to come away to prison, but still allows him to talk with Viola until his superior summarily breaks off the conversation. He seems to be some sort of bailiff or constable, but above the average in ability. In Act V, the "officers" reappear, but only the first one takes the liberty of

---

[42] See J. W. Draper, "Dogberry's Due Process of Law," *J.E.G.P.*, XLII, 563 *et seq.*

speech in the ducal presence. He more fully identifies Antonio as taking part in two naval (or piratical) affrays, and briefly tells of the arrest. The Duke takes his word at face value; but Viola's intercession and the recognition scene with Sebastian seem to save the prisoner from a summary fate. Why Shakespeare should have had two officers may perhaps be asked: one is to identify and one to arrest the culprit, and both would certainly be necessary to subdue and hale to court the high-spirited Antonio: Indeed, the two, like Rosencrantz and Guildenstern,[43] are finely differentiated, although together they speak fewer than twenty lines.

Twelfth Night, like most Elizabethan plays, depicts a wide range of social types, though not as wide as *Hamlet*, for the former does not show the great mass of English peasantry represented in the gravediggers. Nevertheless, the gamut of classes between the duke and the steward was a wide one; and, within this field, Shakespeare gives many types: soldiers and servingmen, shading downward into menials and upward into public servants and courtiers; and he illustrates the clergy and knighthood and the nobility. Thus the upper strata of social Illyria are put before our eyes as a going concern, with their several ambitions and fears and very human struggle for existence. Viola, Sebastian, and Antonio, to be sure, have one foot in the land of make-believe; but, for the most part, even the minor characters (in the words of the Preface to Shakespeare's *Troilus*) "are so fram'd to the life that they serve for the most common commentaries of all the actions of our lives."

[43] *Idem, The "Hamlet" of Shakespeare's Audience* (Durham, N.C., 1938), pp. 22–23.

~ The Lady Olivia

THE Lady Olivia is a realist in a romantic situation: her youth and charm and wealth make her the cynosure of neighboring sheep's eyes, and everyone has plans to marry her off or to be married to her. Thus, while the castaway Viola desperately seeks a husband and protector, the much-bereaved but hardheaded Olivia seeks to avoid wooers, and so gives time for more and more to cluster, buzzing and droning about the honeypot of her attractions until at last she finds a suitable candidate; and then she swiftly follows the ancient maxim of *fortiter in re*. Until she has hit upon her choice, she cannot drive off the others, and so must conceal her plans; she adopts an impenetrable veil of mourning, matches her woman's wit to her instant need, and thus, like Penelope, confuses and evades her suitors. Indeed, she is a realist in a romantic situation; and, as she prolongs this situation, she becomes more and more the axis on which the others' lives and expectations turn: to her own household, her marriage is the all-absorbing question; so also to Orsino and his household, and also to sundry satellites and hangers-on, who sigh and protest devotion in their several ways, disharmonious with one another, and (did they but know it) most disharmonious with the secret aspirations of their mistress.

Although Olivia appears in only six scenes and speaks fewer lines than Viola or Sir Toby, she is truly the crux of *Twelfth Night*. Her role of melancholy mourning—seclusion, veil, and fertile tears—keeps her behind the scenes. Indeed, she appears but once in the first act and not at all in the second; but repeated reference to her makes her a pervading presence, and she is the center of the plots, which, as in contemporary Italian comedy, chiefly concern her lovers. Her part, moreover, seems to have been the final and crowning role of Samuel Gilburne, who for some years had been the leading lady of Shakespeare's company;

168

and perhaps his manly growth in adolescence suggested her somewhat masterful character—so masterful that Manningham, when he saw the performance in 1602 (N.S.), mistook her for a widow. Sixty years later, moreover, when Elizabethan stage traditions were still not quite forgotten, Miss Gibbs chose her role rather than that of Viola. In Riche's *Apolonius and Silla,* her prototype is the Lady Julina, a wealthy, charming, and very self-possessed young widow. This is the only part that Shakespeare at all enlarged from Riche's story; the others he omitted or minimized to make room for his low comedy. Thus, her importance is evidenced in the dialogue, in the plot construction, in the early actors who played the part, and in Shakespeare's treatment of his source.

According to Elizabethan stage convention, the introduction of a character generally gave a clue as to his personality, his place, and his importance in the play; and there is probably no one in Shakespeare who has a more lengthy and elaborate introduction than Olivia. Her appearance is a sort of climax to Act I, most amply and ingeniously prepared for. In the first scene, no less person than the Duke himself declares her overwhelmingly beautiful: "Me thought she purg'd the ayre of pestilence"—her very presence counteracted infection of the plague! His love of her, moreover, utterly subdues him so that passion is tearing him to pieces as Diana's hounds did the unfortunate Actæon. Valentine enters and tells Orsino that his lady has gone into seven years' mourning for her father and her brother, both recently dead, and the scene ends with the lover's continued laments and ecstasies. In the second scene, the Captain again tells of Olivia's double bereavement and of Orsino's bootless suit. Here the Lady is described more prosaically as "A virtuous maid, the daughter of a Count That dide a tweluemonth since." The third scene Sir Toby opens by complaining, "What a plague meanes my Neece to take the death of her brother thus?" Maria urges him to mend his ways; but he is as obstinate as Mrs. Malaprop's "allegory," and, at Sir Andrew's entrance, the merrymaking does not fall into abatement. In the fourth scene, the Duke sends Viola as his John

Alden to woo his love almost *vi et armis*; and, at last in the fifth, the Countess herself appears in state, with Maria as her herald and Malvolio and others dancing attendance—quite a triumphal entry. She is bored but as wary as Queen Elizabeth, and is perhaps a bit ashamed at her renewed interest in Feste and his chatter; but, before she knows it, she is laughing at his jokes, and has forgiven his absence. (What part or lot had a jester in a house of mourning: *ergo*, why not be absent until it is time to laugh again?) At this psychological moment of merriment, doubtless Olivia's first in many months, Maria announces the advent of Viola; Sir Toby reannounces her; Malvolio tries vainly to dismiss her; and thus, with due pomp and reiterated blazon, Olivia's Fate enters upon the scene—or rather, the sister of Olivia's Fate, who inadvertently does his wooing for him. Indeed, though the Countess takes up but part of a single scene, she dominates the act; and her meeting with Viola not only gives it a brilliant climax of color and grouping upon the stage but also starts the major complication, which in the end defeats the well-laid plans of steward and knights and duke. Surely, the playwright Shakespeare, having given Olivia such an introduction, must have considered her crucially important.

Modern critics, allured by the romantic Viola, are inclined to disagree; and disagreeing with Shakespeare is a critical impasse. To a few, she seems more or less significant; to none, very attractive. Dr. Johnson complained that her marriage "wants credibility." Schlegel speaks of "the proud Olivia . . . . entangled by the modest and insinuating messenger of the Duke," as if she were entirely a pawn in the game. Kenny (1864) agrees with Johnson that her marriage is "melodramatic." Ruggles, even more than Schlegel, considers her "devoid of restraints in the indulgence of [her] fancies and passions"— that is, without mastery over herself or others. Oechelhäuser calls the end hurried and unsatisfactory. Conrad admits her the organic center of the play, but does not understand her motives and calls her merely "haughty." More recently, the Arden editors declare her "an admirable foil" to Viola, whom they take to be the heroine: despite her "habit of dignity," she has "something of the spoiled child about her," and she lacks Viola's "readiness to repartee and quick resourcefulness"—this shrewd young lady who manages to dominate her unruly household and her persistent lovers, and finally confounds them all by a marriage of her own choice that leaves her (as she intended) the permanent mistress of the situation! The Tudor editors realize that she is "the central figure" of the play, "endowed with an engaging dignity and humanity"; but they do not seem to understand her shrewd designs. The new Cambridge editors declare her "plainly a self-deceiver," a shallow amateur in melancholy. These opinions are certainly diverse. Olivia seems indeed to have confounded not only Orsino and Sir Toby but also modern commentators—good evidence that she and her schemes are truly feminine in Shakespeare's subtlest manner.

Olivia's mind and education, and something of her character, appear in the very style of her discourse. Her high place and the proprieties of mourning require of her plain speech rather than the skipping repartee of comedy; and this plain speech implies an incisive, direct mind, a will that knows what it wants, and at least the appearance of candor. Indeed, Olivia speaks out anent Orsino's love without fear or equivocation; and commonly her talk is crisp. "If you be not mad, be gone, if you haue reason, be brief." She can be succinct and pointed: "There is no slander in an allow'd foole," and "What is decreed, must be." In a moment of crisis, she rises at once to the occasion: "What is the matter? . . . . Who has done this, Sir Andrew? . . . . Get him to bed, and let his hurt be look'd to." Does this terse competence suggest that she is "devoid of restraints," a "spoiled child," a shallow "self-deceiver"? She will have nothing of Cesario's poetical speech and conventional compliment; she will not even let him call himself her "seruant," after the fashion of the day. This young lady is no soft and clinging vine; and, perhaps for that reason, did not appeal to the Victorian critics. Indeed, her short, sharp speeches have the incisive quality of command rather than the submissive tone of female dependence.

The wide gamut of her allusions, especially in her first

171

scene to give the keynote of her role, show a mind that was widely schooled in serious and practical concerns—indeed, a very Portia. She knows something of law, understands the office of "Crowner"[1] who judged the cause of death, and she can use a betrothal neatly to thwart the purposes of Orsino; the technical terms of heraldry,[2] a very legal science, come naturally to her lips, and she understands itemized inventories[3] such as those made of an estate. Though a peaceful person, she refers to cannon bullets.[4] She is versed in popular science: she can play on the Elizabethan concept of love-sickness;[5] she knows that the moon, right after its ascendant in the heavens, brings woe, and in the fourth, sixth, and eighth signs brings anger;[6] she knows that midsummer was thought to aggravate madness.[7] She has been duly instructed in religion: of course, a "Text" should be prefixed to a homily;[8] the devil in seductive guise tempts souls to hell;[9] and the insane, being "possest" of the devil, "raue."[10] Her education, if not deep, is at least well rounded; and, had she shown some knowledge of the Classics, one might fairly term her a bluestocking like Queen Elizabeth and the Countess of Pembroke. Many Elizabethans, however, especially the Puritans, objected to too much learning in girls;[11] and, since only men might enter the universities, daughters could be educated only by costly private tutors. The preponderance of practical and the absence of Classical allusion in Olivia's discourse suggests that her education had come from her own eyes and ears, from casual reading and from conversation—a fine art in that age[12]—rather than from the assiduity of a learned tutor.

Indeed, Olivia gives evidence of a clear head and a quick mind. She enjoys the combat of wit between Malvolio and Feste; and, though she is too dignified in her mourning to make

---

[1] *Twelfth Night*, I. v. 133.   [2] *Ibid.*, I. v. 294.

[3] *Ibid.*, I. v. 241 *et seq.*   [4] *Ibid.*, I. v. 91.   [5] *Ibid.*, I. v. 88.

[6] *Ibid.*, I. v. 200. Cf. *Batman upon Bartholome* (London, 1582), Lib. VIII, cap. 30.

[7] *Twelfth Night*, III. iv. 58.   [8] *Ibid.*, I. v. 220–21.

[9] *Ibid.*, III. iv. 216.   [10] *Ibid.*, III. iv. 11.

[11] E. Godfrey, *Home Life under the Stuarts* (London, 1903), pp. 98–99.

[12] See J. W. Draper, "The *Conversazione* in Shakespeare's Plays," *Italica*, XXIII, 7 *et seq.*

one in it, she eggs on the contestants.[13] She is competent at worldly-wise epigram: "O world, how apt the poore are to be proud?";[14] and ". . . . youth is bought more oft then begg'd, or borrow'd."[15] She is quick-witted, and instantly invents the stratagem of the ring to oblige Viola to visit her again. She can endure plain speaking, and is not angry when Viola suggests that her fine complexion may be false[16] and that she is "too proud." She can be patient with Feste, and can bide her time with Sir Toby. Indeed, she has poise and self-control. She has also a sense of diplomacy. She knows that bad news requires a lengthy introduction.[17] She is suspicious of eulogy.[18] She can ignore Sir Andrew, checkmate Sir Toby, restrain the Duke, and even get him to countenance her marriage with Sebastian by means of the double wedding—a final master stroke of policy that at once silences his suit forever and makes him give public recognition to Sebastian as her husband. No wonder she runs her household with "smooth, discreet, and stable bearing"![19] Truly, she had some right to think herself capable of ruling her father's lands—and, by the way, a husband.

At the same time, like Queen Elizabeth, she appreciates the lighter side of life; she knows something of drama,[20] music,[21] bearbaiting,[22] and birding.[23] Her speech lacks Sir Toby's traveled elegance; but she knows that mountainous regions are generally "barbarous."[24] Like a true woman, she is interested in clothes—as indeed was Queen Elizabeth—in the fine, transparent cloth, "Cipresse,"[25] and in "graine," the fast red dye derived from the coccus insect.[26] Though she rarely indulges in flowery language, she can on occasion garnish her discourse with a philosophic reference to "Musicke from the spheares,"[27] or a poetic allusion to the "Roses of the Spring."[28] In short, Olivia's conversation shows her candid and forthright and yet tactful, widely but not deeply learned, capable of epigram and

---

[13] *Twelfth Night*, I. v. 80.   [14] *Ibid.*, III. i. 130.   [15] *Ibid.*, III. iv. 5.
[16] *Twelfth Night*, I. v. 233.   [17] *Ibid.*, I. v. 206–7.
[18] *Ibid.*, I. v. 196.   [19] *Ibid.*, IV. iii. 21.   [20] *Ibid.*, I. v. 182.
[21] *Ibid.*, V. i. 114.   [22] *Ibid.*, III. i. 120.
[23] *Ibid.*, I. v. 90–91.   [24] *Ibid.*, IV. i. 48 *et seq.*   [25] *Ibid.*, III. i. 123.
[26] *Ibid.*, I. v. 234.
[27] *Ibid.*, III. i. 111.   [28] *Ibid.*, III. i. 153.

wit, but also capable of holding all her capabilities in check and bending them to her chief purpose.

In Riche's *Apolonius*, the Lady Julina "besides the aboundance of her wealth and the greatnesse of her revenues, had likewise the soveraigntie of all the dames of Constantinople for her beautie"; and Olivia is no less a paragon, rich, noble, and attractive. The Dramatis Personae, added originally by Rowe, describes her as "a Lady of great Beauty and Fortune"; and the lines of the comedy bear this out. Indeed, she is, strictly speaking, more than a "Lady"; she is a Countess, and both Viola and Feste even call her "Princesse."[29] She seems on occasion to use the royal "we,"[30] and she claims power of life and death over Sir Toby[31]—but perhaps this is merely the exaggeration of her anger. Whether or not of royal blood, and whether or not an independent potentate as these words imply, she is at least a Countess, as reiterated passages attest. The first scene introduces her as beautiful, the second as "faire" and "virtuous" and "daughter of a Count." She refers to her "Dowry."[32] She is constantly attended, not only by "fellowes," but also by well-born servitors such as Maria and Fabyan and other "Gentlemen";[33] and the fine liveries and obsequiousness of the former and the fine dress and elaborate deference of the latter would create on the stage an immediate impression of her aristocratic caste. In short, Olivia was a young lady *comme il faut*, rich, noble, accomplished, and beautiful: what more could an expectant husband ask?

She was, however, not to be had for the asking—even by an enterprising duke. Elizabethan ladies, despite legal bonds, despite Biblical monitions and the horror of the godly, and despite their fathers and their brothers (e.g., Brabantio and Laertes) were progressing serenely along the primrose path of female independence. Domestic-conduct books still likened

---

[29] *Twelfth Night*, III. i. 97; V. i. 315. The Venetian senatorial families ranked themselves as princely; but, even if Shakespeare thought of Illyria as a Venetian dependency, this would not apply to its local nobility. Perhaps he thought of Olivia and Orsino as independent princelings of the Holy Roman Empire; but, in that case, Olivia could not inherit her father's title.

[30] *Ibid.*, I. v. 230.　　　　　[31] *Ibid.*, IV. i. 46.

[32] *Ibid.*, III. iv. 67.　　　　　　[33] *Ibid.*, I. v. 70.

woman to "an *Eccho* . . . . [having] but one word for many which are spoken to her";[34] but foreign travelers declared that in fact English women were "almost like masters,"[35] and that they "have much more liberty than perhaps in any other place."[36] Moryson in the course of his journeys over Europe remarked that England was the "Paradice of Women," for there the men treated them "obsequiously."[37] Of course, even at best, this freedom had to be somewhat circumscribed in an age without serious police, when "wanton youths . . . . will not let a maid or a wife passe a long the streetes but they will be medling with her,"[38] and when the double standard of sex morals was the rule. Perhaps *Merry Wives of Windsor* gives the most realistic picture of this independence among the upper *bourgeoisie*.[39] Among the aristocracy, Lady Russel, Lady Sidney, Lady Rich, and others[40]—not to mention Elizabeth herself —furnish obvious examples. Some grew so independent, even going to hunt in "breeches," that James I took alarm and summoned the clergy to put down this monstrous regiment of women;[41] and Stubbes invoked divine imprecations on women who don men's clothes.[42]

This growing independence naturally came more easily to married women and to widows than to maids; and perhaps that is why Niccholes had reason to complain that "The forward Virgins of our age" hastened to matrimony at thirteen or fourteen, and others lingered too long on account of "certaine cautionary worldly respects."[43] Betrothal was generally the prerogative—sometimes a very lucrative prerogative—of the girl's father. The accepted doctrine among the godly was that

[34] R. C[leaver], *Godly Form* (London, 1598), p. 101.

[35] W. B. Rye, *England as Seen by Foreigners* (London, 1865), p. 14.

[36] *Ibid.*, p. 7; see J. W. Draper, "Desdemona," *R.L.C.*, XIII, 336 *et seq.*; and W. Powell, *Tom of All Trades* (ed. *princ.*, 1631) ed. New Shakespeare Society, p. 173.

[37] F. Moryson, *Itinerary* (London, 1617), Pt. III, p. 53.

[38] S. Rowlands, *Greene's Ghost* (London, 1602). Cf. Harrison, *Description of England*, ed. Furnivall (London, 1909), p. 247.

[39] See E. J. Haller, "The Realism of *Merry Wives*," *West Virginia University Philological Studies* (1937), pp. 32 *et seq.*

[40] V. A. Wilson, *Society Women of Shakespeare's Time* (New York, 1925), *et passim.*

[41] *Ibid.*, chapter xvi.

[42] P. Stubbes, *Anatomie of Abuses* (ed. *princ.*, 1585; London, 1836), p. 68.

[43] A. Niccholes, *Discourse of Marriage* (London, 1615), p. 11.

"Children are as the goods of their parents, wholly in their power, to be ordered and disposed by them," especially as to "Making marriage":[44] and the Old Testament and the Church Fathers supported this amply. The board and breeding and dowry of a girl were a great expense to her family; and so the family surely had a right to reimburse itself in the only way it could, by marrying her off in the most advantageous way. Thus "infants in swadling clouts are often maried by their ambicious parents and freendes."[45] Betrothal might be the subject of much "chaffering,"[46] as illustrated in *The Taming of the Shrew* and in the records of the contemporary lawsuits.[47] If Olivia's father, or even an elder brother, had been alive, that lady's independent spirit would have had less scope; and therefore Shakespeare was obliged to make her either a widow, like her prototype in Riche, or an orphan heiress bereft of close male relatives. Indeed, daughters, theoretically at least, had but little standing in an Elizabethan family—so little that William Perkins quite omitted them from his *Christian Oeconomie* (1609), although he speaks of parents, sons, and even servants. In drama, the family must be done away with if the daughter were to shine; and, in *Twelfth Night,* the traditional situation from Italian comedy of the girl and her many lovers receives a new and typically English turn: the girl, like a true Elizabethan feminist, marries herself off without benefit of kith or kin.

According to contemporary English law and custom, an unmarried heiress without a father who was her "guardian by nature" was subject, if she were under fourteen, to a "guardian in socage." The court usually appointed "the *next of Blood, to whom the Inheritance cannot descend,*" perhaps a mother, a half-brother, or an uncle.[48] But apparently, Olivia was older

---

[44] W. Gouge, *Domesticall Duties* (London, 1634), pp. 447–48. See also M. Griffeth, *Bethel* (London, 1588), pp. 172 *et seq.; Catechestical Doctrine* (Oxford, 1846), p. 186; *Conjugal Duty*, ed. R. Wilkinson (London, 1732); Snawsel, *Looking Glasse* (London, 1610); L. C. Powell, *English Domestic Relations, 1487–1653* (New York, 1917); and J. W. Draper, "Brabantio," *Eng. Studies*, XXII, 193 *et seq.*

[45] Stubbes, *op. cit.*, pp. 99–100.   [46] Godfrey, *op. cit.*, p. 118.

[47] C. J. Sisson, *Lost Plays* (Cambridge, 1936), pp. 14 *et seq.*, p. 80 *et passim.*

[48] C. Viner, *General Abridgment* [1742–56], XIV, 170 *et seq.*, M. Bacon, *New Abridgment* (Philadelphia, 1811), III, 413.

than fourteen: she certainly seems older, and Sir Toby is clearly not her legal guardian. Her father, moreover, according to a common custom, had appointed her brother[49] guardian in his will; but the brother's death had brought these plans to naught. Even if Sir Toby, moreover, had been Olivia's guardian, he could not have forced a husband of his choosing on her; for, in this regard, he had only the negative power of a veto.[50] Thus Shakespeare, for the necessary purposes of the plot, has made the maiden Olivia her own mistress: her natural guardian was dead; the guardian appointed in her father's will was also dead —we must suppose too suddenly to name his own successor— and thus Olivia was left a petty counterpart of Queen Elizabeth, a young and affluent Countess; and the audience would easily understand her in this light.

Not without reason did the law provide guardians for unmarried girls; and Olivia's situation was beset with uncertainties and dangers. She must somehow shield herself from the unwelcome attentions of fortune hunters and of fools like Sir Andrew; and she ran a serious risk even of abduction and forced marriage[51] to some miscreant who wished only to squander her patrimony as soon as wedlock gave him control of it.[52] This danger was so real that Queen Elizabeth passed an act even to reinforce the statute of Henry VII which made such an abduction a felony.[53] Portia's father in *The Merchant of Venice* is solicitous to provide for her marriage with his posthumous consent; Brabantio shields Desdemona from Roderigo; and Laertes and Polonius warn Ophelia against the dangerous advances of the Crown Prince. In fact, a daughter was a family asset that required constant and careful tending; and Olivia in her position as self-guardian had a most exacting role. She adopts a screen of modest retirement that to the Elizabethans would doubtless seem a proof at once of her proper maidenly reserve and of her shrewd sagacity: if she accept the Duke, she has a master; if she refuse him face to face, she insults him; but, if she will

[49] Viner, *op. cit.*, XIV, 166 *et seq.*   [50] Viner, *op. cit.*, XIV, 184.

[51] *Ibid.*, XIV, 191 *et seq.*   [52] Niccholes, *op. cit.*, p. 18.

[53] Viner, *op. cit.*, XV, 296 *et seq.*; Bacon, *op. cit.*, IV, 539; Sisson, *op. cit.*, pp. 12 *et passim.*

not see him for a reason that all commend, she holds him checkmate. Thus she maintains the sacred atmosphere of conventual seclusion, but without the restrictions of an actual convent; and so she gets herself the maximum protection, with the minimum of restraint, and all this with the approval of Mrs. Grundy. Who shall say that Olivia was not astute?

Like Queen Elizabeth, the Countess promises herself a permanent virginity, and uses as her seal the chaste Lucrece.[54] Her "vaile" proclaims her maiden modesty[55]—perhaps made of transparent "cipresse"[56] so that she can observe her little world. She weeps daily, and eschews all company. In fact, she displays the most approved appurtenances of sorrow; and, if "the liues of those that dye, consist in the memory of those that liue,"[57] she is paying her full obligation to her brother and her father. Her declaration, however, that she will weep for seven years is rather more than propriety required.[58] Doubtless, she made it in the shock of her first grief at the double bereavement; but, as time wore on and her youth reasserted itself, this rigid mourning became more and more a matter of convenience: it held the importunate Duke at bay while she made plans and gathered her forces to meet the onslaughts of impending matrimony. Well might Manningham at an early performance mistake this artful young lady for a widow. Meanwhile, the suits of Sir Andrew and Malvolio develop; the curtain rises; the coy Olivia, lured from her mourning humor by the wit of Feste, falls all at once in love with Viola; and the comedy trips merrily on its way.

In preparing for the quadripartite wooing of Olivia, Shakespeare was obliged to circumvent the same social limitations as Menander and his Latin followers. In Greek and Roman times, a respectable girl lived in seclusion and was married by her parents; and, in order to depict honorable but romantic love,

---

[54] *Twelfth Night*, II. v. 92.

[55] *Ibid.*, I. v. 165; R. Brathwait, *English Gentlewoman* (London, 1631), pp. 82 *et seq.*

[56] *Twelfth Night*, III. i. 123; Cf. M. C. Linthicum, *Costume in the Drama of Shakespeare* (Oxford, 1936), p. 119 n.

[57] Brathwait, *op. cit.* (ed. 1615), p. 113.

[58] T. R. R[ogers], *Anatomie of the minde* (London, 1576), line 49; and T. Overbury, *The Mourners Meane* (London, ? 1618).

178

the playwrights had to postulate, as in Terence's *Andria*, a virgin of good family, shipwrecked or stolen from her home, and thus a subject for proper and legal marriage, and yet on the outskirts of a free and easy demimonde where she can meet her lover in person and fall in love. Elizabethan girls were not so strictly kept as those of Greece and Rome and Renaissance Italy and Spain; but their fathers, especially in noble families, arranged their marriages; and, therefore, Shakespeare had to have Olivia's father and brother die in order to give her freedom of choice; and the fact that he went to all this trouble to do so shows that his depiction of her use of this freedom was a major matter in the comedy. The strong-willed but shrewd Olivia is a dominating figure for whom he carefully cleared the stage. This is the situation, then, with which the main plot opens: Olivia *contra mundum*, supported in her anomalous position by her mourning and her wit, dangling like ripe fruit just out of reach of the boorish Sir Andrew, the elegant Orsino, and the impossible Malvolio—and then a little gust twists off this fruit into the astonished lap of Sebastian.

According to the Captain's statement in the second scene, Olivia, when the play began, had already been repulsing Orsino's suit for more than a month. He had seen her, apparently more than once;[59] but she hardly knows him by sight, for she fears that Cesario may be he in disguise.[60] Indeed, Orsino's love was dangerous and required dexterous manipulation. Like so many of the petty nobles of Italy and the Holy Roman Empire, the "Duke" or "Count" is apparently an independent ruler in his own right.[61] If perchance he were Olivia's feudal suzerain, he might claim by law her guardianship and so a voice in the disposal of her hand; and, even as an independent equal,[62] his title of "Duke" implied a power greater than hers that might force her to submission.[63] At times, indeed, Orsino could threaten dangerously.[64] Despite all this, Olivia has determined to reject him, consonant with Cleaver's admonition not to

[59] *Twelfth Night*, I. i. 23. [60] *Ibid.*, I. v. 295.
[61] *Ibid.*, I. ii. 26–27; III. iii. 30 *et seq.*
[62] *Ibid.*, V. i. 158–59.
[63] *Ibid.*, I. v. 208–9. [64] *Ibid.*, V. i. 122 *et seq.*

marry "aboue thy degree."[65] As a suitor, the Duke's position is somewhat embarrassing: unable to press his claims in the conventional way through a parent or near relation, he is obliged to risk the contumely of a rebuff by addressing the lady herself. Of this difficulty Olivia takes full advantage by refusing to be seen; and, furthermore, though she admits his excellencies,[66] she insists she "cannot loue him."[67] As she grows enamored of Viola, she becomes more insistent that she will none of him, and in fact gives him no audience until the final scene after she has been safely betrothed to Sebastian. At first sight, this seems strange behavior on her part, for the match was obviously appropriate and to everyone's advantage. She promises to give Viola "reasons" for her decision[68] but never does so, and the only clue to her motives, beyond her own shrewd and independent character, is a remark that she made to Sir Toby which he quotes early in the play:

> Shee'l none o'th Count, she'l not match aboue hir degree,
> neither in estate, yeares, nor wit: I haue heard her swear t.[69]

This statement, apparently delivered with a convincing oath, would surely have told an Elizabethan audience—who saw plenty of feminism in actual life—just why the Duke was *non grata* as a wooer: he is so much her superior in "estate," and perhaps also in "yeares,"[70] that he would dominate any such partnership; and, worst of all, he thinks of women as distinctly subservient to men,[71] and proposes to be the "one selfe king" of his wife's every thought and feeling.[72] Thus Shakespeare, by giving Olivia the independence of Elizabethan ladies, motivates the old story, which required that she refuse the very eligible Duke, and choose instead a wandering youth of here and everywhere. The Countess is determined to dominate her husband; and so she will not wed a husband who both can and will dominate her. Some of Orsino's very virtues—his high

---

[65] Cleaver, *op. cit.*, p. 143 *et seq.* De la Primaudaye advises a husband ten years older than the wife, *French Academy* (London, 1586), p. 496.

[66] *Twelfth Night*, I. v. 257. [67] *Ibid.*, I. v. 260.

[68] *Ibid.*, I. v. 309.   [69] *Ibid.*, I. iii. 102–4.   [70] *Ibid.*, II. iv. 35.

[71] *Ibid.*, II. iv. 99 *et passim.*   [72] *Ibid.*, I. i. 44.

position, age, and lusty manhood—are to Olivia the best reasons
for refusing him.

Sir Andrew's suit required of Olivia less tact, and yet some
vigilance; for either Sir Toby might claim to be *in loco parentis*
and so try to betroth her as he pleased, or he might even connive
at an abduction. A Countess to the manner born, Olivia will not
even consider the *nouveau riche* Sir Andrew; and, as even he at
times realizes,[73] his case is hopeless. When her uncle brings
him, an unbidden guest, to grace her hall, she tries to evade
him with the same technique that worked so well with Orsino;
but he is less decorously considerate, and he and Sir Toby make
themselves very much at home; therefore she cannot quite
ignore him. She uses Maria and Malvolio to meet the situation
and put down nightly roistering; but Maria has set her cap
for Sir Toby, and so is not too strong in her reproofs; and Malvolio's interposing merely arouses the enmity of Fabyan, and
unites the household against the steward. In short, Olivia can
avoid accepting the knight's attentions only at the high price of
enduring his riot in her hall. Nevertheless, she persists, though
it must have been clear to her that such a situation could go on
forever. Finally, by sheer accident, he gets into her presence,[74]
and can only gape speechless before the accomplished Viola.
At last he is forsaken even by Sir Toby, and lapses in the duel
episode from Olivia's lover to his protector's gull and dupe. Sir
Andrew's prolonged visit makes one realize why old-fashioned
hospitality was declining among the Elizabethans, and why
Portia's father required her wooers under oath to quit the
house at once on failing the casket test. Just as Orsino's good
qualities ruled him out, so did Sir Andrew's bad ones—indeed,
so much so that the Countess never deigns even to give him
audience.

Of Malvolio's suit, she never even knows until the play
is practically done. Sir Andrew, as a fool and coward, was
personally impossible; Malvolio, as a "Coystril," a mere menial, is socially impossible. He is introduced, moreover, like
Sir Andrew, as a "Foole"—not exactly a "natural" fool as Sir

---

[73] *Ibid.*, I. iii. 18, 97 *et seq.*   [74] *Ibid.*, III. i. 85 *et seq.*

Andrew is, but a fool for the nonce because he is "sicke of selfe-loue."[75] The audience, furthermore, is occasionally reminded that he is an ass,[76] a brainless "Woodcocke,"[77] and, as he himself admits, a "most notorious gecke and gull."[78] All this springs from his "ouer-weening"[79] disposition that makes him aspire to wed the Countess and rule her domicile and demesnes. These hopes doubtless sprang partly from his choleric pride and self-conceit,[80] and partly from the fact that Olivia, on being left unprotected, had found great need of him. Indeed, it is just possible that in real Elizabethan life she might have married him; and this fact shows him less of a fool than his adversaries declare, but also makes him more dangerous to their way of life, and so gives further motive to their animosity. In any case, Olivia, since she was not aware of his ambitions, made no particular plans to counter them. Indeed, her defense against the others encouraged Malvolio by enlarging his authority in the household; and this in turn defeated him by arousing the resentment of Sir Toby and Maria, who make him ridiculous in order that Olivia may surely reject him. Thus, his love-making was ended before it ever really began.

The quadripartite triangle comprising the love affair of Orsino and Olivia with Viola and Sebastian is the least realistic episode in the play; but Shakespeare inherited the situation from his source, and he must justify it as best he could in terms of Elizabethan mores and current psychological belief. The Duke's ambassador, by his status, speech, and manners, must be a gentleman; and Olivia is ready to react from her strict and lonely mourning. Dante's story of Paolo and Francesca and Longfellow's of John Alden illustrate the danger that the marriage broker runs that he will capture the affections that he is supposed to seek for his client. But, in *Twelfth Night*, the go-between in her own person and in that of her twin brother, gains the love of both the intended principals. Olivia's strategy in this case is quite different from that with her other

---

[75] *Twelfth Night*, I. v. 88.
[76] *Ibid.*, II. iii. 123.   [77] *Ibid.*, II. v. 83.   [78] *Ibid.*, V. i. 362.
[79] *Ibid.*, II. iii. 142 *et seq.*; and II v. 31.   [80] *Ibid.*, II. iii. 145.

lovers: Orsino, she politely evades; Sir Andrew, she brusquely ignores; Malvolio as a lover never occurs to her; but Viola, and then by accident Sebastian, she woos and weds with no minced words and little restraint of action. The twins obviously surpass her in neither estate nor age, and she is so much in love that she takes a chance on their wit. She declares her passion to Viola apparently at their second meeting, is refused, but, like Orsino, will not so be answered.[81] Again she urges, and once more is repulsed.[82] Yet again, with a priest all ready, she comes upon her love—this time, not Viola but her twin brother—and the two are legally betrothed posthaste dispatch.[83] One judges that Sebastian was as smitten with her at first sight as she had been with Viola—at least, one hopes so. Of course, at her next meeting with Viola who knows nothing of the wedding, she is again repulsed, and for a moment thinks that her husband has played her false. Then luckily, the complication of the twins is disentangled; Sebastian declares himself the lucky bridegroom, and all is well. Indeed, the Countess' love affairs were growing too complicated for her to manage;[84] a summary wedlock with Sebastian was the obvious way to cut the Gordian knot, and she cleverly persuades the Duke to join with her in a double wedding that will commit him to a public acceptance of her marriage and so ward off all future complications. She handsomely offers to defray the cost of the wedding;[85] and the cost will not be light; but politically it is worth the price. Each of Olivia's lovers pays a forfeit for paying her attentions: Orsino suffers from love-melancholy, and has to endure the ignominy of public refusal; Sir Andrew is bilked roundly by Sir Toby; Malvolio suffers gulling and imprisonment; but Viola, who does not pursue the lady of her own free will, suffers perhaps the most, for she must woo another for the man she loves; and she deserves the reward of the happy ending. Olivia no less so.

Psychology and mental states are at once the cause and the

---

[81] *Twelfth Night*, III. i. 113 *et seq.*   [82] *Ibid.*, III. iv. 199 et seq.

[83] *Ibid.*, IV. iii. 25 *et seq.* J. W. Draper, "Signior Brabantio," *English Studies*, XXII, 193 *et seq.*

[84] *Twelfth Night*, V. i. 105 *et passim.*   [85] *Ibid.*, V. i. 332 *et seq.*

result of human action: Iago's dangerous choler seems to have been native to him, and governs his doings in the play;[86] Hamlet's melancholy humor is not natural to him, but arises from the events and situations to which he is subjected.[87] So it is in life, and so a dramatist must show character and action reacting mutually. Olivia, like Hamlet, hardly appears on the stage in her normal humor; and, even more like Hamlet, her normal humor is apparently sanguine though events have made her melancholy. At first, this melancholy, like Hamlet's when he first appears, is "natural," the result of grief at a recent death; later, when she jests with Feste, she shows a glimpse of her innate sanguine temper—as Hamlet shows his natural self for a moment in his first scene with Rosencrantz and Guildenstern. Then, like Hamlet, the whirligig of events has its revenges and submerges both Olivia and Hamlet into a far more serious "unnatural" melancholy, arising in the one from unrequited love, and in the other from thwarted purpose. As a woman, the Countess should be phlegmatic, like Maria; but as a Countess, she might properly be choleric or sanguine; and her independent character suggests one of these latter temperaments. She is too much the diplomat and too tolerant of Sir Toby to be greatly choleric; and choleric pride would hardly forgive Viola's rejection of her love.[88] She is more probably sanguine; and the sanguine temper best accords with her hopefulness in trying circumstances, her "faire" appearance,[89] her high position,[90] and especially her susceptibility to love[91] as soon as Feste had dispersed the clouds of her melancholy.

Olivia's speech, though not fast for the Elizabethan stage,

---

[86] J. W. Draper, "The Jealousy of Iago," *Neophilologus*, XXV, 50 *et seq.*

[87] *Idem, The "Hamlet" of Shakespeare's Audience* (Durham, N.C., 1938), pp. 175 *et seq.*

[88] C. Dariot, *Iudgement of the Starres*, tr. F. Wither (London, 1598), sig. D 2 *et passim.*

[89] *Twelfth Night*, I. ii. 35; III. i. 97; cf. Vicary, *Anatomie*, E.E.T.S., Ex. Ser., LIII, 41; *Booke of Arcandam*, tr. W. Warde (London, 1592), sig. M 2 r; Dariot, *op. cit.*, sig. D 2 v; T. W[alkington], *Optick Glasse* (London, 1631?), pp. 116–17.

[90] Dariot, *op. cit.*, sig. D 2 v.

[91] T. Cogan, *Haven of Health* (London, 1589), sig. Hh 2 v; N. Coeffeteau, *Table of Humane Passions* (London, 1621), p. 551; Walkington, *op. cit.*, p. 17; Burton, *Anatomy of Melancholy*, Part III, Sec. 2, Mem. 2, p. 1; J. Ferrand, 'Ερωτομανία (Oxford, 1640), p. 64.

presents a clear contrast to Viola's slow utterance: in no scene do her verse passages show a preponderance of slow speech; her general average in the play is 1 to 1½, and, in Act IV, scene i, her passion can increase her speed to 1 to 3—. She uses such slurs as "spirit," "heavens," and "thou'ldst," each in one syllable, and as "flatterer," "murderous," "tyrannous," and "th'unmuzzled," in two syllables. She is slowest when she is puzzled over Malvolio's smiling madness, but more than regains her speed later in the scene. Her tempo seems to express the balanced restraint in which her precarious situation obliges her to hold herself—a sanguine temper tinged with enough choler to make her independent, and with the melancholy that begins to arise from her unrequited love for Viola. In short, the very rhythms of her speech seem to express the impact of the plot on her humor and character, and so imply her fundamental realism.

Olivia's double reaction from melancholy at her brother's death to the sanguine at Feste's jokes, and from a fresh melancholy at her unrequited love for Viola to her sanguine, not to say festive, spirit at the end, is clearly substantiated by the popular psychologists of the age. In the early part of the play she is naturally distressed over the deaths of her two late protectors; and death was a recognized cause for natural melancholy.[92] The very extremity of her mourning, however, fordid itself, very much as the extremity of Romeo's love-melancholy for Rosaline opened the way for his sanguine affair with Juliet.[93] Moreover, if the play may be considered as set in May[94]—and Feste's reference to approaching summer[95] seems to bear this out—then the season of the year favored the sanguine temper.[96] For months Olivia has been living as a cloistress and weeping daily; and then Feste comes back from his sojourn at the Duke's and dares to bandy wit at her very sorrow; and she is tricked into laughter, and so recoils to her natural, sanguine self. But the sanguine complexion was hot and moist and ardent, and there-

[92] Burton, *op. cit.*, Part I, Sec. 2, Mem. 4.
[93] John Cole, "Romeo and Rosaline," *Neophilologus*, XXIV, 285 *et seq.*
[94] See Appendix A, p. 257.   [95] *Twelfth Night*, I. v. 21.
[96] Sir T. Elyot, *Castell of Helth* (London, 1541), leaf 71 v.

185

fore given to love. Just at this lucky moment the personable Cesario, despite the efforts of knight and steward, leaps all civil bounds and enters Olivia's presence. Of course, she loves him at first sight. Orsino's wooing had been inopportune, when melancholy closed her eyes to him; but, as soon as Feste cures her, she falls in love, like Titania, with the first man she sees. Thus, her feelings join with her independent nature in making her select the twins as the object of her love. The beginning of Riche's romance has a parallel situation: Apolonius, when he first meets Silla on the way home from the wars, has too much martial choler, according to Riche, to fall in love with her; but in Constantinople under different influences, he loves first the Lady Julina and later the persistent Silla. Thus Shakespeare would seem to have transferred from the Orsino of his source the psychology for his Olivia.

The Countess, however, has no sooner achieved this fortunate recovery than her rejection by Viola plunges her into the throes of unrequited love; and so she is once more "addicted to melancholly."[97] She has, however, the presence of mind and strength of will to conceal her malady from the world; and, aside from Viola, whom perforce she tells, only Feste and Maria know why she is "out of quiet."[98] She has a momentary qualm[99] about Cesario of whom she knows almost nothing, but she easily convinces herself of his "fiue-fold blazon" of heraldic quarterings. She will not marry above herself, but she must not marry too far below, and ancestry determined social rank. She could not well inquire of Orsino or even of Sir Toby; and so she trusts, like a modern American girl, to her own instincts, and luckily they do not lead her astray. Indeed, in the last act, after she has taken the irrevocable step, Orsino of his own accord assures her of Sebastian's gentility.[100] The Countess is badly smitten: like Desdemona, she is more than half the wooer; she stoops to stratagem to bring her lover back into her presence; and, when he is "hardly" entreated to return, she breaks the laws of propriety to "come to him" rather than waiting with maiden modesty for him to be ushered in to her.[101] The violence

[97] *Twelfth Night*, II. v. 191.   [98] *Ibid.*, II. iii. 131.
[99] *Ibid.*, I. v. 277 *et seq.*   [100] *Ibid.*, V. i. 279.   [101] *Ibid.*, III. iv. 63.

186

of her love and the danger of her situation justify the hasty betrothal that seems so improbable to modern critics who know neither Elizabethan social life nor Elizabethan psychology. Suddenly, in the last act, when she thought that all was well, Viola, unaware of the betrothal, renounces her, cleaves to the Duke, and seems to bring all her plans to naught. Olivia is outraged; but Sebastian enters, claims her as his wife, and so the complication is happily resolved. As the comic end approaches, the Countess should doubtless be portrayed as changing once more to her natural sanguine humor; but Shakespeare has crowded so much material from Riche in the last act that her lines have little space to show it.

If a comedy is to be convincing and significant, the final wedding bells should seem to lead to a happy married life. Sir Toby and Maria, both phlegmatic, would not be sufficiently dynamic personalities to run great risk of marital discord; the fairy princess, Viola, like all fairy princesses, of course becomes the perfect wife; and Orsino's virtues, set forth even by Olivia, give ample warrant of his success as a husband. But what of the brave Sebastian and his strong-minded Countess? Here surely was the tinder for a marital conflagration. Sebastian, however, being his sister's twin, had enough in him of the fairy prince to guarantee success at anything; and Olivia, likewise, if she could negotiate the dangers of an unprotected maidenhood and an unassisted spousal, could surely rise to the demands of simple matrimony. The Elizabethans, moreover, would see ampler reasons than all this to look forward to her happy marriage: Sebastian seems to represent the fortunate balance of humors that gave the harmony of perfect physical and mental health; and Olivia is innately sanguine. This humor was "the paragon of complexions,"[102] made one "liberall, faithfull and mild,"[103] and was especially adapted to wedded bliss.[104] Domestic-conduct books generally agree that the wife should be subject to the husband;[105] but many great ladies of the age found the out-

---

[102] Walkington, *op. cit.*, p. 111.   [103] Dariot, *op. cit.*, sig. D. 2 v.

[104] Ferrand, *op. cit.* (ed. 1645), p. 93.

[105] See, for instance, Cleaver, *op. cit.*, pp. 82 *et al.*; and R. Brathwait, *English Gentlewoman* (London, 1631), p. 41.

ward forms of submission quite consistent with the actuality of rule. Lady Mary Boyle, like Olivia, managed a common-law marriage with her lover, and then forced her father to accept him.[106] Whately felt that the wife should be "an equall yokefellow" to the husband.[107] Vaughan, with the examples of Queen Mary and Queen Elizabeth in mind, even writes in favor of woman's rule;[108] Hopton remarks that a noblewoman who marries beneath her should keep her high place and title;[109] and some great ladies of the age clearly dominated their husbands.[110] Surely, Olivia, who, under all the disadvantages of youth and maidhood, could "sway her house" with "smooth, discreet, and stable bearing,"[111] was entirely equal to the added responsibility of a mere husband; and Elizabethan men from their own experience doubtless accepted her in that light. Olivia, moreover, without father or brother, had little choice but to be independent; and, in so charming a young lady (and a countess withal), much could be overlooked.

In *Twelfth Night*, Shakespeare takes the dull and conventional figure of Lady Julina from Riche's Byzantine romance, makes her an independent English noblewoman like Lady Suffolk, Lady Lake, or Bess of Hardwick, and so at once motivates the plot and creates a realistic portrait. Olivia is perhaps the climax of the playwright's studies in the independent woman. At first the type appears crudely in Kate the Shrew, who tries by might and main to escape her married fate; but, transported to a country house where her new-fangled ideas had little scope, and cured of her choleric pride,[112] she succumbs to proper submission. So also, on a purely physical plane, is perhaps an early draft of Helena, who, with equal determination, pursues her husband and gets him by a trick.

[106] E. Godfrey, *Home Life Under the Stuarts* (London, 1903), chapter ix.

[107] W. Whately, *A Care-Cloth* (London, 1624), p. 73.

[108] W. Vaughan, *Golden-groue* (London, 1608), sig. S 4 v *et seq.*

[109] A. Hopton, *Concordancy of Years* (London, 1612), p. 195.

[110] V. A. Wilson, *Society Women of Shakespeare's Time* (New York, 1925), pp. 206 *et seq.*

[111] *Twelfth Night*, IV. iii. 19 *et seq.*

[112] See J. W. Draper, " 'Kate the Curst,' " *Journal of Nervous and Mental Diseases,* LXXXIX, 757 *et seq.*

Portia accepts her father's will, but manages to get the man she loves; Juliet is more rebellious to her parents, but surrenders all to her lover; and even Beatrice, though she leads the man a merry chase, seems quite submissive in the end. But Olivia, for all her grand passion, never quite succumbs; and, like Mistress Page and Mistress Ford in a humbler social class, she proposes even after marriage to be her own master, and with a cleverness for which critics have given her little credit, without help of friends or relatives—in fact, in spite of them—she marries whom she will.

In Riche's story, Viola is the heroine, all the events center about her courtship of Silla, and the Lady Julina (Olivia) is little more than an obstacle for her to overcome. Riche, therefore, begins his tale in Cyprus, and the Lady Julina appears later as a mere incident to the plot. Shakespeare shifts the whole center of gravity: he gives the Lady Julina not merely two but four lovers, like a heroine in Italian comedy; and her wooing, rather than Viola's, becomes the structural crux of the piece. Her decision to marry Sebastian governs the fate not only of these four lovers but also of Sir Toby, for he is thus obliged to safeguard his future through Maria rather than through Sir Andrew, and also of Viola, for she has no chance to marry Orsino as long as he pursues Olivia. The Countess, as more or less intentional arbiter of the main action, must be shrewd and determined and quick-witted; and Shakespeare found prototypes for just such a feminine figure in many contemporary noblewomen. He must, moreover, keep the audience's sympathy for this self-willed lady; and so, instead of putting her in the dubious position of rebelling against her male relations, he erases all of them from the scene, except the unprepossessing Sir Toby. He also makes two of her lovers, Sir Andrew and Malvolio, quite impossible; and, finally, he makes Olivia herself beautiful, young, and charming, so that, as in the case of Viola, we forgive all, not because we know all, but because forgiving a pretty woman is so much pleasanter than carping at her frailties—or rather, in Olivia's case, her woeful lack of frailties. Indeed, she rules the plot as Shakespeare revised it;

189

and any effort to dethrone her throws the whole comedy out of joint. How can Viola be the heroine, and Sir Toby or Malvolio the comic hero, as most critics would suggest, when this hero and this heroine have little or no relation with each other in the plot? The identity of the hero is possibly open to question; but undoubtedly the heroine, as the early actresses who chose the role well knew, is clearly the Countess Olivia. Whereas Shakespeare reduced the role of Viola from his source, his chief additions—Toby, Andrew, Maria, Feste, Malvolio—all center around Olivia; whereas he filled out Viola's not-too-convincing part with the facile stuff of stage convention, he made Olivia a realistic portrayal of a current type; and, to accent her part further, he gave her as fully and carefully prepared a grand entry as he gave any character in all his plays. Olivia is far from a wooden convention, as some critics seem to think; she is a vital and realistic force in a comedy of manners—a woman whose decisions (as a countess' decisions should) rule the fortunes and lives of those about her and so determine the plot. She can quietly make up her mind and bide her time and have her way, and doubtless she proved an able administrator of her domain. Indeed, she is perhaps the most psychologically true-to-Elizabethan-life of Shakespeare's long list of great ladies; and yet, especially in her grand passion, she is very human—in short, a counterpart of Queen Elizabeth herself, but luckier in loving a Sebastian rather than a Leicester or an Essex.

❧Feste, the Fool

ESTE is a fool; but, if he ever committed any folly, he has apparently long since married and repented at leisure. Indeed, when he settled down and commenced fooling in earnest, he seems, according to some critics, to have turned philosopher beneath the guise of his motley; and, for all his workaday gaiety, moreover, he is a shrewd appraiser of persons and something of a manager of affairs, even of the affair between Olivia and Sebastian. His profession and outward character are like his name, festive; and this festival guise helps to give the comedy that illusion of romantic unreality that blinds the uninitiated not only to its essential realism but also to Feste's own essential truth to life. He is a gleeful stage manager to the *comédie humaine* of Shakespeare's Illyria; and critics have been too busy enjoying the performance he puts on to look much behind the scenes or to inquire deeply into his life and character, even though he takes curtain calls before the audience in seven scenes and speaks over three hundred lines. They enjoy the effect, but miss the means—so subtle is Shakespeare's art. Ulrici takes the jester to be a mere Shakespearean Democritus, adroit only in merriment. Gervinus, on the hint of Viola,[1] further observes how nicely he adapts both speech and action to his auditors. Ruggles likewise describes him as a "wise, cool-headed jester," a "respecter of times and persons"; and Weiss declares him the only character of true poise and "sobriety" in the play; but none of them explains the serious purpose that governs this discretion. More recently, Davey calls him "a singing, merry-making, convivial fool, yet withal somewhat of a scholar and philosopher";[2] but the Arden editors think him lacking in Touchstone's philosophic depth and "a much less original creation." Warde believes him "covetous" and "petty," and the sort of

---

[1] *Twelfth Night*, III. i. 60 *et seq.*

[2] S. Davey, *Trans. Roy. Soc. Lit.*, XXIII (N.S.), 140.

person who is "tolerated rather than appreciated,"[3] despite
the fact that the Duke demands his presence, that Olivia is
angry at his going away, and that Maria begs him to join in
the guying of Malvolio. His "covetous" behavior Bradley explains as due to his "degrading" social status, indeed "little
better than a slave," that forced him to such shifts.[4] The new
Cambridge editors repeat that he is "one of the most philosophical" of Shakespeare's clowns and "the master-mind and
controller of *Twelfth Night*."[5] Drs. Mueschke and Fleisher
compare him, somewhat distantly, to Carlo Buffone in *Every
Man Out of His Humor*.[6] Critics, in short, find him a clever
fool, perhaps even a philosopher, and a moving force in the
comedy's intrigue; but they say little of his social status, his
personality, or his motives, and that little is mere assertion
rather than careful analysis of the evidence within and without
the play.

Feste is Shakespeare's own creation, without prototype in
the comedy's known sources; and, as Shakespeare's own creation, he is surely worth such illumination as the literary and the
social background of Elizabethan fools and foolery can supply.
His wit and word-play sometimes make the dialogue hard to
interpret; but, unless his raillery has point in fact, its Attic salt
lacks savor, and, therefore, an underlying fact may be inferred even within an ambiguous double meaning. Thus a
serious study of the text in the light of contemporary fools
and fooling in literature and in life should reveal those finer
implications that were obvious to the Elizabethans but are lost
on modern ears; and from such a study should emerge something of Feste's biography, a good deal of his technique as an
entertainer, a juster *aperçu* of his motives, his actions, and his
attitudes toward those about him. Thus his character should
stand revealed.

---

[3] F. Warde, *Fools of Shakespeare* (New York, 1913), pp. 78, 80, 96.

[4] A. C. Bradley, "Feste the Jester," *Miscellany* (London, 1929), pp. 207 *et seq.*
(*ed. princ., Book of Homage to Shakespeare*, ed. Gollancz, 1916).

[5] *Twelfth Night* (ed. Quiller-Couch and Dover Wilson), (Cambridge, 1930), pp.
xix, xxvi.

[6] P. Mueschke and J. Fleisher, "Jonsonian Elements in 'Twelfth Night,' " *P.M.L.A.*,
XLVIII, 725–26.

192

The Elizabethan fool was both a tradition in drama and an actual figure in the life of the age; in literature and in life, he had undergone a complex evolution in England and on the Continent. The stage fool came down from the Vice of the Medieval drama, through such figures as Cacurgus in *Misogonus* to the Elizabethan theater; and, though Feste jocularly compares himself to "the old vice . . . . with dagger of lath,"[7] yet he has little in common with this degraded representation of Satan, except the fact that both take a more active part in the plot than did most clowns of the Renaissance stage.[8] In the sixteenth century, the influence of the *zanni* in Italian *commedia dell' arte*, and the more realistic influence of the stupid English rustic, somewhat affected the type.[9] The clown became a sort of burlesque chorus to the play, a sardonic commentator on the action; he is portrayed as loving fine clothes and good living; he is a practical joker, a coward, and a braggart; he may be a comic lover; he is likely to be proficient at acrobatics, singing, and dancing. These are among the ingredients that go to the making up of Falstaff;[10] and Feste shows about half of these characteristics. His talk, moreover, combines the two jocular styles of the Elizabethan stage fool—rude vernacular and grandiloquent bombast; and his humorous technique borrows freely from the twenty-odd devices attributed to the type, especially their use of nonsense, paradox, perversions of words, mock-Latin, comic proverbs, and chop-logic.[11] Of course, most of these effects are among the universal vehicles of humor current in life as well as on the stage; and so Feste's use of them does not prove that he is entirely an outgrowth of this literary tradition. Indeed, several major elements of his role distinguish him from it rather clearly. An old play lists "three kinds of fools . . . . An innocent, a knave-fool, a fool politic."[12] Most stage fools were "innocents," that is, half-wits or country

[7] *Twelfth Night*, IV. ii. 124–26. Cf. G. L. Kittredge, ed. *As You Like It*, "Introduction," p. xiv.

[8] Olive Mary Busby, *The Development of the Fool in Elizabethan Drama* (Oxford, 1923), pp 29–30.

[9] *Ibid.*, chapter i.

[10] J. W. Draper, "Falstaff, 'Great Fool,'" *M.L.Q.*, VII, 453 *et seq.*

[11] Busby, *op. cit.*, chapter iv.   [12] *Wit Without Money*, II. ii.

clowns like Launcelot Gobbo; but Feste as a shrewd court fool is "politic" rather than innocent, and there are "barely a dozen" court fools in all Elizabethan drama outside Shakespeare,[13] and practically all of them are later than Feste. Shakespeare's fools, furthermore, are much more highly developed than those of his brother playwrights;[14] and Feste's part in the plot is greater than that of the conventional stage fool.[15]

Feste, therefore, as one might expect in Shakespeare, stems less from the theater than from life. Far from being a country boor, he is sophisticated, worldly-wise, and even learned in a fashion; far from being an innocent, or a "natural," he appears to the consensus of opinion[16] as sage, if not serious, and even philosophic. One should therefore seek his prototype among the fools, not of the stage but of the courts, an ancient and time-honored, if not honorable, profession.[17] Since the Norman Conquest, if not earlier, the English kings and nobles had employed for amusement in their households not only harmless lunatics, whose custody they got by a writ *de idiota inquirendo*,[18] but also clever entertainers who used the cap and bells as a livelihood and a basis for intrigue, and often, under the protection of its immunities, rose to great power.[19] In the Renaissance this type grew common: such was the famous Will Somers, fool to Henry VIII,[20] and Tarlton, fool to Elizabeth. Such a court jester had Feste been to Olivia's noble father who "took much delight" in him;[21] and now, by inheritance, he has become the Countess' "corrupter of words."[22] Not only do his wit and wisdom prove his superabundant sanity, but Olivia herself assumes that he can use his "right wits" whenever he will.[23] Such was the sort of fool actually played by Robert Armin, who was by profession both court fool and stage fool, and for whom this part was written when first he joined Shakespeare's com-

<hr>

[13] Busby, *op. cit.*, p. 13. [14] *Ibid.*, pp. 33 *et seq.* [15] *Ibid.*, p. 31.

[16] Cf. T. W. Baldwin, *Organization and Personnel of the Shakespearean Company* (Princeton, 1927), p. 313.

[17] Busby, *op. cit.*, pp. 8 *et seq.*

[18] Enid Welsford, *The Fool, His Social and Literary History* (London, 1935), p. 159.

[19] *Ibid.*, p. 138. [20] *Ibid.*, p. 159.

[21] *Twelfth Night*, II. iv. 14.

[22] *Ibid.*, III. i. 36–37. [23] *Ibid.*, V. i. 313.

pany in the spring of 1600.[24] Indeed, as court fool,[25] he even published and republished a book on his professional colleagues and their witticisms, anecdotes, and escapades.[26] He was doubtless the greatest living authority on court-foolery; and, in creating for him the part of Feste, the dramatist surely intended to capitalize his professional fame and bring to the common public some of the quips and cranks with which he regaled the great.[27] The present study makes no claim that the part of Feste is a biography of Armin;[28] but it does suggest that this role, perhaps the first portrayal of a court fool in Elizabethan drama, evolved, not from mere stage convention, but from life as Armin knew it and as Shakespeare himself saw it in contemporary fooldom.

What references we have to Feste's early life come from the Epilogue—if Shakespeare wrote it and if we may take it at face value. Most critics follow either Steevens in thinking it a mere "nonsense ditty,"[29] or else Goodall in calling it a "philosophical" exposition of life in general; but the fact that the story it tells is phrased in the first person singular suggests that, as Farmer believed,[30] it is a sketch of Feste's own biography. If this be true—and it is hard to contradict such prima facie evidence—then a brief review of its statements is in order. In paraphrase it says: when I was a child, my follies were trifles in the common course of nature; but, when I grew to be a man, I found that men shut their gates against knaves and thieves; and, when I married, I found that playing the bravo and the swaggerer brought in no money, and that drunkards got merely addled brains. Apparently, this realization led Feste to seek respectable steady employment as court jester. Many of the famous jesters, both on the Continent and in England, seem to have sprung from humble origins. Gonella, the reputed fool of Niccolò d'Este, was the son of a Florentine shopkeeper;[31] the famous Brusquet seems to have started as a quack

---

[24] Baldwin, op. cit., Plate III; and "Shakespeare's Jester," M.L.N., XXXIX, 451–52. See also Appendix A, p. 257.

[25] Welsford, op. cit., p. 162.   [26] Baldwin, Organization (ed. cit.), p. 303.

[27] Welsford, op. cit., pp. 162, 244, 284.   [28] Little is known of his life.

[29] Twelfth Night (ed. Furness var.) pp. 313–14; and Warde, op. cit., pp. 98 et seq.

[30] Twelfth Night (ed. cit.), p. 316.   [31] Welsford, op. cit., p. 128.

doctor in Avignon and turned to buffoonery as more lucrative;[32] Chicot, the fool of Henry IV, was, to be sure, a wellborn Gascon, but fell, through poverty, to fooling;[33] his colleague at court, Maître Guillaume, started life as an apothecary at Louvain.[34] In England, Scogan[35] and Heywood[36] had gone to Oxford; but Somers, before entering the service of Henry VIII, had been servant to a Northamptonshire gentleman;[37] Tarlton seems to have commenced swineherd as a boy;[38] and Armin was the son of a Norfolk tailor.[39] Feste's picture, therefore, of his knavish youth somewhat corresponds with realistic fact.

From these small beginnings, Feste has risen to wealth and perhaps to power, if not quite to gentility. He is "an honest man and a good housekeeper,"[40] his house being apparently next to a church.[41] He has enjoyed high favor under the local Count, Olivia's father,[42] and seems to have taken unto himself considerable independence, so that he comes and goes at will. Although the early fools were classed with "subservingmen," bakers, brewers, and scullions,[43] and so were supposed to stay in their masters' palaces or risk a whipping,[44] yet in time they rose in the world, and, for all Maria's warnings,[45] Feste absents himself without serious consequences. Indeed, in summer, minstrels sometimes traveled, "visiting palaces of other noblemen."[46] Scrofula, moreover, buffon of Borso d'Este, had a house of his own.[47] Many Elizabethan jesters were not required to live at court or to wear motley;[48] and Armin, from October 11, 1600 to his death in 1615, was a resident of St. Botolph's, Aldgate, in the City.[49] The Epilogue, if it may be

[32] Welsford, *op. cit.*, p. 149.   [33] *Ibid.*, pp. 151–52.

[34] *Ibid.*, p. 154.   [35] J. Doran, *History of Court Fools* (Boston, n.d.), p. 148.

[36] *Ibid.*, p. 152.   [37] *Ibid.*, p. 138.

[38] *Ibid.*, pp. 173–74.   [39] Baldwin, *Organization* (*ed. cit.*), p. 152 n.

[40] *Twelfth Night*, IV. ii. 10; III. i. 27 *et seq.*

[41] *Ibid.*, III. i. 7 *et seq.*   [42] *Ibid.*, II. iv. 14.

[43] *Cyuile and Vncyuile Life* (*ed. princ.*, 1579), ed. Roxburghe Library (London, 1868), p. 40.

[44] Doran, *op. cit.*, p. 291.   [45] *Twelfth Night*, I. v. 3 *et seq.*

[46] J. Q. Adams, *Life of Shakespeare* (New York, 1923), p. 100.

[47] Welsford, *op. cit.*, pp. 130–31.   [48] Doran, *op cit*, p. 177.

[49] Emma M. Denkinger, "Actors' Names in the Register of St. Botolph, Aldgate," *P.M.L.A.*, XLI, 95.

trusted, refers to Feste's marriage, and Sir Andrew, to his "Lemon."[50] If he was married, he had good precedent both in literature and in life: in two versions of the Durham morris dance, the fool has a wife;[51] and both Scogan[52] and Tarlton[53] were married. Thus, Feste's private life suggests that he was far from being the "slave" that Professor Bradley, without documentation, terms him.

The exact social status that he had achieved is difficult to define: like that of Iago, it seems to have been on the borderland of gentility; and certainly he makes common cause with Sir Toby and the gently born Maria and Fabyan against the parvenu Malvolio. Moreover, he presumes, and is permitted, to call everyone *thou*—even the Duke and the Countess—except the touchy Malvolio and the drunken Sir Toby. Perhaps this is jester's license; but the others often call him by the *you* of polite equality—all except Malvolio and the fool Sir Andrew. The Duke refers to him as "fellow"[54] and "my good Fellow";[55] and the Countess, except for one occasion when she is startled and displeased,[56] consistently calls him *you*. All this suggests that Feste, like Tarlton and Armin, had achieved from his professional status a certain social recognition. In the Middle Ages, the fools had been hardly more than outcasts,[57] and the *zanni* of Italian Renaissance comedy were little better; but the actual condition of the court jester had improved both in Italy[58] and in England. The fool often ruled in the servants' hall;[59] Jack Oates, the jester of Sir William Hollis, aspired to consort as much as possible with gentry.[60] Archibald Armstrong, who amused James I with his humor and horseplay,[61] was once granted the freedom of the City of Aberdeen; he meddled in politics, got valuable patents, and accompanied Prince Charles to negotiate the Spanish match.[62] Feste then might properly associate with a knight, a servingman, and a lady in waiting.

[50] *Twelfth Night*, II. iii. 28.

[51] Barbara Swain, *Fools and Folly During the Middle Ages and the Renaissance* (New York, 1932), p. 67.

[52] Doran, *op. cit.*, p. 126.

[53] *Ibid.*, p. 178.

[54] *Twelfth Night*, II. iv. 50.

[55] *Ibid.*, V. i. 12–13.

[56] *Ibid.*, V. i. 309.

[57] Swain, *op. cit.*, p. 54 *et passim*.

[58] Welsford, *op. cit.*, p. 136.

[59] Doran, *op. cit.*, pp. 182–83.

[60] Welsford, *op. cit.*, pp. 162–63.

[61] Doran, *op. cit.*, pp. 195 *et seq.*

[62] Welsford, *op. cit.*, pp. 171 *et seq.*

Feste is not only an artist in wit and entertainment but also in extracting their condign monetary rewards. Olivia's bounty supplies him with daily bread and with "Ginger . . . . hotte y'the mouth."[63] To supplement these emoluments and maintain his private residence, he levies for current jokes many an odd "testrill" (sixpence) upon Sir Andrew and Sir Toby,[64] and tribute from Sebastian,[65] and repeated "expences" from Cesario,[66] and double largess of "gold" from the Duke.[67] Thus Feste's profession of foolery was decidedly remunerative, and his management of it shows him a prudent and perspicacious fool. The giving of such favors was a common convention of the age; no less authority than James I advised his son to cast "coin" occasionally among his pages.[68] Even the Medieval fool, who occupied a much lower plane than the fool of the Renaissance, had his gratuities: Bellzebub in the St. George plays gets money;[69] in *The Sage Fool's Testament*, the jester leaves his master "All my money";[70] Hitard, the fool of Edmund Ironside, left his property to Cantebury Cathedral;[71] and Rahere, professional entertainer to Henry I, was able to found the church of St. Bartholomew the Great in London. In France the same is true, especially as one comes down into the Renaissance: the second fool in *Six Manières de Fols* is portrayed as rich; Brusquet found foolery more lucrative than medicine or law;[72] in 1622, the female fool, Mathurine, received a pension from the King of twelve hundred livres;[73] and l'Angely, the jester of Louis XIV, made a fortune by his fooling, combined perhaps with politics.[74] A successful court jester might live in luxury until his vein ran out, and then he might die in want, like Bernard Bluet of the ducal court of Savoy;[75] and this uncertainty doubtless induced many fools to make hay while the sun of favor shone. In Tudor England, Heywood declares in his *Wytty and Wytless* that a fool was better off and securer

---

[63] *Twelfth Night*, II. iii. 115–16.   [64] *Ibid.*, II. iii. 27, 34, 36.
[65] *Ibid.*, IV. i. 19–20.   [66] *Ibid.*, III. i. 44 *et seq.*   [67] *Ibid.*, V. i. 28.
[68] James I, *Workes* (London, 1616), pp. 167 and 187.
[69] Swain, *op. cit.*, pp. 67–68.   [70] *A Booke of Precedence*, ed. Furnivall, p. 76.
[71] Swain, *op. cit.*, p. 55.   [72] Welsford, *op. cit.*, p. 149.   [73] *Ibid.*, p. 153.
[74] *Ibid.*, p. 157.   [75] Welsford, *op. cit.*, pp. 155–56.

than a husbandman; and some of the court fools drew regular salaries,[76] such as the Marquis of Ferrara gave Gonella.[77] The wardrobe accounts show payments to fools;[78] and Tarlton, who was prudent to the point of avarice, appointed guardians in his will to take care of the valuable "cattels" he left his son.[79] King James's Archie became rich, and in 1611 was granted a pension of two shillings a day for life.[80] Tarlton, moreover, was so anxious to do well by himself that, as titular parson of Sherd, he is said to have melted the parish bell to sell the metal for money.[81] Certainly Feste's wealth, and his efforts to acquire it, were in accord with the lives and characters of contemporary fools, who feared with good reason that their gala day might soon be set.

Feste can hardly have been young; but he still has a good leg,[82] and can cut a caper and dance a jig. Whether he wore the conventional cap and bells and motley of his vocation is not clear.[83] Even in the days of Henry VIII, Will Somers did not always wear motley;[84] in the reign of Elizabeth, fools often discarded it.[85] Feste's declaration to Sir Andrew, "I did impeticos thy gratility" seems to mean, as Johnson says, "I did impeticoat thy gratuity";[86] and that might imply that Feste wore the long dress of the Medieval Vice,[87] and possibly he also carried the Vice's dagger of lath.[88] But perhaps Feste was merely habited in the long blue coat of the old-fashioned Tudor servant,[89] or possibly in some castoff habiliments of his late lord and master. On the other hand, Viola's reference to his "tabor"—regularly accompanied by a fife—suggests that he may have been dressed like the picture of Tarlton in the British Museum.

[76] *Ibid.*, p. 158.   [77] *Ibid.*, p. 128.

[78] *Ibid.*, p. 170.   [79] Doran, *op. cit.*, pp. 175 and 181.

[80] Welsford, *op. cit.*, pp. 171 *et seq.*

[81] Doran, *op. cit.*, p. 177; cf. Busby, *op. cit.*, pp. 47–48; and cf. the avaricious cook in Dekker's *If It Be Not a Good Play*.

[82] *Twelfth Night*, II. iii. 23.

[83] *Ibid.*, I. v. 55. This reference seems to be merely metaphorical.

[84] Busby, *op. cit.*, p. 83.   [85] Doran, *op. cit.*, p. 177. Cf. p. 291.

[86] *Twelfth Night*, II. iii. 29.   [87] Busby, *op. cit.*, p. 82.

[88] *Twelfth Night*, IV. ii. 124–25.   [89] Busby, *op. cit.*, p. 82.

Feste, if not educated, at least has a bowing acquaintance with learning. He can chop logic in a fashion,[90] like the clowns in the Old French *sotties* and in Heywood's interludes; he knows something of Latin,[91] Spanish,[92] and Italian;[93] he refers to Mercury[94] and the Myrmidons,[95] and knows that Pythagoras believed in the transmigration of souls[96] and that sleep was a recognized cure for insanity;[97] and he has sufficient grasp of metaphysics to play on the axiom, "Whatever is, is."[98] Surely he has seen something of the quadrivium and the trivium; or else, like Shakespeare himself, he had a mother wit that needed but little formal schooling to pick up what knowledge he required. Quite so the actual jesters of the age, though generally lowborn, often took to themselves the limbs and outward flourishes of learning: Scogan[99] and Heywood[100] seem to have gone to Oxford, and Somers quoted Latin to his master.[101] One may be sure that Queen Elizabeth and James I were no less learned in their tastes than was Henry VIII.

Many fools did not hesitate to advise their noble masters even in politics, or at least took an active part in court intrigue. The *sotties* of the reign of Louis XII had put serious satire into the mouths of fools; and Chicot gave Henry IV shrewd political advice.[102] The German fools of the sixteenth century dared even to touch on religious controversy.[103] Sir Thomas More's fool, Henry Patterson, tried to persuade his master to acknowledge royal supremacy.[104] Tarlton, who had the Queen's ear, not only as jester but also as groom of the bedchamber, made the most of his influence at court.[105] Archibald Armstrong meddled in Jacobean politics, both foreign and domestic.[106] Feste, however, for all the avarice that critics have found in him, apparently did not use his arts for politics or sell his influence for the use of others. He does not even plead the Duke's suit to Olivia, and, indeed, insists on being well paid

90 *Twelfth Night*, V. i. 19 *et seq.*   91 *Ibid.*, I. v. 53–54 and 312.
92 *Ibid.*, IV. ii. 15.   93 *Ibid.*, I. v. 41 *et passium.*   94 *Ibid.*, I. v. 95.
95 *Ibid.*, II. iii. 31.   96 *Ibid.*, IV. ii. 52 *et seq.*   97 *Ibid.*, IV. ii. 97–98.
98 *Ibid.*, IV. ii. 17–18.   99 Doran, *op. cit.*, p. 148.   100 *Ibid.*, p. 142.
101 *Ibid.*, p. 143.   102 Welsford, *op. cit.*, pp. 151–52.
103 *Ibid.*, p. 139.   104 *Ibid.*, p. 161.   105 Doran, *op. cit.*, p. 175.
106 Welsford, *op. cit.*, p. 171.

RICHARD TARLETON, COURT JESTER
From Harleian MS 3885

merely to announce Orsino's visit.[107] Perhaps Shakespeare meant definitely to imply that Feste was above such machinations; and Armin might have resented such a suggestion as a slur on Tarlton and himself. More likely, this aspect of the jester's life was omitted by sheer default, for Shakespeare shows little political interest in his comedies until after the accession of James I.[108]

The foregoing survey of Feste's antecedents, way of life, social status, wealth, personal appearance, and probable education shows him, like Tarlton and Armin, the usual type of Renaissance court fool, except that he does not seem to have dabbled in politics. One may perhaps infer, therefore, that the wit of his conversation and his actions in the play are likewise similar to the wit and the doings of Tarlton and of Armin himself. In either case, an analysis of his technique of entertainment would seem to be in order.

Feste is the most musical of Shakespeare's jesters;[109] and he can adapt his repertoire to hearers of such varied tastes as Sir Toby, Sir Andrew,[110] and the Duke.[111] In fact, he has made himself and his singing indispensable to two noble households. Warde describes him as a combination fool and minstrel;[112] but skill in music was a common stock in trade for the stage fool,[113] and also for the actual court jester: Heywood[114] and Tarlton[115] sang; and Armin, who must have been able to sing to take the part of Feste, doubtless learned his music from Tarlton who was his foster father.[116] Feste, moreover—and, therefore, Armin—could also dance, or at least cut a caper, for the jig at the end of the play was presumably accompanied by some such action; and skill in dancing and even acrobatics also belonged in the stock in trade of the stage fool.[117]

Feste's chief claim to favor, however, was certainly his wit,

[107] *Twelfth Night*, V. i. 29 *et seq.*

[108] J. W. Draper, "Political Themes in Shakespeare's Later Plays," *J.E.G.P.*, XXXV, 61 *et seq.*

[109] Busby, *op. cit.*, p. 67; and Warde, *op. cit.*, p. 78.

[110] *Twelfth Night*, II. iii. 33 *et seq.*   [111] *Ibid.*, II. iv. 50 *et seq.*

[112] Warde, *op. cit.*, p. 78.   [113] Busby, *op. cit.*, chapter iv.

[114] Doran, *op. cit.*, pp. 154–55.   [115] Doran, *op. cit.*, pp. 173–74.

[116] Welsford, *op. cit.*, p. 284.   [117] Busby, *op. cit.*, chapter iv.

both persiflage and daring practical jokes. His pointed raillery is quite in the tradition of the stage fool; and, since Armin unquestionably augmented Shakespeare's lines ad libitum, the text may well be in his tradition also as court fool. Feste has the sagacity of the finished and perfect fool, a virtuoso in the art of courtly entertainment, who can select from his repertory of effects what style or technique he will to fit the person or occasion. He can use music or speech or action; he entertains the Duke and Sir Toby with songs; he fends off Maria with impudence; he woos Sir Andrew with innocuous nonsense, and outwits his mistress with syllogistic paradox; he knows that he cannot entertain Malvolio at all, and so he entertains himself at Malvolio's expense. Like other stage fools, he remembers proverbs aptly[118]—"*Cucullus non facit monachum*,"[119] and he can run off a neat epigram, extempore, on drink, on pleasure, on foolery, on what you will.[120] He wins the Duke's praise for his paradox and oxymoron[121]—common devices of court fools,[122] and he can play on double meanings and mistake the word[123] with as nimble a wit and as innocent a face as Falstaff himself. Yet, withal, he never lapses, as most fools did,[124] into the mere obscene.

Feste, to be sure, does not dabble in politics; but he has a generous share of the impudence that went with his calling. Like the Mantuan dwarf, Nanino,[125] he indulges in daring parody.[126] The Joyous Societies of Valois France even aimed their shafts at the royal government, and Brusquet did not stop at gross effrontery.[127] So Feste, on his very first appearance, undertakes to prove to his noble mistress that she is a fool,[128] and has the hardihood to say that the soul of the brother she mourns is in hell; but luckily he has calculated well, and gets her to laugh, for all her mourning, and so saves the situation: such was the witty defeat of the wise King Solomon at the hands

[118] Busby, *op. cit.*, p. 77.
[119] *Twelfth Night*, I. v. 53–54.
[120] *Ibid.*, I. v. 130–33; II. iv. 75–76; III. i. 39; IV. i. 22–24; IV. ii. 45–46.
[121] *Ibid.*, V. i. 16 *et seq.*
[122] Busby, *op. cit.*, p. 72.
[123] *Twelfth Night*, III. i. 3 *et seq.*
[124] Swain, *op. cit.*, p. 63.
[125] Welsford, *op. cit.*, p. 136.
[126] *Twelfth Night*, I. v. 38 *et seq.*
[127] Welsford, *op. cit.*, p. 149.
[128] *Twelfth Night*, I. v. 37 *et seq.*

of the fool, Marcolf, in Medieval story.[129] Stone, a jester of
James I, was whipped for calling a certain lord a "fool";[130] and
Armstrong was at last dismissed from the court of Charles I for
ridiculing Archbishop Laud.[131] Feste was indeed a privileged
character. Triboulet, like Feste, on occasion mimicked the
clergy;[132] and Tarlton himself masqueraded as a parson.[133]
Indeed, Feste works this vein with enough actual and pretended
learning to amaze Sir Andrew, to trick Malvolio, and to make
the critic Hutson think him originally trained for Holy
Orders.[134] His more significant raillery, like that of Swift, is
aimed at the foibles and shams of mankind; his very name,
suggestive of the Italian *festa* or *festare*, is the perfect expression of the holiday mood in which kings clothed the serious
business of their courts. Viola compliments him as "wise enough
to play the foole"[135] and to adjust his fooling, like his songs,
to his varied audience. Indeed, he shows considerable acumen
in judging the aims and motives of those about him, and so
keeps himself in the good graces of his betters, and lives
shrewdly by his wits. In the exercise of his profession, he was
certainly no fool.

He does not, however, confine his comedy to mere words.
The fool in Tudor drama, unlike the Vice of the morality
plays, had generally become a mere chorus with little part in
the plot;[136] and court fools, moreover, were likely to take unto
themselves a sort of choral, or editorial, role of comment mal-
apropos on passing incidents;[137] but Shakespeare presents Feste
quite realistically as plotting for himself, and also as taking
part in the plot of Maria and her henchmen against the luckless
Malvolio; and his part in these affairs demands proper expli-
cation.

Feste cannot be very young; he has a house, if not a family;
he has a taste for "ginger" and the condiments of life: surely he
has no wish to be cast forth on an unfeeling world; and yet,
when the play begins, he has just risked his place in the sun of

[129] Swain, *op. cit.*, pp. 32–34.   [130] Doran, *op. cit.*, p. 196.
[131] *Ibid.*, pp. 204–5.   [132] Welsford, *op. cit.*, p. 147.
[133] Doran, *op. cit.*, p. 177.   [134] *Twelfth Night*, ed. Furness var., p. 405.
[135] *Ibid.*, III. i. 60 *et seq.*   [136] Busby, *op. cit.*, pp. 29–30.   [137] *Ibid.*, p. 38.

Olivia's favor by running away for a matter of days to the court of a neighboring Duke.[138] He does this, furthermore, at the very time that the successive deaths of Olivia's father and her brother have left her in an anxious and even dangerous position, with an importunate nobleman demanding her hand in wedlock and the riot belowstairs of Sir Toby and the suitor he has chosen for her. Feste went off without leave or notice, and he has been "long absent."[139] Indeed, he has the assurance to suggest that he expects to spend as much time with the Duke as with the Countess;[140] but perhaps this is merely an intimation of their coming marriage. On his return in the first act, Maria proffers her good offices with Olivia, and asks for a confession of his recent doings; but Feste declines her mediation and tells nothing. Seemingly, Feste was indeed a fool!

At first sight all this seems quite inexplicable, for Feste was truly in a parlous state. The laws against vagabonds and runaway servants were severe;[141] and Maria cogently suggests that he may well be "turned away"[142] for his French leave; and, as she further intimates, loss of place for a servant in those days was "as good as hanging." Furness is much disturbed by this passage;[143] and, indeed, though hanging was the legal punishment for a servant who stole from his master to the value of forty shillings,[144] Feste apparently did not deserve anything beyond the "moderate castigation"[145] usual for minor misdemeanors. The reference to "hanging," therefore, would seem to allude to the ultimate consequences of his loss of place; for "cast" servants had little choice but to steal or starve. The "incertaintie of service"[146] filled the roads and cities with vagabonds, who, as public nuisances, were treated with great severity; and "hanging" was liable to be their sad and impotent conclusion. Servingmen were prudently advised to provide them-

---

[138] *Twelfth Night*, II. iv. 10 *et seq.*

[139] *Ibid.*, I. v. 17. [140] *Ibid.*, III. i. 38 *et seq.*

[141] See C. Whibley in *Shakespeare's England* (Oxford, 1917), II, 489 *et seq.*

[142] *Twelfth Night*, I. v. 17 *et seq.* [143] *Ibid.*, I. v. 60.

[144] Harrison, *Description of England* (London, 1587), Bk. II, chapter xi.

[145] M. Bacon, *New Abridgment* (Philadelphia, 1811), IV, 292.

[146] H. Peacham, *Coach and Sedan* (London, 1636), sig. C 3; also J. W. Draper, "Falstaff's Robin and Other Pages," *Studies in Philology*, XXXVI, 446 *et seq.*

selves with some other resource for a livelihood,[147] or to save, if possible, for a rainy day, like Adam in *As You Like It*.[148] "A young Servingman, an olde Beggar"[149] was a current saying; and masters, overburdened as they were with hungry mouths,[150] would dismiss a servant for the least infraction; and then he must live as he could.[151] Some, moreover, ran away because their "wages cannot suffice so much as to find them breeches."[152] Indeed, servants were little better than serfs, but attached to a master rather than to the land; and anyone who enticed a servant away—as Orsino had possibly lured Feste— was subject to legal action by the master.[153] The House of Este used to loan its court fools to cheer friends in illness; German and Italian nobles used to exchange fools with their friends;[154] and in England there were neighborhood fools who went from house to house like the Medieval minstrels;[155] but Feste was none of these; he had deliberately run away.

Such folly would strike Elizabethans at once as strange, especially in a competent and settled fool. Surely he must have ample reason to desert the lucrative semi-sinecure that he enjoyed amidst the creature comforts of Olivia's luxurious establishment. Why then did Feste, who clearly valued the fruits of good living and was, moreover, a householder in the community, jeopardize his future by running off? The Elizabethans doubtless saw the reason without being told: Orsino's suit had been pending for some time, and Feste early came to the conclusion that the charming and lovesick Duke would win his mistress' hand. At least, he hints as much,[156] and such an assumption was most natural. Professional policy required that he visit this Duke,[157] thus he risks the present to secure the future. Of course, he will not explain this to Maria, partly because she

[147] *Cyuile and Vncyuile Life* in *Inedited Tracts*, ed. cit., pp. 91–92.

[148] G. Markham in *Inedited Tracts*, ed. cit.; also J. W. Draper, "Shakespeare's Rustic Servants," *Shakespeare Jahrbuch*, LXIX (1933), 87 et seq.

[149] Markham, *op. cit.*, p. 177.

[150] See J. W. Draper, "The Theme of *Timon of Athens*," *M.L.R.*, XXIX, 20 et seq.

[151] Markham, *op. cit.*, pp. 142 et seq.; and L. B. Wright, *Middle Class Culture* (Chapel Hill, 1935), pp. 444–45.

[152] Harrison, *op. cit.*; Bk. II, chap. xi.   [153] Bacon, *op. cit.*, IV, 593.

[154] Welsford, *op. cit.*, pp. 131 et passim.   [155] Welsford, *op. cit.*, p. 164.

[156] *Twelfth Night*, III. i. 40 et seq.   [157] *Ibid.*, II. iv. 78 et seq.

might tell Olivia, partly because he does not want the others in the hall to realize how he has anticipated them, and partly because he feels, and rightly, that his mother wit is quite equal to allaying the anger of the Countess. She comes in and speaks to him severely; he braves her displeasure, wittily proves her a fool, and dares suggest that her lamented brother is in hell. She laughs at his paradoxes, and Feste is forgiven.

Feste early guesses Olivia's passion for young Cesario—as he had also guessed Maria's designs upon the single blessedness of Sir Toby.[158] He slyly warns Cesario that the self-willed and calculating Olivia intends to rule her husband;[159] and he rightly judges that Orsino's "changeable"[160] melancholy will speed his recovery from Olivia's refusal. In fact, Feste, except perhaps for Olivia, is the shrewdest person in the play. When he has once made up his mind which way his wind blows he sets his sail accordingly, seeks and obtains Cesario's good opinion of his fooling (as he had the Duke's) and, when the two knights set upon the youngster to do him injury, Feste runs off to "tell my Lady straight,"[161] for he knows that she will be furious if they harm her lover. He cannot know that Cesario is actually a girl, or that the valiant knights are by mistake attacking her brother, who turns the tables on them and proves much more of a knight than they. As a matter of fact, Feste loses his pains with Cesario as he did with the Duke, for Olivia actually marries the twin Sebastian; but even so, the fool had played safe, and loses nothing by his policy.

Feste takes part not only in the major plot of Olivia's love affairs but also in the guying of Malvolio. He feels that the steward has, of course, no chance as a suitor for the Countess; and, if Malvolio did have a chance, Feste believes, as Maria and the other gentles do, that it should be nipped betimes. Though he takes some pains to impress even Sir Andrew, he hardly cares what he says or does to Malvolio: indeed, did not Malvolio at the crucial moment of his return from absence-without-leave take the occasion to cast aspersions on his jester's skill? And Feste, like Will Somers,[162] was not without a high regard for

---

[158] *Twelfth Night*, I. v. 20 and 26–28.   [159] *Ibid.*, III. i. 34.
[160] *Ibid.*, II. iv. 79–80.   [161] *Ibid.*, IV. i. 30.   [162] Welsford, *op. cit.*, p. 168.

his professional attainments. He allies himself with the "disorders" belowstairs, and joins Sir Toby in taunting Malvolio.[163] Of course, Maria easily persuades him to impersonate the curate and befool the would-be count; and he continues to plague him even after the others have departed.

It is a brilliant dialogue at cross-purposes. Malvolio entreats "good Sir Topas" (*vice* Feste) to be his messenger to "my Ladie." Feste answers with an exorcism to the "hyperbolicall fiend" with which Malvolio is possessed, and rebukes this talk of "Ladies." The steward declares his wrongs and his sanity of mind and cries out against the "hideous darkness" of his prison; but the pseudo parson merely goes on berating the fiend, and insists that the prison is "transparent as baricadoes" and "lustrous as Ebony." Malvolio reaffirms his sanity and the darkness of the place; and to this Feste with his best clerical manner responds in a high, moral tone: "there is no darkness but ignorance"; and he learnedly refers to "the Ægyptians in their fogge." Malvolio seems to believe in proof by iteration, and again repeats that the house is "darke," that he is "abus'd," and is not "madde," and begs the learned clerk to try his wit with a question. Feste borrows from Pythagoras an inquiry about the transmigration of souls. Malvolio returns the orthodox Christian denial to the tenet; but this fine clergyman declares that his patient must agree with the Pagan philosopher "ere I will allow thy wits. Fare thee well." In a moment he returns in his own person, and, perhaps because he is fearful of Malvolio's future anger, is more sympathetic to the prisoner's plea. Then he changes his voice and is once again Sir Curate, and advises "sleepe," which cured crazy Lear.[164] As curate he rebukes himself (as jester) for holding discourse with a madman; as fool, with a change of voice, he promises to depart at once. Malvolio, beseeching, calls to him, "Foole, foole, foole I say," and begs him to fetch a candle and paper; and the fool innocently asks, "But tell me true, are you not mad indeed, or do you but counterfeit?" But he promises to bring materials

[163] *Twelfth Night*, II. iii. 103 *et passim.*

[164] See J. W. Draper, "The Old Age of King Lear," *J.E.G.P.*, XXXIX, 537–38. Sleep and music were recognized cures for madness.

for writing, and so goes off with a song. This is Feste's tour de force of raillery: for those who sympathize with Malvolio, it is ruined; but, for the Elizabethans, it must have been the *summa* of comic dramatic irony. In a later scene, with a very human touch of malice, Feste tells the steward of his impersonation. He had too much *amour propre* not to put this finishing touch on his performance; and Malvolio must have been chagrined indeed to have been fooled by a mere fool, whom he accounted a very fool indeed.

Feste is clearly modeled on the actual court fool. Though sprung from humble origins, he has acquired some education, a house, and perhaps a wife, comparative wealth, and a privileged social status in which he may discard motley and come and go as he will. Like all those that dwell in the half-world of insecurity, he has developed a keen eye to the main chance; but he is wise enough not to dabble in politics, and chooses rather to found his career on his singing, his sharp repartee, and his piquant impudence. He joins in the practical jokes on Malvolio; he woos the Duke for reasons of obvious policy; and, for like reasons, he helps Olivia woo Cesario, and even on occasion becomes her trusted messenger.[165] Over all this plays the lambent sparkle of his badinage. Like so many clever people, he lives on two planes of being, an outward façade of professional raillery, and a serious inner urge for the good things of the great world to which he was not born. He is truly chameleon-like, and eats the air promise-crammed—chameleon-like in his varied wit to half a dozen sorts of people, and planning and plotting that the promise of his future livelihood may be fulfilled, as in the end under Olivia and Sebastian, it seems to be fulfilled to the merriment of all.

Shakespeare thought of character in terms of bodily humors and planets, which dominated contemporary science. The covetous, like Feste, were thought to be melancholy,[166] and melancholy might produce a bitter wit;[167] but the frolicsome Feste,

[165] *Twelfth Night,* IV. i. 8–9.
[166] C. Dariot, *Iudgement of the Starres,* tr. F. Wither (London, 1598), sig. D 2 r.
[167] A. Laurentius, *Preservation of the Sight,* tr. Svrphlet (London, 1599), pp. 85 *et seq.*

as he himself avers, is no cold "dry" fool. Singers and artists were thought to be phlegmatic;[168] and, moreover, phlegmatic persons of short stature, like Feste,[169] were thought to be "apt to conceyue."[170] He has, moreover, something of a sanguine temper, and also takes umbrage at Malvolio with choleric directness. His character, therefore, seems to show, like Mercutio in *Romeo and Juliet*, that mercurial combination of the humors that made one ingenious[171] in quick reply, and gave skill in rhetoric, "imagination," and "curiosity [oddity] in writing."[172] The mercurial type flits from humor to humor, and would naturally adapt itself to those about it.[173] Our Feste, then, seems outwardly at least to be a mercurial fellow, in vivid contrast to the ardent melancholy of Viola and the Duke, to the fine balance of Sebastian, to the phlegmatic humors of the two knights and Maria.

The fool tradition that came down from the Middle Ages saw the world as topsy-turvy, and all society as fools, except the fool;[174] and *Twelfth Night*, seen from one angle, is a comedy of all-too-human fools whom Shakespeare depicts as fooled to the top of their several bents, Feste perhaps the least of all. Olivia fools Orsino by refusing him; and Viola fools him and marries him; Sebastian unwillingly makes a fool of himself and of Olivia by letting her lead him to the altar; Olivia fools Sir Toby and Sir Andrew; and they fool Malvolio; and Feste, in this world of chance and caprice and change, though fooled as to Olivia's marrying the Duke, is perhaps less of a fool than any of the rest. There are two noble fools, Orsino, who thinks he can win Olivia, and Olivia, who thinks she can win Viola; two knightly fools, Sir Toby who thinks he can marry off his niece, and Sir Andrew who thinks he can espouse her; a commoner fool, Malvolio, who thinks he can wed a

---

[168] Dariot, *op. cit.*, sig. D 4 r.   [169] *Twelfth Night*, IV. ii. 8.

[170] T. Hyll, "Art of Phisiognomie" in *Contemplation of Mankind* (London, 1571), leaf 125 r *et seq.*; cf. *Booke of Arcandam*, tr. Warde (London, 1592), sig. M 3 r *et seq.*

[171] T. Hyll, *Schoole of Skill* (London, 1599), leaf 50 v.

[172] Dariot, *op. cit.*, sig. D 4 v.

[173] *Ibid.*, sig. D 1 r. See J. W. Draper, *The Humors and Shakespeare's Characters* (Durham, N.C., 1945), chapter vi.

[174] Swain, *op. cit.*, p. 14.

Countess; and a fool-by-vocation, Feste, who knows the others for what they are: such is this gay Illyrian world of realistic foolery, quite in the tradition of *The XXV Orders of Fooles* and Tarlton's *Jests* and Armin's *Nest of Ninnies*. *Twelfth Night* is also a play of foils and vivid contrasts: Viola and Maria and Orsino who seek marriage, over against Olivia and Sir Toby who seek to avoid it; the contrasting humors of the several figures; and above all the two arch-fools of the comedy, Feste and Sir Andrew, the court fool and the fool-courtier whose difference may be phrased in Feste's own remarks, "Better a witty fool than a foolish wit."

❧ Plot Structure and Characterization in *Twelfth Night*

CHAPTER ELEVEN

THE detailed study of the characters in *Twelfth Night*, which has taken up the foregoing chapters, has served to explain the several personalities in the play, to define the degree of realism in each, the degree in which each arose from Shakespeare's source, and the fashion in which each is integrated in the tissue of the plot. In short, this has been an intensive examination of details from the point of view of the individual characters. It now remains to examine the larger matters of plot structure, methods of characterization, time and place of setting, interplay of realism and convention in the style, and finally the significance of theme. As the Greek root of the word *drama* implies, a play is a *doing*, and the interweaving of deeds creates plot; deeds imply doers, who must somehow be differentiated, and related by adequate motives to the things they do. All this must happen in some time and place when and where such people could do such things; they must talk about themselves and each other and their deeds in a way appropriate to this time and place and in accordance with the theatrical conventions that the audience accepts. Above all, these more or less realistic people must express in their speeches and actions some fundamental principles and truths of life, or else the play can have no basic reality and no general significance. Of these five topics, the present chapter proposes to discuss the first two, plot structure and characterization in *Twelfth Night*.

Until the nineteenth century, critical comment is too scattering and vague to indicate clearly the interpretation of plot or character or theme. In 1662, for instance, Pepys condemned the piece as "a silly play, and not related at all to the name or the day";[1] a century later, Dr. Johnson, on the other hand, praised

---

[1] *Twelfth Night*, ed. Furness var., pp. 377–78.

"the graver part" as "elegant and easy" and the low comedy as "exquisitely humorous," but all this tells us little. The Romantic critics of the nineteenth century make the play what they will, interpret it in terms of their own Romanticism purely for its emotional values of fantasy and humor, and seem to find no general significance. Schlegel and Hazlitt, for example, praise it for its "ethereal" and "poetic cast." (Is Sir Toby Belch "ethereal"?) Kenny declares the plot insufficiently motivated and therefore pointless; and Montégut calls the piece "a somewhat grotesque masquerade"; the editors of the Arden text, more or less following Dowden, find it, like the comedies that precede, a combination of humor and romance, an expression of the very joy of life. Unlike Kenny, they think that it displays "technical mastery" and faultless integration of plot, but they do not explain this excellence of structure or show on what vital theme it centers; indeed, they call the piece "a Twelfth Night extravagance in which there is no demand for rigid realism." The Tudor editors have a like attitude: "In Illyria, as in the Forest of Arden, anything may happen." This is "a world of poetry, of beauty, of dreams," with apparently no more meaning than a dream. More recently, Professor Parrott sees the play as "lacking in consistency," and yet declares: "Perhaps no comedy of Shakespeare exhibits so clearly his mastery of his craft as the way in which he interweaves and complicates these plots and brings them at last together in a most natural and happy solution."[2] Welsford calls the comedy "a poem of escape" given over to "deliberate unreality";[3] and the new Cambridge editors refer to its "irresponsible extravagant fooling," comparable to the " 'musical' farces of to-day." Indeed, this is a long and tortuous road that criticism has traveled since Dr. Johnson called "the graver part" so "elegant and easy." How can the intricacies of comic dramaturgy display at once "technical mastery" and inconsistency? Most critics stress its "unreality"; and yet the foregoing chapters have shown that most of the characters were common types of the London streets. The whirligig of time, in fact, has clouded this realism,

[2] T. M. Parrott, *William Shakespeare*, A Handbook (New York, 1934), p. 149.
[3] Enid Welsford, *The Fool* (London, 1935), p. 251.

and so has taken from *Twelfth Night* its significance of theme, and reduced it from the respectability of comedy of manners to the demimonde of farce in which all verisimilitude and meaning are sacrificed to a momentary laugh. Sometimes one feels that Shakespeare's chief, though unintentional, detractors are his modern critics. Strangest of all, they reiterate that the master holds the mirror up to very nature and humanity itself, and yet they reduce some of his major works to mere grotesqueries.[4] Especially strange that a play that immediately precedes *Hamlet* and the problem comedies should have no rhyme or reason. Fantasy and wit pervade all Shakespeare; but dramatic dependence merely on these effects, rather than on deeper matters of character and theme, belongs to his early experiments, to *Love's Labour's Lost* and to *Romeo and Juliet* rather than to *Hamlet*, *Macbeth*, and *King Lear*. The last century or more has burdened *Hamlet* with a plethora of meanings; for *Twelfth Night*, it has found none. The play, apparently, happens nowhere, concerns unreal people, and is full of sound and laughter signifying nothing. Would it, therefore, be fitting to describe it as "a tale told by an idiot"? Surely, this is a direct challenge to explore more carefully its general aspects.

The major plot of *Twelfth Night* is clearly the story of Olivia and her four or five lovers: Orsino, Sir Andrew, Malvolio, and Viola-Sebastian. Of these, Shakespeare's source supplies the first and the last; he himself added the other two, and so gave the play the repeated motif of lovers contending for the *prima amorosa*—a motif common in the *commedia dell' arte* of the age. He had already used it secondarily in *The Merchant of Venice*, in the wooing of Bianca in *The Shrew*, and of Ann Page in *Merry Wives of Windsor*; but, in *Twelfth Night*, it takes the center of the stage. Olivia reacts to each lover, and he to her reception of him. She merely ignores Sir Andrew, and he can hardly be persuaded to continue his suit, and finally yields to the desperate remedy of the duel, which leaves him worse off than before. Malvolio's suit the Countess does not even guess, so great is its presumption; Maria gulls the steward

[4] See J. W. Draper, *The "Hamlet" of Shakespeare's Audience* (Durham, N.C., 1938), chapter xi.

into belief that his lady secretly favors him, very much as Sir Toby and Fabyan gull Sir Andrew; and, as the result in the one case is the comic duel scene, the result in the other is the steward's ridiculous strutting before the Countess and his consequent baiting as a madman. To Orsino's suit, Olivia shuts her doors—or, rather, leaves them open only wide enough for Viola to enter; and Orsino, following polite convention, pursues her as best he can with importunate embassies, until at last he meets her face to face, takes his direct refusal, and believes for a moment that his marriage broker has betrayed him. Viola, who never wished to woo the Countess for herself, and only half-wished to woo her for the Duke, achieves the lady's love, and inadvertently passes it on to her twin brother. This is an ironic embarrassment of success that nearly ruins her plans to win the Duke for herself. Thus, the courtships of Sir Andrew and Malvolio conclude in the ridiculous, as courtships should when a fool and coistrel woo a rich and personable Countess; the courtship of Orsino, which normally should have been successful (as Feste expected) ends in the Duke's marriage to another; and Viola's courtship for Orsino ends in gaining Olivia's love for herself and by chance transmitting it to Sebastian. The two aristocratic pairs of lovers, of course, come to a serious and happy end; but the fool and the steward are discomforted.

The detailed episodes of this major plot arise naturally from the personalities and social planes of the characters concerned, and also grow reasonably from one another. Sir Toby motivates Sir Andrew's aspirations; and, of course, a shrewd and spirited girl would quash them. Maria similarly motivates Malvolio's hopes; but Olivia, of course, would not fall to marriage with an impudent servant. The Duke might reasonably expect (after a proper coy refusal) to gain the lady; but she is too independent to subject herself to such a husband. Sebastian, however, is just the man she wants; and he is clever enough to recognize a good match when he sees it—or innocent enough to be led to the altar without much forethought. Thus, each of the love affairs is reasonable in conception and in out-

216

come—Sebastian's perhaps the least, but Shakespeare had little time to show us his inner thoughts and motives. The love affairs of Sir Andrew and Malvolio provide several great comic scenes, and these are properly integrated in the course of action: Sir Andrew's foolish riot in the hall is the logical result of his character and Sir Toby's, and his ludicrous duel with Viola is the natural consequence of his earlier failure to catch Olivia's attention, of his own silliness, and of Sir Toby's taste in practical jokes. A lover who still pursues after all is lost save honor risks being a laughingstock. Malvolio's finding the letter and preening himself upon it is the natural result of Maria's plot. He consequently appears before his lady arrayed with an incongruous impropriety more glaring in that age of formal etiquette than any modern audience could realize. He postures before the Countess and quotes incoherent phrases from the letter, and, of course, is shut up as mad, for Feste to guy and torment. In short, each episode of the main plot grows from the characters and from the episodes that precede; and one feels no straining to effect the brilliant comic scenes, for they come into being in the natural course of the action. The plot is nicely integrated within itself and with the characters who do the deeds and the great comic passages that they recite.

The minor plots consist of Viola's love affair with the Duke, and of Maria's with Sir Toby; and both of these arise from Olivia's mourning, for this mourning kept Viola from serving Olivia as she first planned, and it also brought Sir Toby and Sir Andrew to the Countess' household and into conflict with Malvolio, and so gave Maria her opportunity to trick the steward and so win the knight as her husband. Thus, the minor plots develop from the major plot; and, furthermore, each minor plot in its course and in its conclusion is linked with the chief action.

Viola's love affair with the Duke is of necessity more passive than Olivia's, for she can say or do little to advance her suit; and Orsino is quite consumed with the pursuit of Olivia. Like Rosalind with Orlando, she tells her love under the guise of a fiction, and discourses sadly of an imagined sister's passion, which is in truth her own. Her position as go-between helps her into Orsino's affections; and, when the strong-minded Olivia refuses him, he naturally reacts toward a passive creature whom he has ruled as master and so can hope to rule as mate— or so he thinks. Thus, the working of the Olivia plot determines the conclusion of Viola's love affair, for Olivia's refusal of the Duke delivers him to Viola.

The other minor plot is likewise closely integrated to the central action. Maria, dowerless but shrewd, is in a situation quite opposite to Olivia's: she has no lovers, and only her wit to supply the want of them. Sir Toby is a knight and a man of the world, and his advent in the household with Sir Andrew spells *opportunity*. He soon understands her purpose, having doubtless known many young women in his day, and by way of answer and amusement sets Sir Andrew to practice love-making on her. She is chagrined but not discouraged. The riot in the hall, however, may cast Sir Toby out; and Maria tries vainly to quiet him. Malvolio enters and upbraids them all. Here is a common enemy: what better can serve to unite Sir Toby to Maria? She quickly sees her chance, and the result is her plot to discomfort the ambitious steward. This little conspiracy both amuses Sir Toby hugely and accomplishes his purpose of removing a rival aspirant from Sir Andrew's way. Of course, he is delighted with Maria, and begins to treat her, if not with respect, at least with an admiring intimacy that is even more to her purpose. Sir Andrew's suit, as time goes by, seems clearly doomed to failure. Olivia, moreover, does not value her uncle's company and would gladly see him depart; but Sir Toby does not wish to leave behind him the easy life of his niece's hall, and the one tie that can give him security in this establishment is Maria. She is Olivia's indispensable abigail, and, moreover, she has charge over "Cakes and Ale" and presides at the buttery bar. Maria, therefore, is the obvious and only substitute in his scheme of future ease; and she doubtless knows as much. If she can defeat Malvolio for him, will not her wit prove useful in other exigencies? Thus, Olivia's refusal of Sir Andrew resolves the Toby-Maria plot; and the thin knight's ignominious defeat at the hands of Sebastian makes the fat knight all the more open to Maria's consolations. Of course, they marry and, we trust, live happily ever after.

Sebastian's quest of a career, Shakespeare might have made into another minor plot; but either space or interest lacked. Moreover, he had lately developed this theme in Bassanio and Orlando. Sebastian seems even less energetic than these two in providing for himself, and when he has been shipwrecked with little means or fortune can think of nothing better to do than casual sight-seeing; he is even more impractical than Orlando.[5] Certainly, he was wise to jump at Olivia's proffers; for, though a good swordsman and a thoroughly nice boy, he seems to have no initiative to carve for himself. Olivia, therefore, is doubtless just the right wife for him, and will take the place of Antonio and Adam and of Portia and Rosalind to guide him through life's pitfalls. His career does not constitute even a minor plot: he is simply there to provide Olivia with a husband, and he does it.

Thus the three plots of the play are reasonable, not only in each separate course of action, but also in relation with one another. They all arise from Olivia's mourning, which gave her independence, sent Viola to Orsino's palace, and brought Sir Toby with Sir Andrew into Olivia's household and so into the orbit of Maria's scheme of things. All three plots end similarly in marriages that provide a happy future for the six participants —both wedded bliss and reasonable security of tenure in their social spheres. Only the impudent gulls, Sir Andrew and Malvolio, are quite properly left out; and even they are not much the worse for the wear and tear of events. These three plots, moreover, in their course of action, impinge on one another: Olivia's vis-à-vis refusal of Orsino gives the Viola plot its happy ending, and her refusal of Sir Andrew helps to persuade Sir Toby to accept Maria. Thus the intrigue is skillfully interlocked, and each part contributes to the others. In short, the comedy has unity and structural coherence.

The presentation of these plots is typically Elizabethan:

[5] J. W. Draper, "Shakespeare's Orlando Inamorato," *M.L.Q.*, II, 179 *et seq.*

each has a different tone and is interlarded with the others so as to produce the maximum of contrast. The antecedent action that took place before the curtain rose is reduced to the lowest possible terms, so that as many comic episodes as possible are presented viva voce on the stage. In the Olivia plot, the two deaths that make the Countess her own mistress, her vow, and her initial refusal of Orsino are all that comprise the pre-play; and none of these would have offered much chance for comedy. In the Maria plot, the advent of the two knights in the house is the only episode that takes place before the curtain rises: and, as the commonplaces of Elizabethan life would have made clear the relation of Sir Toby and Sir Andrew, it needed practically no exposition. The earlier life of Viola and Sebastian is purposely left vague: romantic characters do not need, as Sir Toby and Olivia do, to have their roots in social actuality. In short, only Olivia's initial situation required careful exposition, and the deaths that set her free and the devices by which she maintains this freedom are repeatedly set forth so that the veriest groundling would understand how she happened to be choosing a husband for herself.

The plot structure, therefore, is both well conceived and essentially Elizabethan; but it could not be so well reflected in the play's theatrical effects; for Olivia, the structural center of the piece, appears in few of the more striking scenes. Indeed, she cannot appear with Orsino until the very end when she refuses him point-blank; she cannot appear with Sir Andrew, whose company she eschews; and her vow of mourning and her dignity as a Countess will not permit her to take part in any of the more uproarious fun. Shakespeare, to be sure, makes us feel her presence by the repeated reference of others even when she is not on the stage; but her scenes with Viola and Sebastian are neither very poetic nor very witty—how could they be when she is more than half the wooer? Thus the most brilliant passages in the play concern, not its structural center, but Sir Toby and Sir Andrew and Maria and Malvolio, figures that Shakespeare added to the plot, rather than the core he derived from Riche's story. Our modern "star" system on the stage has accentuated this difficulty, for the "star" prefers to take a comic role such as Sir Toby or Malvolio; and, since the rise of Romanticism, the leading lady is likely to take Viola. Thus the main part is subordinated to two peripheral roles, both of which chiefly belong to quite separate minor plots; and, on the modern stage, therefore, the perfection of structure is more or less concealed. The crucial scenes of the comedy should be Olivia's falling in love with Viola, which does occupy the climax of Act I, and her betrothal with Sebastian, which, however, is not shown upon the stage at all. The difficulty is that Olivia, like Hamlet, is of necessity so passive that she cannot act until the very end: she is an unmarried woman and in mourning; and, as true comedy of manners required, Shakespeare refused to sacrifice realism for an extra laugh. Thus in the comic effect of the play, Olivia is overshadowed by her lovers and her servants and even her own jester. Modern democracy, furthermore, has thrown the play still further out of focus by giving Malvolio a meretricious tragic sympathy; some actors have actually played him as if we should weep rather than rejoice at his confusion. In short, time has emphasized the original disparity between the perfect structure and the comic values of the scenes.

This plot, in its main outlines, is not highly original. Shakespeare took the middle of Riche's story, cut off the beginning, and condensed the end into a single rapid scene. Then he enriched the central portion with two added lovers and their private concerns that form two minor plots. The additional lovers made the plot basically that of contemporary Italian comedy in which rivals claim the hand of a single lady;[6] the original story supplied the common convention of mistaken identity in an exaggerated form;[7] and, on this somewhat commonplace texture, Shakespeare embroidered his comic scenes. Perhaps the fact that the fundamental situations of Olivia and Sebastian and Viola were rather well worn explains the playwright's comic emphasis on Malvolio and Feste and the knights

[6] Cf. O. J. Campbell, "Italian Background for the *Merry Wives of Windsor*," *University of Michigan Publications* (Ann Arbor, 1932), p. 89.

[7] J. W. Draper, "Mistaken Identity in Shakespeare's Comedies," *Revue Anglo-American* (1934), pp. 289 *et seq.*

—the realistic figures that were entirely his own; and it is perhaps a tribute to his genius that these characters that are entirely his own are the truest to life and the most comic and amusing in the piece. On the other hand, if Olivia's position as the center of wooers be conventional, her shrewdness and independence of character certainly are not—especially not in the Italy of that day;[8] and, if her scenes lack the highest brilliance of poetry and of wit, yet she remains a subtle (though unappreciated) example of character portrayal—a typically Elizabethan heroine of an Italian comic intrigue.

The problem of characterization in serious drama is difficult at best, for the successive episodes of the plot require a constant yet varied motivation that must be based in traits already established in each character concerned. The dramatist, therefore, could most easily conceive of plot and character together since they so constantly interact; but, where the plot, as often happens in Elizabethan plays, is borrowed from a well-known story— and consequently the incidents are fixed beforehand in the minds of the audience—the difficulties are greatly aggravated; for, the plot being a given quantity, these problems must be solved through characterization alone. This may even present, as in Desdemona,[9] insuperable inconsistencies. If the episodes, moreover, require several separate traits—in short, a complex personality—then the character must show all these traits in every major speech and action. Thus, in Act I, a character cannot be a moral coward like Macbeth, in Act II, a miser like l'Avare, and finally an intriguing villain like Richard III; but his miserliness and his villainy must color his moral cowardice, just as the tints in a good painting all reflect one another, for, in actuality, the light in a room, glancing from each object to all the others, gives to the eye a complex blend of colors. No wonder that so few dramatists have managed to create even a handful of truly complex characters, and that most plays either ignore the problem and so fall to the rank of farce or melodrama, or else content themselves with portraying simple

[8] *Idem*, "Desdemona," *Revue de littérature comparée*, XIII, 337 *et seq.*
[9] *Ibid.*

types, either traditional stage types such as the Victorian "heavy villain," or social types such as the feminist heroines of Shaw, or embodiments of a single vice or virtue such as Tartuffe.

The dramatist who is creating his own plot can weave a simple chain of incidents about a miser or an upstart tradesman and produce, like Molière, a thoroughly consistent play setting forth a simple type. Indeed, Victorian drama regularly made its chief roles such simple types as the "juvenile lead," the "heavy," and the golden-haired ingénue, and relegated "character parts" to minor choral figures whose traits and reactions would not affect the plot. Shakespeare often uses types traditional to the stage, especially for his more romantic figures; and, in *Twelfth Night*, Viola, with her vague past, her fortunate outcome in the plot, and her golden future, is a proper heroine, the Juliet-Miranda of the comedy. Sebastian is an incipient "juvenile lead," and comes out the hero, as far as a duel and an accidental marriage can make him one. Their link with stage convention further appears in that they are concerned in the artificial device of mistaken identity, a timeworn trick inherited from Classical comedy, and Viola, moreover, follows the common convention of the heroine disguised as a page. Indeed, the prepossession of the nineteenth-century stage for Viola can perhaps be explained in part by her approximation to the recognized theatrical type of the young ingénue. As a matter of fact, being largely compounded as she is from elements in Shakespeare's source and elements of stage convention, she seems less Shakespeare's own, less significant, less lifelike, and less vivid than any other major figure in the piece.

Of the simplest sort of type that expresses throughout but a single trait, like a figure in a morality play, Shakespeare presents few examples, and none in *Twelfth Night* unless it be Sir Andrew; but even his stupidity shows such variety and finesse and is so well grounded in his social background that he belongs rather to the social type, like Molière's Bourgeois Gentilhomme. Sir Andrew, in short, is the rich gull of dubious ancestry, a common upstart type in Elizabethan London. Orsino is the wellborn lover, a disappointed Romeo, elegant and charming, but beclouded with melancholy. He somewhat approximates the stage type of "juvenile lead," but seems a bit too realistic as a Duke and as a lover. He is the Renaissance nobleman, a figure of the age rather than merely of the theater. Fabyan is the servingman, fearful of his place; Antonio and Viola's sailor are faithful friends of low degree; and Curio and Valentine are faithful henchmen, such as should serve a Duke. These are mainly social types. The complex personalities, moreover, such as Sir Toby, Malvolio, and Olivia, all fit into some recognizable social group; and, indeed, this ubiquity of social setting is quite to be expected in a comedy of manners. *Twelfth Night*, in short, is a precise reversal of the Victorian plays in which the crucial figures in the plot are common types expressing merely a theatrical convention, a single exaggerated trait, or a well-known social group, and in which the complex reality of life is relegated to one or more of the minor characters. In *Twelfth Night* the minor characters generally blur into the background as mere types, and most of the chief figures who make the plot and react to it are painted full length as complex personalities. Just so it should be in significant drama.

These complex personalities, who transcend a single term or epithet, comprise a surprisingly large number of the characters. Maria is not a mere waiting maid, or the mere expository confidante of old French comedy; beside her relationships with Olivia, she is the wooer of Sir Toby, and the practical jokester of Malvolio. In the first of these parts she shows loyalty and discretion; in the second, feminine guile; in the third, quick-witted cleverness. She judges her mistress and Sir Toby and Malvolio all aright; and, playing on their feelings and their foibles, she archly bends each to her purposes. Her character is at once diverse and unified, for discretion and feminine guile and cleverness are but different aspects of this same quality by which she gains her ends. Malvolio, likewise, has several clear-cut facets to his character: the faithful steward, the impudent parvenu, the lover of sorts, and something of the fool —a more diverse and daring combination than Maria, but possible in the social whirligig of the time. Feste, moreover, is no mere simple fool, in either sense of the term. But *imprimis*, the highborn Olivia, with one auspicious and one dropping eye, in equal scale weighing delight and dole, surveying with sidelong gaze the landscape of her lovers and meanwhile laughing with Feste, scolding Sir Toby roundly, and discreetly ruling her household and herself—at once mournful and merry, innocent and keen-witted, direct in speech and devious in action, circumventing alike uncle and duke and steward, a very Queen Elizabeth—Olivia, like the King in *Hamlet*, is a Shakespearean portrait too subtle for the Victorian critic used to the crass ingénue and the crasser "heavy." Also a complex personality is Sir Toby, who plays uncle to Olivia, go-between to Sir Andrew, baiter to Malvolio and to Viola, and finally husband to Maria. Such also is Feste, who plays both fool and wise man in the comedy, and plays all the characters for all that he can get—a money-making fool in contrast to the prodigal Sir Andrew. Indeed, if the number of complex characters be any index of a comedy's excellence, *Twelfth Night* deserves to rank among the greatest ever penned; for Shakespeare has bestowed this crowning reality of life on no less than five of its characters, and not only on figures of his own invention—Sir Toby, Maria, Malvolio, and Feste—but also supremely on Olivia whom he borrowed from Riche's stiff and artificial story, and made, by a triumph of creative skill, a very living Elizabethan countess.

These characters not only motivate the plot but also furnish striking contrasts with each other. *Othello* presents two jealous husbands on contrasting social planes,[10] and *King Lear* shows two families composed of filial and wicked children; so *Twelfth Night* has three clever women obliged by untoward circumstance to find husbands for themselves: Viola, Maria, and Olivia. Viola by shipwreck, Maria by lack of dowery, and Olivia by the deaths of her father and her brother, are all cast upon the world to fend for their own futures. Maria, having a secure and comfortable home, is in a less parlous state than

---

[10] J. W. Draper, " 'Honest Iago,' " *P.M.L.A.*, XLVI, 724 *et seq.*

Viola, and her poverty and lack of noble rank make her less of a shining mark for trouble than is her noble mistress; but she lacks the romantic glamour of the one and the wealth and title of the other, and so risks being overlooked by mere insignificance. All three achieve success, as they should in a true comedy, where in Act V flawless (or only slightly spotted) husbands are to be had for the taking. Of course, Maria as befits her lesser station, achieves a spouse a trifle less than flawless; and, though she gains the dignity and prestige of the married state, she yet remains a waiting woman, with small chance that Sir Toby will better her condition. Viola marries her duke and, of course, lives happily forever after; and Olivia follows the Wife of Bath's advice and gets a husband whom doubtless she can rule. From another point of view, this is a play of fortune hunters, realistic and romantic, sensible like Maria and, like Malvolio, impudent; and Fortune favored those with whom Shakespeare and his audience sympathized. Viola, Olivia, Maria, Sir Toby, Orsino, Sebastian, even Feste with his itching palm, all win success; but Sir Andrew loses his money and Malvolio his "face." The comedy also shows a contrast of military figures: Sir Andrew, the bragging coward; Sir Toby, the realistic soldier no better than he should be; Viola, who against her will plays soldier in the duel; and the ideal Sebastian who saves the situation and marries the Countess, all inadvertently. The comedy does not lack for parallels to make its contrasts sharp.

Drama requires an initial instability of equilibrium, or else no events would naturally transpire; and high comedy, based on character, demands that this inequilibrium be fundamentally apparent in the major personalities: a not-too-violent incongruity must appear between their abilities and their ambitions or between their characters and the place in life in which they find themselves. This last is especially evident in *Twelfth Night*, where, indeed, every man is out of his humor. The two knights should be choleric, hot, and dry, but are in fact phlegmatic, cold, and wet; the steward should be phlegmatic and has in fact the pride and ambition of choler; the Duke, as a duke, should be sanguine, hot, and moist, but the melancholy of unrequited love has made him cold and dry; and Olivia, who should as a woman be passive and phlegmatic, is melancholy and sanguine. In the end these incongruities are generally resolved: Sir Toby looks forward to an easy future; Malvolio has no choice but to let himself be entreated to a peace; Orsino's happy marriage doubtless brings him back to the sanguine humor proper to a duke; and Olivia, having had her way in courtship, probably continues to have her way in marriage. Indeed, this is a comedy of transverse humors, in which the knights and gentles are phlegmatic or melancholy, and the heroine and menial-in-chief are sanguine and choleric.

The fact that Shakespeare's characters are more or less patterned after definite humors might suggest that to Elizabethans they all seemed simple types; but this is not necessarily true. Some show a combination of humors like the mercurial Feste and the lovelorn Duke; and, even if a single humor consistently rules a character's every act, choler and phlegm and melancholy had so many variants and acted in so many different ways that a highly individualized personality might result. A choleric person, for example, was essentially wrathful and easily provoked, but incidentally he might also be proud, obstinate, and shrewd; and his sex, age, the time of the year, and the general situation might influence his humor. Some readers may also feel that Shakespeare's use of an outworn psychology precludes the realism of his characters: in the first place, Galenic medicine was not altogether foolish or it would not have flourished for so many centuries; and, in the second, the terminology even of a pseudo science may serve to express observed truth with some accuracy; and Shakespeare had no choice but to use the known terms and concepts of his age.

Indeed, Shakespeare's use of the humors gives unity to characters whose complexity might otherwise make them verge on impossible inconsistency: Olivia's sanguine merriment with Feste redeems her from the melancholy of her mourning, and so makes possible her sudden passion for the Duke's handsome messenger; and fickle melancholy seems to explain the Duke's sudden transfer of his love from Olivia to Viola—like Romeo's sudden change from Rosaline to Juliet. Sir Andrew's phlegm explains his stupidity, his cowardice, and his dullness in feats of love; in fact, it is the common denominator of the fractional parts that compose his personality. Only choleric pride could motivate Malvolio's initial rudeness to his betters, his outrageous expectations, and the fall that overtakes him. To the Elizabethans, the humors, which were common knowledge in every household, must have supplied a running commentary on the play's psychology and motives. Their incongruity to a character's situation or social aspirations starts the plot in motion; their well-known patterns guide the actions and the reactions of various characters to these actions; and the outcome of this pattern supplies an inevitable end. Thus Malvolio, as an incongruously choleric servant, would be inflated with pride to raise himself above the status of his birth; this incongruity would express itself in ridiculous words and deeds; and such pride could end only in a fall. This is a comic parallel to the tragic career of Coriolanus, also impelled by choleric pride.[11] These recognized humor-patterns that form the very nexus between plot and character are essential to interpreting a serious play of the period, for they are the very heart of its organic unity.

All this background, theatric, social, and psychological, is essential to the understanding not only of the larger matters of dramaturgy, but also of the fine details of dialogue; and, in Shakespeare's dialogue, every phrase expresses the reaction of character on character. Sometimes the dramatist leaves these nice reactions to be shown purely by facial expression, pose, or gesture; but sometimes the dialogue reflects these passing feelings. It is so in the famous Garden Scene. The two knights are hidden behind the box tree. Malvolio struts down the walk "practicing behauiour." He soliloquizes on his chances of marrying the Countess, and the following commentary from the three eavesdroppers expresses their several feelings: Sir

[11] J. W. Draper, "Coriolanus," *West Virginia Philological Studies* (1939), p. 22 *et seq.*

Toby, as uncle and would-be disposer of Olivia's hand, is shocked at Malvolio's social presumption, and calls him "an ouer-weening rogue"; Fabyan, who is in the plot for mere sport, warns Sir Toby to be quiet, and comments on Malvolio's ridiculous posturing; and Sir Andrew, always the exaggerated mimic of Sir Toby and the cheap braggart, swears that he could "beate the Rogue." Sir Toby, fearful that Malvolio will hear and all the fun be spoiled, calls for silence. So the scene continues, a monologue with annotation apropos, expressive of each individual.

Sometimes the reactions shown in the dialogue arise, as so often in life, from misunderstanding of the speaker; and the expression of this on the stage is one type of dramatic irony, a brilliant and realistic effect on which *Hamlet*, *Othello*, and *King Lear* are largely built. Its comic use appears in *Twelfth Night*, especially in the crucial scene when Malvolio presents himself cross-gartered and simpering before his distraught mistress. Even the occasion from which the scene arises has an ironic twist: the Countess, unmindful of his tender aspirations, sends for him to act as messenger to her lover (quite as the Duke used Viola); and he enters with a facial expression and a costume utterly inappropriate not only to his ambitions but also to the purpose that she has in mind. His speech is so allusive to the counterfeit letter that it is utterly elusive to Olivia. Maria has prepared her to believe him mad; and there follow forty lines of perfect dialogue at cross-purposes, in which Olivia thinks him more and more insane, and Malvolio thinks that he is pleasing her. A servant enters to announce Viola's return. Sir Toby, Fabyan, and Maria enter and taunt the steward who openly scorns them and finally flings off the stage with a last contemptuous speech. Thus the comedy of the piece grows from the characterization, for the whole scene depends on Malvolio's choleric pride and ambition, on the sportive zest of his detractors, and on the ulterior purposes of Sir Toby and Maria. In this one scene, the conflict between Malvolio's humor and his social class creates a comic irony that arises, therefore, from both situation and character.

In short, Shakespeare's characterization in *Twelfth Night* is within itself consistent even in the most complex personalities; and, furthermore, it is perfectly integrated with the plot and with the comic effects of the dialogue. Just as in life we express our characters in our every word and act—in handwriting, in gesture, in the very way we walk across a floor—so Shakespeare by the most varied and subtle means portrays those shifting nuances that we term personality. Occasionally a figure tells plainly what he is, as the Duke Orsino declares his love-melancholy in the initial scene. Sometimes one figure describes and explains another, as Maria does Sir Andrew. More subtly, we see these figures express themselves in an unguarded speech or action, as when Malvolio postures down the garden path or Viola shows her terror at the duel; and, most subtly of all, we see the reactions of Malvolio's affectation and of Viola's fears on those around them, each according to his point of view and character. Thus, a single incident, like a pebble tossed into a glassy pond, throws out a widening circle of waves that strike the edges and then return again upon the place where the pebble sank. So drama, in its reactions of plot and character, expresses in human terms the eternal interaction of relativity: and surely no comedy does so with more brilliance and more delicacy than does *Twelfth Night*.

Some critics, like Professor Stoll, believe that Shakespeare's characters are mere compounds of theatrical convention and not at all a reflection of real life; and some, like Professor Hart,[12] suggest that he was such an exuberant poet that he must have been a poor playwright, and so, even in his own day, required a professional producer to cut and revise his writings to make them actable "theatre." Of course, Shakespeare used the conventions of the stage; of course, he was a great poet; and, like enough, his plays sometimes had to be revised to fit special needs, such as an abridged version for use on tour. But, to suppose that Shakespeare, like Eugène Scribe, was so much the merely clever playwright that he could be nothing else, or that he was so little the playwright that an anonymous adapter

---

[12] A. Hart, "Did Shakespeare Produce His Own Plays?" *M.L.R.*, XXVI, 173 *et seq.*

had to revise his poems before they could be staged—either of these extremes is as gratuitous and unfortunate an assumption as to think that he was so ignorant a country boor that Bacon, or Sir Walter Raleigh must have written these plays that Ben Jonson and his other friends accredited to William Shakespeare. Surely the Elizabethans knew the striking character types and situations of their own society as well as any of us; and they saw his comedies as realistic reflections of themselves "framed to the life."[13] The present study certainly suggests that they knew whereof they spoke. The characters of *Twelfth Night* owe but little to theatrical convention, and it remains for the next chapter to show that Shakespeare's style, witty or poetic, does not conflict but accords with the other aspects of the comedy. Had Shakespeare neglected the higher possibilities of comedy of manners for the theatrical legerdemain of farce or the purely lyric effects of closet drama, he would hardly have presented at least five complex and lifelike personalities that far transcend the simple types of stage convention as listed by Dr. Forsythe[14]—simple types that would likewise have sufficed for mere poetic dialogue. He would, moreover, have taken his simpler characters from these stage types, or made them mere morality-personifications, instead of drawing so many from contemporary life; he would not have developed their inner selves with such finesse in terms of the accepted psychology of humors; he would not have troubled to integrate so nicely character with plot and with the nuances of dialogue; he would have depended more on facile and striking surprise and less on the more lifelike subleties of dramatic irony. Our ignorance of Elizabethan social life has obscured his realism; our ignorance of the theory of humors in its psychological ramifications has obscured the subtle unity and depth of his characterization; and only by relearning these backgrounds as the Elizabethans knew them can we interpret the plays as the Elizabethans saw them. Of course, no fine art can completely reproduce the intricacies of real life, but drama expresses more

[13] See the Preface to the 1609 Quarto of *Troilus and Cressida.*
[14] R. S. Forsythe, *Shirley's Plays* (New York, 1914).

of its simultaneous facets than any other aesthetic medium; and Shakespeare's dramas express these intricate relations of man to man and man to his environment more fully and more vividly than the works of any other dramatist. This is the supreme virtue of his plays and the very crux of his subtle insight, and to gainsay this quality is to gainsay his highest excellence. He saw life steadily, and also saw it whole.

The Setting, Style, and Theme of *Twelfth Night*

IVING drama, like a plant with its roots in the soil from which it draws vitality, must grow from a setting that is, if not recognizably realistic, at least governed by recognizable principles of life—a *somewhere* in which such people could live and breathe and in which such things could happen. This should be true of *Twelfth Night*. The two Italian plays that have been taken as its source are set respectively in Naples and in Genoa; and Riche lays the scene of his *Apolonius* in Cyprus and Constantinople; but none of these settings has any considerable realism of local color. Hazlitt describes the setting of Shakespeare's comedy as being "of a pastoral and poetical cast"; and most critics take its milieu as a "land of dreams." Producers, driven to a decision by the necessity of scenery and costume, have sometimes followed Riche and made the play Greek, or have more often taken "Illyria" as the coast of Classical Illyricum and given it the contemporary costumes of Venice, which ruled the Adriatic isles.[1] According to the text, the action takes place partly on a seashore, and partly in a near-by "City" that is sufficiently ancient and important to have "memorials" worthy a traveler's notice;[2] and the name of this country, or city-state, is repeatedly given as "Illyria." Shakespeare had earlier used the adjective *Illyrian* in *Henry VI*: "Bargulus [Bardyllis] the strong Illyrian pirate";[3] but, as Bardyllis was mentioned by Cicero as a contemporary of Philip of Macedon, this reference is clearly to ancient Illyricum and not to the obviously Renaissance "Illyria" of *Twelfth Night*. Most commentators seem to take "Illyria" as a romantic variation of the name of the Roman province; and

[1] *Twelfth Night* (ed. Furness var.), p. 4 n.
[2] *Ibid.*, III. iii. 24 *et seq.*
[3] *Henry VI*, Part II, IV. i. 108.

233

Godwin referred it to the coast line of that province, modern Dalmatia.

As a matter of fact, Illyria to the Renaissance was just as definite a place as Naples or Genoa, though doubtless less widely and intimately known. A dialogue, *Concerning Dysentery and Intermittence of the Pulse,* dated shortly after 1550, in which the speakers are the well-known physicians, Amatus Lusitanus, Andreas Laguna, and Barkosius, alludes to an "Illyrian monk" whom Amatus had recently cured of a malignant fever.[4] The region referred to was not coextensive with ancient Roman Illyricum, which stretched from the Adriatic to the Danube and included nearly all of modern Yugoslavia, but appears in the standard contemporary atlas of Ortelius as modern Slovenia and Croatia,[5] a comparatively small section east of Istria and Venice, and running from the Adriatic coast northeast across the mountains to include more or less of the upper valleys of the rivers Save and Drave. It was bounded on the north by the Hapsburg Duchy of Styria and the Kingdom of Hungary, and to the east and south by Slavonia, Bosnia, and Dalmatia, the last of which seems sometimes to have been included in its boundaries. In Roman times, therefore, this region was rather to the north of the Province of Illyricum, and was part of Pannonia or even Noricum; but Constantine, in reorganizing the Empire, created the enlarged Diocese of Illyricum, and included in it this territory. In the fifth century, the Ostrogoths overwhelmed it, and lingered there for a time on their triumphal way to Italy; and later it was a border province of Charlemagne's Empire. In the seventh century, the Croatians, a Slavic people, pressed into it from the south and east; and, ever since, it has been at the crossroads of South Slavic, Italian, German, and Hungarian cultures. In the Middle Ages, it was within or on the borders of the Holy Roman Empire; but culturally the coast line was under the influence of Venice, which ruled the adjacent islands; and even within its

---

[4] See H. Friedenwald, "A Sixteenth-Century Consultation," *Bull. Hist. of Med.,* IX, 206.

[5] A. Ortelius, *Theatrum Orbis Terrarum* (Antwerp, 1579). The map of Illyria was made in Vienna in 1572 and first appeared in the 1573 edition.

234

borders were a few towns, such as Capella and Bachri, with suggestively Italian names. During the tenth and eleventh centuries, Croatia was a kingdom which family alliances brought under the rule of Hungary, and which proved a source of contention between that country and Venice. In the fifteenth and sixteenth centuries, the advancing power of the Turks turned Croatia into a border mark of the Hapsburg dominions; and, as elsewhere in Europe, the local nobility by degrees lost their ancient feudal privileges. In 1812, Napoleon, with ancient Illyricum in mind, combined Dalmatia, Croatia, and adjacent regions into his Illyrian Province; and the term Illyrian Kingdom was applied to the northern part of this region on its restoration to the Hapsburg Empire in 1815. Thus, for over two thousand years, *Illyricum* and *Illyrian* have been intermittently applied to part or all of the region northeast of the Adriatic Sea; but, apparently in Shakespeare's time, the name generally referred to a smaller section east of Istria, the territory of the Croats and the Slovenes.

In the sixteenth century, the Holy Roman Empire included "part of Croatia";[6] and, as the local nobles still clung to some of their feudal independence, Shakespeare's conception of Orsino as waging war is not incongruous; but it would have fitted contemporary Italy quite as well. In the Empire, however, the Salic Law would hardly have allowed Olivia's accession to her father's title—certainly not if she were, like Orsino, a semi-independent ruler. The upper classes in the comedy show the cosmopolitan culture that had spread over western and central Europe from Renaissance Italy. One might expect that the proximity of Venice might lend local color as it did in *The Merchant of Venice* and *Othello*;[7] but *Twelfth Night* has no reference to the Rialto, or the magnificoes, or the "officers of night": in fact, the pleasure capital of Europe and Queen City of the Adriatic does not once appear; and the propriety of Venetian costuming, especially for the plainer folk, is there-

---

[6] See Dr. Edward Brown in John Harris, *Navigantium atque Itinerantium Bibliotheca* (London, 1705), II, 320.

[7] J. W. Draper, "Some Details of Italian Local Color in *Othello*," *Shakespeare Jahrbuch*, LXVIII, 125 *et seq.*

fore questionable. It would probably be most suitable for the would-be fop, Sir Andrew. Certainly, the independence of Orsino and Olivia does not suggest the subjection of a Venetian vassal state.[8] The name Orsino connects the comedy with Tuscany and the Papal dominions, where the Orsini, Dukes of Bracciano, had long been a famous noble family; and Shakespeare must have known of the Duke Orsino who was Florentine ambassador at the English court in the winter of 1600–1601.[9] The dramatist, however, may not have realized whence the Orsini took their title; and Papal and Florentine details that would locate "Illyria" in central Italy are quite lacking. Thus, the vaguely Italian atmosphere of the piece cannot be localized in any one region. If Sebastian and Viola, furthermore, were supposed to come from Manzolino[10] in the valley of the Po, this adds yet another Italian background.

Indeed, the more one examines the local color of the comedy, the less definitely Italian and the more cosmopolitan it seems. The dialogue, though it has scraps of Latin, French, and Spanish, yields no Italian but "Madona," Sir Andrew's "ducates," and Sir Toby's reference to a *viola da gamba*; and all these references had become international with the spread of Italian culture in the Renaissance. Orsino's "gallies"[11] suggest the Mediterranean, for ships propelled by oars were impractical on the rough Atlantic. The names, moreover—Viola, Curio, Feste, and Antonio—suggest Italian background; but Sir Toby Belch and Sir Andrew Aguecheek are definitely English, and Italian names were affected outside Italy. In short, Shakespeare's "Illyria," despite actual proximity to Venice and the Venetian colonies in Dalmatia, is hardly more Italian than was any other part of Renaissance western Europe. In judging the local color of the play, the critic is therefore reduced merely to "Illyria," and must seek in the text for its Italian, native, and English elements.

The Illyria of Shakespeare's day was, of course, essentially Slavic in its population, mores, and native character, though its

[8] On the local nobility in states subject to Venice, see Harris, *op. cit.*, II, 320.
[9] See G. Sarrazin, *Shakespeare Jahrbuch*, XXXII, 167–68.
[10] See Appendix B.　　　　　[11] *Twelfth Night*, III. iii. 30.

nobility might show some gloss of Italian and perhaps Hungarian or Germanic cultures. Shakespeare's knowledge of the Slavs was apparently almost nil, and his London audience was equally ignorant. One, therefore, could not expect much in the way of Croatian local color, and the reference to "the old hermit of Prage"[12] is about as near to it as he comes. The maritime allusions in the play—shipwreck, "gallies," naval fights, and the traveled references of Sir Toby and Maria—though not as impossible as the coasts of Bohemia, fit Croatia rather poorly, for its mountains rise steeply from its shore line and cut off from the sea the pastoral and agricultural interior. Apparently, no episode of the plot and none of the characters are particularly Croatian; for they would fit, not only England but also (except for the feminist, Olivia) most other parts of Europe that were emerging from the economic and social conditions of feudalism to the Renaissance. In short, if the Italian atmosphere of the play is superficial, the Slavic atmosphere hardly exists at all, and the larger aspects of the piece are international. In fact, the play is as cosmopolitan and international as the Renaissance itself.

The style of the dialogue, whether blank verse or racy prose, follows the conventions of current English drama; but most of the allusions, though they seem Elizabethan at first sight, would fit as well any other country of western or central Europe, including Italy or Croatia. References were widely current to the Greek and Latin classics, to the Galenic or other sciences, to sport, to social classes and conditions, to such things as a "stone-bow" or a velvet gown. One might expect to find, as in *Macbeth*,[13] a special effort at local color in the opening scenes, but one rather finds motifs common to contemporary Europe if not to all mankind and even fairy lore: music, love, hunting, death, and mourning, a shipwreck, concern over a drowned brother, and over the needs of the survivors. Even the third scene, which seems so typically English, between Sir Toby and Maria and Sir Andrew, is universally Renaissance

[12] *Ibid.*, IV. ii. 15.
[13] J. W. Draper, "Historic Local Color in *Macbeth*," *Revue Belge*, XVII, 43 *et seq.*

in its elements and allusions: the plague, Olivia's mourning, Sir Toby's roistering and his girth, Sir Andrew's cowardice, stupidity, and ducats, and then the ample comic illustration of that roistering and that stupidity until both knights dance off, presumably to bed. All these are universal motifs phrased for the most part in terms that are no more English than the vivid use of the English language would require. Croatians certainly ate mutton and doubtless knew caper sauce; they had pictures of girls, doubtless with curtains before them to keep the dust off; they danced current court dances, and enjoyed "Reuels"; and some Croatians probably danced as ludicrously as Sir Andrew and some laughed as slyly as Sir Toby. The same is true of the last scene in the act, which also seems so English. The "brissle" of a broom, the "colours" or flag of an army, "gaskins," the wide hose of the period, a "Botcher" or mender of clothes, "Cannon bullets," "bird-bolts," Mercury, Diana, and so forth, were doubtless as well known to Croatia as to Italy and England. Sir Toby's reference to "pickle herring," the office of "Crowner," and a "Sheriffes post" seem typically English; and yet even these were not impossible in Croatia. The use of French and Spanish elsewhere in the play seems to accord better with England than with Croatia; and Puritans, cross-garters, yellow stockings, and "Westward hoe" seem thoroughly English; but the "Elephant" might as well be an inn in Messaline as in London; the "belles of S. Bennet"[14] might refer to the chimes of any church dedicated to St. Benedict, and such were to be found all over western Europe. A "bum-Baylie"[15] was, like the "Crowner," probably characteristic of England; but he must have had his counterparts hither and yon. Such games as cherry-pit[16] and whipping the "parish-top"[17] doubtless existed widely; and, though the ballad "Please one, and please all"[18] was known to contemporary London, such ballads were doubtless to be found high and low throughout the Continent. In short, when Godwin calls this play "thoroughly English,"[19] he ignores the fact that most of it is, if not

14 *Twelfth Night*, V. i. 38.
15 *Ibid.*, III. iv. 175.   16 *Ibid.*, III. iv. 119.   17 *Ibid.*, I. iii. 42.
18 *Ibid.*, III. iv. 26.   19 *Ibid.*, p. 22 n.

universal, at least cosmopolitan of its age; for it reflects common customs and universal folklore and the international culture that had spread north and west from Italy and was overwhelming that earlier international culture of the feudal Middle Ages.

In short, Shakespeare announces a definite geographical locale for the setting of his play, and then makes no attempt to live up to it. Perhaps he intended it merely as an excuse for his generalized Renaissance background. His choice of Venice for the setting of a play is easily understood, for Venice was the dear, damned, disreputable town, the capital of gaiety and fashion; but why should a dramatist use Croatia about which the Elizabethans knew little and cared less? One suspects that he chose it because he did not wish to be constrained to a region too well known, and he wanted to write a comedy that would apply over the length and breadth of the Renaissance world, that would be as effective on tour in Germany as in England. At all events, the comedy reflects but little that is merely Italian or merely English: it is pan-European; and truly its appeal has turned out to be universal in time as well as place.

The producer's problem of costume and scenery yet remains. Classical Grecian dress seems obviously out of order; the play belongs neither to those times nor to that country. Shakespeare's fundamental conception of it in terms of contemporary themes and character types calls for a contemporary Renaissance milieu upon the stage: Renaissance Greece was Turkish, and the play is clearly not Oriental. The lack of Slavic local color in the lines throws some doubt on the propriety of Croatian costume. Venetian dress, as pictured for example in Vecellio, might pass for the courtly figures; but other Venetian local color is notably absent: for instance, Orsino is politically too independent to be conceived of as a vassal of the Venetian state, and the real Orsino came from central Italy. Thus finally one is reduced to the actual practice of Shakespeare's company—Elizabethan costume—and Elizabethan costume is particularly fitting for a cosmopolitan play; for, if we may believe Portia as she com-

239

ments on her English suitor, it was itself a cosmopolitan conglomerate of national fashions:

How oddly he is suited! I think he bought his doublet in Italy, his round
hose in France, his bonnet in Germany, and his behaviour every where.

Closely allied to the setting of a drama is the style of
its composition, for both are largely taken up with the detail
of the dialogue. The former has to do chiefly with concrete
touches, allusion, simile, and metaphor; the latter, with versification, sentence structure, wit, wordplay, epigram, and various figures of speech. The text of *Twelfth Night* shows a wide
variety of styles in prose and poetry, and a brief survey of styles
both in themselves and in their contrasting effects would seem
to be appropriate.

These styles are generally the same as in most high comedy
of the age: lyric, as in the introductory scene in which Orsino
tells his love and woes; matter-of-fact exposition, as in the second scene in which Viola takes stock of the situation after her
shipwreck; wit and low comedy as in the third, leading up to
rollicking horseplay and deep belly laughter. Later, of course,
the proportion of action increases at the expense of the lyric and
expository styles, and the play becomes a mixture of comic dialogue and comic episode. The groundlings had to be amused or
they would spoil the show, and their low intelligence demanded
constant variety; and, furthermore, the tradition of Medieval
drama, with its comic interludes in serious religious pieces, gave
precedence for rapid contrast on the Elizabethan stage. *Twelfth
Night*, therefore, like most plays of its period, presents a ka-
leidoscope of styles.

An audience, in part inattentive and of low intelligence,
required a clear and careful exposition of the initial situation
in the play, and Shakespeare explains Olivia's unusual and
anomalous position in three successive scenes. The language
problem also made such repetition necessary. For centuries,
Latin had been the vehicle for ideas and exposition, and Elizabethan English, as the language of the crowd rather than of
the closet, was too loose in syntax and too inexact in diction to

lend itself to the niceties of accurate statement. Indeed, English hardly developed an expository style until the time of Dryden and the Royal Society. Thus, both his audience and his language obliged Shakespeare to reiterate and again reiterate the facts of Olivia's bereavement and her consequent independence, and likewise to assure the listener again and yet again that Sir Andrew is a rich fool and a coward. Indeed, the difficulty in expressing previous events and backgrounds essential to an understanding of the play perhaps explains why Elizabethan dramatists eschewed the highly unified effect of Greek dramaturgy, which concentrates upon the last of a chain of episodes, and tells the others only in expository retrospect.

The passages of comic action, such as Sir Andrew's dancing, Malvolio's strutting and picking up the letter, Viola's duel, and Feste's capering in the finale, are matters of histrionic rather than literary style. One can only suppose that the Elizabethan actor, on the outer stage in the midst of the pit, got full artistic measure from pose and posturing. Of course, such scenes could sometimes be a vivid auxiliary to the exposition, for nothing could better express Sir Andrew's doltish self-esteem than his angular capering. The scene in which Malvolio finds the letter is a mixture of incongruous action, dramatic irony, and witty comment: the action is Malvolio's, for the other characters lie concealed; the dramatic irony arises from his ignorance of trick; and the witty comment is Maria's and Sir Toby's, for Malvolio rarely lowered himself to wit. The steward enters, preening himself upon his expected fortune. He minces forward in assiduous caricature of formal elegance. He weighs and considers and reflects upon his lady: "What should I think on't?" He is "a rare Turkey Cocke," and "iets vnder his aduanc'd plumes," and pensively regards his aspirations "To be Count Malvolio." What a perfect parody of the airs and graces of the pushing middle classes censured by Hamlet as treading on the very heels of courtly fashion! Malvolio proceeds to an imaginative picture of his future life as Count: he fondles in prospect the folds of a "branch'd Veluet gowne": he cultivates an eye of Jove to threaten and command a much-subdued Sir Toby, while the real Sir Toby, hidden in the box tree, doubles his fists in prospect; he briefly pays Sir Andrew his disrespects. Then he comes upon the letter. He stoops most elegantly, picks it up elegantly, and elegantly considers the handwriting. He breaks the seal, first begging permission of the wax. (Like Osric, he undoubtedly complied with his dug before he sucked it.) Reading aloud ranked as a liberal art; and Malvolio's rendition of the missive is doubtless semi-oratorical. He comments on it, with footnotes by his unseen auditors. He strikes a pose and cogitates the matter, gives thanks to "Ioue," and takes an elaborate *congé*. A perfect blend of comedy in speech and action if adequately played—a perfect expression of Malvolio's character—and any audience, like Sir Toby, would not miss "this sport for a pension of thousands to be paid from the Sophy."

The lyric style is Shakespeare's usual foil to the wit and horseplay of the more laughable scenes. In *The Merchant of Venice*, dominated by the serious characters of Antonio, Bassanio, and Portia, this high poetic style seems dominant; and the greater romanticism of the plot also occasions this: but, in *Twelfth Night*, though Orsino and Viola are often poetic in their talk, Sir Toby, Maria, and especially Feste give the dialogue a lightsome prosy bent; and, moreover, the comedy contains two of the most famous butts in all drama, Sir Andrew and Malvolio, so that the dialogue shows the poetic as distinctly secondary to a witty style in prose. Perhaps the poetry of the play can best be analyzed in Orsino's opening scene, and in the first encounter between Viola and Olivia. As befits a Duke, Orsino most of all uses rhetorical heightening. His figures are rich in metaphor and simile: music is the "food of Loue," appetite is a living thing; the excellence of the beloved is like the highest "pitch" that a falcon's flight can attain; the organs of love are "soueraigne"; music is like a breath of wind; Olivia is a "Cloystresse"; and Orsino's capacity for love is as great as the sea. He alludes to the story of Actæon and to the "rich golden shaft" of Eros; he gives an apostrophe to the "spirit of Loue"; and, in a realistic and timely hyperbole, he

242

declares that Olivia would purge the air even of the plague. The pun on "hart" and the concluding epigram supply a touch of wit; but the scene as a whole is highly serious poetry. The entire passage, moreover, is in blank verse, and its stately rhythm is enriched with complexly interwoven alliterations of *s* and the vowels, contrasting with other sounds. There is also subtle onomatopoeia both in the melody and in the meter: "That strain agen, it had a dying fall," and "O spirit of Loue, how quicke and fresh art thou." In short, the scene, like any lyric, depends largely on figures of comparison and of sound; and Shakespeare shows a subtle mastery of both. The tempo, as indicated by the slurrings required by the meter, seems—as in most Elizabethan plays—fairly fast, but with slower interludes for emphasis;[20] and this systole and diastole of changing speed weaves a subtle pattern in the lines—if only actors would heed it.

The love-making between Olivia and Viola in Act I, scene v, is an artful stepchild of the lyric style; for Viola, who, as Orsino's proxy, is supposed to say the pretty speeches, does not really wish to win Olivia for him. To be sure, she uses many figures, and the proper kinds—metaphor, simile, and allusion —but some are overstrained and artificial and many had been made trite by contemporary sonneteers. The passage opens with a ten-lines-long conceit comparing Viola's memorized love speech to a sermon; and some of the following metaphors, though intellectually clever, do not give the right emotional tone for amorous discourse: love-making is prosaically compared to a business negotiation; Olivia's veil is a curtain before a picture; her complexion is likened to cochineal dye. Nature is somewhat tritely personified; and Olivia's inventory of her charms is almost a parody of the waning sonnet craze. Trite also are the hyperboles, "groanes that thunder loue," and "sighes of fire." Indeed, quite properly, almost half the lines are prose, and the only very musical passage is Viola's threat to build a "willow Cabine" at Olivia's gate and sing there songs of disappointed love. As in Pope's verse, the in-

[20] See Appendix, p. 264.

243

cisive rhetoric of parallel structure and anaphora largely takes the place of music. In fact, the passage is intellectual rather than sincerely emotional, for it is taken up with a love affair which neither the lady nor the lover's proxy really cares to pursue. *Twelfth Night* is too much concerned with loves of a merely prudential cast to have much lyricism outside the songs of Feste. Surely, this is an answer to any who would say that Shakespeare sacrificed his dramatic effects to his poetic.

The fourth style in the play, the witty, dominates most of the scenes and shows great variety of techniques, for nothing wears out faster than a joke, and so good comedy must continually change the devices by which it tickles the audience to laughter. One of the passages of purest wit, with little admixture of comic action or poetry or exposition, is the short introduction to Act II, scene iii, between Sir Toby and Sir Andrew:

To. Approach Sir *Andrew*: not to bee a bedde after midnight, is to be vp betimes, and *Deliculo surgere*, thou know'st.
And. Nay by my troth I know not: but I know, to be vp late, is to be vp late.
To. A false conclusion: I hate it as an vnfill'd Canne. To be vp after midnight, and to go to bed then is early: so that to go to bed after midnight, is to goe to bed betimes. Does not our liues consist of the foure Elements?
And. Faith so they say, but I thinke it rather consists of eating and drinking.
To. Th'art a scholler; let vs therefore eate and drinke.

Sir Toby beckons the somewhat wobbly Sir Andrew out upon the stage and opens with a paradox and an erudite allusion to the standard Latin grammar of the day. Sir Andrew sottishly replies and makes a parody on the metaphysical axiom that "whatever is, is." Sir Toby, still in a learned mood, at once picks it up as if it were the third statement, or "conclusion," of a syllogism in logic, and with an incongruous simile declares that he hates bad logic as he does "an vnfill'd Canne." He then proceeds to a ridiculous parody of a logical (in this case, illogical) syllogism, and concludes with an epigram that is at

244

once paradoxical and ironic: "to go to bed after midnight, is to goe to bed betimes." Since the early Middle Ages, logic had been a regular part of elementary education immediately following Latin grammar; and any Elizabethan of the least intellectual pretensions would understand the parody.[21] Then, in a *non sequitur* completely without transition, Sir Toby turns to the learned field of alchemy; and, using the catechistical method of the Church, he asks whether "our liues" do not "consist of foure Elements,"—earth, air, fire, and water—which were thought to make up all matter. "Our liues" has an obvious double meaning: it signifies either all living things, or lifetime before death. Sir Toby uses it in the former, but Sir Andrew, who cannot fathom his friend's subtleties, mistakes it for the latter, and remarks that life "rather consists of eating and drinking." Such a misunderstanding, of course, constitutes dramatic irony. Sir Toby compliments him sarcastically on his learning, and comes for once to a truly logical conclusion: "let vs therefore eate and drinke." These dozen lines which initiate the revelry contain nearly all of the finer species of wit: parody, allusion, *non sequitur*, paradox (combined with oxymoron), epigram, incongruous simile, double meaning, veiled sarcasm, and dramatic irony; and most of them appear in several lights and aspects. The command of such varied effects as custom cannot stale is evidence of artistic mastery. This little passage is a tour de force, and its writer was indeed a virtuoso.

Quite as comic but quite different is the initial scene in Act III between Viola and Feste. When the jester talked with Sir Andrew, he palmed off on him mere nonsense; but Viola was an interlocutor worthy of his steel; and, by a process that the Elizabethans called "mistaking the word," he twists each statement that she makes into another meaning. He is a slick and slippery prestidigitator of language, and, like Polonius, can run a poor phrase through all its paces. He juggles with double meaning, paradox, and odd allusion, and in his own practice

---

[21] See A. H. Gilbert, "Logic in Elizabethan Drama," *Studies in Philology*, XXXII, 527 *et seq.*; and T. W. Baldwin, *Shakspere's Small Latine and Less Greeke* (Urbana, Ill., 1944).

shows that "wordes are growne so false, I am loath to proue reason with them"—a touch of cynical satire that the Elizabethans would have appreciated. He will give Viola no direct answer until she tips him, and then winds up with a fine parody of courtly euphemisms. (He will not use "Element" because it is "ouer worne.") In the dialogue previously analyzed between Sir Toby and Sir Andrew, learned parody incomprehensible to one speaker was the foundation of the comic effect, and the other figures of speech were merely for variety. Here the foundation is an intentionally twisted double meaning in which both speaker and hearer enjoy the joke along with the audience, and the parody and other figures are merely secondary. Thus Shakespeare can use one or another comic device for his major effect and use the rest for variety and secondary support. The one gives unity, the others piquancy. This is the eternal problem of all artistic styles, to maintain the basic singleness of tone and yet avoid the monotony of wearisome repetition. This ideal is possible only to the master of many effects; and such was William Shakespeare.

Shakespeare's variations of style, however, do not, as Professor Hart implies, exist merely for their own sake, like a pretty tune. The comedy in the Sir Andrew scenes depends largely on his ignorance; in the Feste scenes, largely upon his shrewdness: thus, the very type of the wit is an adjunct of the character who speaks and often also of the character to whom it is addressed. Orsino's lyric style is more effective and sincere than Viola's when she woos Olivia for him, because Orsino's love is more sincere and so does not seek refuge in trite or artificial phrases. Shakespeare's styles are indeed the limbs and outward flourishes of the very characters themselves; and, as the previous chapters show, their metaphors and allusions reflect their several educations and past lives. In *Twelfth Night*, the dominant style is comedy per se, and it runs the whole gamut from suppressed guffaws at Sir Andrew's dancing to the intellectual relish of Feste's wit and the irony of Viola's somewhat labored adorations. The expository passages are only a necessary evil, and the poetry but an incident proper to dukes and their love affairs.

Most of the scenes are a daring commixture of comic techniques and styles in which the playwright relieves the ludicrous with the witty and these in turn with comic intrigue and action— truly a tour de force of styles.

Of the five artistic elements of drama, the last—the theme —is a sort of summation of the others in their interrelationship. In a serious play, as in life, certain types of people must react to a given situation in certain definite ways; the setting must have helped to produce this situation, and helped to make the people what they are; and the styles in which they speak and move and gesture are the expressions of their several characters reacting to these situations. In short, in true comedy and tragedy, as distinct from farce and melodrama which ignore the realities of life, all five elements of the play are interwoven; and the fundamental principles of human nature and of cause and effect must be exemplified in this interweaving. Otherwise the action would run counter to nature and so be unconvincing. If unity be the essential basis of true art, furthermore, then a comedy or a tragedy should illustrate some single principle, some basic human urge which works itself out, as it would in life, variously in the various major characters according to their several situations and personalities. If, on the other hand, one sees no coherence within the plot or between plot and character, then the play (as in the case of farce and melodrama) has no fundamental meaning; and the majority of critics, therefore, who follow the Romantic interpretation of *Twelfth Night* and see in it no more reality of motive than in a masquerade, thereby reduce the play to the level of farce; and, indeed, the theme of *Twelfth Night* is a subject usually cursorily dismissed.

Love is, of course, the subject of most comedies, and Bathurst,[22] Professor Craig,[23] and others have so interpreted *Twelfth Night*. Certainly Olivia has manifold wooers, and there are also the courtships of Maria and Viola; but, if love were the theme, would not at least one of these courtships, as in *Much Ado*, follow normal Elizabethan convention? But in each

[22] *Twelfth Night* (ed. Furness var.), p. 380.
[23] Hardin Craig, *Shakespeare* (New York, 1931), p. 309.

case, the girl, unaided and unadvised, chooses the man, an unusual procedure in actual Elizabethan life. In *Twelfth Night*, neither father nor brother nor next of kin bestows the hand of Viola, Maria, or Olivia. Moreover, is it really love in any strict sense between Maria and Sir Toby, or between Olivia and most of her wooers? Immediate practical considerations seem rather to be the mainspring of their courtship; Olivia herself in her final choice is governed by such motives and by accident as well as by her passion. Viola is perhaps a Juliet in the play; but it certainly lacks a Romeo. Indeed, the whole comedy has a worldly-wise and humorous tone far removed from *Love's Labour's Lost* and *Romeo and Juliet*, and comparable rather to *The Shrew*.[24] It has no balcony scene, and its purple passages are built upon parody and satire rather than on passion: the guying of Sir Andrew and of Malvolio, and Viola's mock duel. The two conspiracies against Malvolio and against Viola that comprise most of the plot are hatched, partly for the fun they give Sir Toby, but mainly to secure his future position in the household, and incidentally to secure Maria and Fabyan and Feste too.

The plot, to be sure, centers in the problem of Olivia's marriage; but most sensible Elizabethans would have agreed with the Countess of Champaigne that marriage and love were unrelated. Marriage as an institution concerned the direct continuing of a legitimate family line, the safeguarding of its interests and its future; and every member of the family, down to the humblest servitor, had an interest to protect more or less identical with the general family interest. This was the natural development in the Middle Ages and the Renaissance of the old tribal life; economic instability and pressure forced the members of the group to depend on one another. Of course, the Elizabethans would think of Olivia's marriage in terms of such family policy, and of the interests of the individuals in the family whose future it would govern. This is not the story of a Juliet's or an Orlando's love, its realization and the conse-

---

[24] J. W. Draper, " 'Kate the Curst,' " *Journal of Nervous and Mental Diseases*, LXXXIX, 757 *et seq.*

quences, but of the very realistic struggles and intrigues over the betrothal of a rich Countess, whose selection of a mate determines the future of all the major and most of the minor characters. Had she taken Orsino, her normal choice, the differing hopes of Viola, of Sir Toby, and of all her lovers other than the Duke would have been wrecked. The choice of Sir Andrew would have disappointed the other lovers, ruined Malvolio, and ultimately herself. Her choice of Malvolio would have been equally disastrous. This is not a play of passion, but of marriage in its most prudential aspects, the very antithesis of *Romeo and Juliet*. Olivia suffers little, and we have no great compassion for her. In fact, her chief difficulty is in evading unwelcome importunities. The tone of the play is certainly not tragic, nor even romantic; indeed, it is a comedy of manners, realistic on the whole and genially satiric.

Perhaps the theme of *Twelfth Night* is youth versus age, with Viola, Sebastian, Olivia, Orsino, Sir Andrew, and perhaps Maria representing youth without parental guidance, Sir Toby and Malvolio representing age—also without guidance. Youth, except in the case of Sir Andrew, wins its way and rightly so, for it is a better way than that of scheming age. But if this were indeed the theme, the period of life of the characters should be more emphasized; and Olivia, who is young, schemes much more cleverly than Sir Toby or Malvolio. In 1877, Furnivall noted "the shadow of death and distress across the sunshine" of the play: Olivia's father and brother are just dead; presumably Viola's parents are also dead, and she and Sebastian have just been saved only by a miracle. Youth and old age and death enter into the play, as they must in all depictions of life; but none of them governs the course of the plot or dictates its outcome.

Twelfth Night is rather the comedy of the social struggles of the time: Orsino wishes to fulfill his duty as head of the house and prolong his family line by a suitable marriage; Maria wants the security and dignity of marriage to a gentleman—a difficult accomplishment in view of her lack of dowry. Feste and Sir Toby want the security of future food and lodging;

Viola and Sebastian hope to reassume their doffed coronets; and Sir Andrew and Malvolio are arrant social climbers, who long to acquire a gentility that neither can possess. In short, this is Shakespeare's play of social security; and, in time of peace, marriage was the chief means by which this prize was gained or lost—one's own marriage, or the marriage of one's friend, over-lord, or master. The universal urge of all humanity is said to be survival; and this in turn resolves itself into food, lodging, and a mate. Every important character in the play is scheming for one or all of these: even Feste is looking to his future when he runs away to court the Duke who seems about to wed his mis-tress; and Fabyan in making Malvolio ridiculous is paying the steward back for denouncing his bearbaiting to Olivia. Every major action in the plot is governed by this urge; and the con-clusion shows all the characters with whom the audience would sympathize rewarded with as much certainty of future as one can hope for in this world.

The changes that Shakespeare made from his source in Riche's story give definite support to the theory that he intended social security to be the theme of the comedy. In Riche, Silla (Viola) has the protection of a royal father at whose court Apolonius (Orsino) has been visiting, and she deliberately fol-lows her lover to Constantinople; nothing of this appears in Shakespeare. In Riche, Julina (Olivia) is a widow, and as such does not occupy the uncertain social status of an unmarried young heiress without protection of a father or a brother; in Shakespeare, Olivia has only Sir Toby, who is more of a danger than a protection. In Riche, Silvio (Sebastian) is not ship-wrecked, and leaves home merely to seek his errant sister. Riche's story, therefore, is merely a love romance: Julina's marriage to Silvio had no apparent motive of social security on either side, nor did Silla's marriage to Apolonius. Thus Shake-speare's interest in the theme of social security seems to account for his major changes from his source. This reconstituted plot requires a group of characters who will show the dangers of Olivia's position, a persistent noble suitor who will not be gain-said, a presumptuous menial who aspires to be Count, and a self-seeking uncle who (as was common in that age) insists on a suitor calculated to his own advantage. Thus the main plot concerning Olivia's lovers (suggested in part by the conventional action of Italian comedy) was necessary to illustrate this social theme. Likewise, the shipwreck of Viola and Sebastian, and the seeming fact that they are orphans bring into their lives an insecurity that was not in Riche's story.

In the Introduction to his *Twelfth Night*, Kittredge remarks: "The significance of a study of sources lies in the opportunity it gives to see Shakespeare at work"; and, if the foregoing interpretation of the play be correct, one can reconstruct somewhat the steps by which Shakespeare conceived of the play, starting with Riche and with the universal theme of security that the uncertainties of a transitional age must have made especially arresting. This theme required, as has been shown, the revisions and additions to Riche's plot that Shakespeare made, and theme and plot together fixed the personalities of the characters: the Duke must be amorous but too dominating for Olivia and yet attractive enough for Viola; Viola and Sebastian must be charming and romantic; Malvolio must be an efficient but presuming servant; Sir Toby's part in the plot requires his genial cynicism and self-seeking disregard for his niece's future; Sir Andrew could be only a fool to linger so long in a hopeless suit; and, above all, Olivia herself must be the clever, independent woman of the age, old for her years but definitely in love. Some of these characters approximate well-known stage types: Viola and Sebastian, the romantic lover; Olivia, like Beatrice, the independent woman; Sir Toby, perhaps a sort of *miles gloriosus* resting at home on his laurels. The setting of the play, a generalized realism of the contemporary Renaissance, and the style of each scene, must follow as essential corollaries; and thus the composition of *Twelfth Night* appears, not as a fantastic accident, but as a well-wrought comedy of manners, as inevitable in its whole and in its parts—in plot, character, setting, style, and theme—as Aristotle himself could have desired.

The theme of social security appears elsewhere in Shakespeare. In a corporate, national sense, it is the theme of the political tragedies such as *Macbeth* and *King Lear*; and it more or less underlay the earlier history plays. In the comedies, moreover, various characters here and there seek to protect their respective futures, but this theme is sporadic and implicit rather than general throughout a given play. Bassanio, for example, seeks marriage largely because it is the obvious, if not the only, way to recoup his fallen fortunes; but certainly Antonio, in signing the bond, does not seek social security. Petruchio is providing for his future and that of his family line when he marries and tames Kate; but, until the cure is safely done, his choice of a wife does not suggest future security. Benedick also is taking something of a chance; and Romeo certainly never thinks of security at all. These marriages are either very daring or most romantic or both; and the prudential motive that governed such matters in actual Elizabethan life hardly appear in them. Even Orlando and Rosalind, who are in a parlous way, with no visible means of support, do not espouse each other for any practical reason: a kind Providence at the end of the comedy luckily restores the lady's father to his domains, and so provides cake and honey for their future days. Indeed, this theme of social security allies *Twelfth Night* less with the more carefree and romantic comedies that go before than with the serious plays that follow—with *Macbeth*, written on the security of a state governed by God's Anointed as opposed to the anarchy of a regicide-usurper's rule;[25] with *King Lear*, written on the security of an undivided realm as opposed to the ruin of disunion.[26] In the contemporary problem plays, this same theme appears: in *Measure for Measure*, the Duke's announced object is to secure his dominions against growing lawlessness; and in *All's Well That Ends Well*, Helena, like Maria, seeks and finally wins the security of a noble husband.

Indeed, this theme was most appropriate to the Elizabethan stage, for the old families, whose sons crowded to the court and to the law clubs and so to the theaters, were suffering from a

[25] J. W. Draper, "*Macbeth* as a Compliment to James I," *Englische Studien*, LXIII, 207 *et seq.*

[26] *Idem*, "The Occasion of *King Lear*," *Studies in Philology*, XXXIV, 176 *et seq.*

sharp decline—a political decline in the face of rising royal power that, through the law courts and the civil service, was strangling their feudal privileges, an economic decline in the face of a rising merchant class enriched in foreign trade. The landed aristocracy, moreover, were traditionally burdened with wide family obligations, obligations to tenants and vassals, and the ancient custom of keeping open house to travelers. Thus, they sank deeper and deeper into debt, and, in fact, for all their old castles and broad acres, were hardly better off than Viola and Sebastian and Sir Toby. A theme, therefore, so timely and so striking, especially to such an audience, could hardly fail of its effect; and its realism must have been as obvious as the theme of Ibsen's *Doll's House* was to the generation for which that play was written. In *Twelfth Night*, the great nobles, Orsino and Olivia, are not affected by this economic strain; to them social security is merely a matter of providing suitable heirs to the family name and fortune and enjoying happiness in wedlock. Some years later, in *Timon*, Shakespeare worked out to its full conclusion this theme of social security, or rather insecurity, and showed the ruin of a noble line through economic pressure.[27] *Twelfth Night* then is a play on social security in the family, and from this, Shakespeare stepped upward to social security in the state; but the theme is not carried to the bitter end as it is in *Macbeth* and *King Lear* and *Timon*: Orsino and Olivia are too permanently and safely affluent, and their respective marriages provide something of this affluence for their spouses and also for Maria, Sir Toby, and Feste.

The present interpretation of *Twelfth Night* finds the action of the play a complex but well-integrated unity with the minor plots dependent on the major in both commencement and conclusion, and with the episodes developing on the whole naturally and reasonably from the initial situation, from the characters, and from one another. The personalities are highly diversified both in humor and in social types; the part each plays would have seemed to an Elizabethan audience either

---

[27] J. W. Draper, "The Theme of *Timon of Athens*," *M.L.R.*, XXIX, 20 *et seq.*

realistically motivated or so glamourously romantic as to be imaginatively acceptable. The methods of characterization are as diverse as the characters themselves: the personalities express their traits in talk, gesture, and action, in physique, age, and humor, and also appear in the attitude of others toward them. The setting is "Illyria," not a Land of Nowhere (indeed an actual region on contemporary maps), but so little known to the Elizabethans that it could be used to reflect the generalized conditions of the Renaissance, its elegance and brilliance, and its problems of social and economic change. The style of the play is expository, or lyrical, or witty, as the particular scene required—some characters pithy in speech, some elaborate or prolix, as they would be in life. The theme is social security, generally attained through marriage; for security in that age, as today, was generally an economic matter, and the wealth that gave economic safety was usually gained (or was supposed to be, at least) by inheritance or family alliance. Thus, three pairs of heroes and heroines achieve their desires, and the action at last slows down to a static equilibrium in which all who deserve it live happily ever after. The play is all of a piece; the threads are perfectly interwoven; each character does what such a person might be expected to do, and this is also what he should do to further the plot; and all their careers illustrate the comic solution of a single significant theme—significant in all ages but especially in the changes and chances of Shakespeare's time. Above all, the laughter of the piece, supplied partly by the action, partly by the style, arises without strain from the plot and the characters, and is expressed in a swift and brilliant dialogue replete with epigram, allusion, and fine ironies, somewhat elusive to the modern ear. Such is the comedy of *Twelfth Night*.

The interpretation of a masterpiece is clearly the most important thing about it, for this interpretation is, or ought to be, an expression of the very meaning that a great mind intended to convey, not a mere reading in by some critic, distant in time and place, of his own ideas. The metrics, dates, sources, and other facts incidental to Shakespeare's plays have been methodically and scientifically studied, but all these painfully collected data —and indeed all scientific methods—are generally cast aside when the modern critic comes to the ultimately important business of interpreting a given play. He is very likely to ignore entirely the two most pertinent types of fact: the inner life of the characters expressed in the psychology of the time, and their outer life, expressed in terms of the social idiom that Shakespeare and his audience were used to. Without these data to guide him, he wanders fancy-free over the field, strewing obiter dicta up and down, deciding on nice matters of character and theme with no attempt to collect the essential evidence, or even to footnote from contemporary writers his statements on disputable points. As a consequence, Shakespearean interpretation shows a maze of inconsistency, and the serious student reaches a hopeless feeling that either the plays mean nothing (and therefore Lamb's *Tales* are practically as good!) or that one meaning is as good as another (as if the theory that the earth is flat were quite as true as the belief that it is round). Thus the Shakespeareans have reduced Shakespeare to a mere *Arabian Nights* teller of stories, with occasional purple passages of wit or poetry. In fact, a whole school of modern criticism, stemming from Professor Stoll, asserts that neither Shakespeare, nor any other dramatist, has any serious meaning: playwrights are mere manipulators of theatric tricks that play on our emotions, and, thus comedy and farce are practically one. The present writer, on the contrary, makes bold to state that the major plays of Shakespeare actually possess the reality (and the Elizabethan realism) that the Elizabethans themselves found in them, and that the plots express deep human motives worked out according to true principles of life. In short, they are what the world has always called great drama. To demonstrate this belief, regarding one play at least, he has tried to gather all pertinent materials both in and outside *Twelfth Night*, has tried to marshal these materials with logical nicety, and has set them forth as clearly as he can in a systematic treatise. His conclusions show plot, character, and theme so perfectly fitted in an artistic unity that each part helps to prove his conclusions in the rest;

and he ventures to set forth the whole as an approximation of Shakespeare's meaning in the play. At times, he has himself been surprised at the results to which the evidence led, just as one sometimes picks up a piece in a picture puzzle, hardly expecting it to fit in and yet finding that it does. He takes no credit for the consequent interpretation of the whole; for, if there be credit, it is (like the interpretation itself) Shakespeare's. Indeed, he hopes and believes that the conclusions of this present volume are not the child of his own ingenuity, but of the supreme artist's creative imagination.

Appendix A

DATE, SEASON, AND TIME
ANALYSIS OF THE PLAY

DESPITE the absence of early quartos, the date of *Twelfth Night* is rather well established. The *Diary* of the barrister John Manningham records a performance early in 1602 (February 2, 1601, O.S.); but, as the "many contemporary allusions"[1] attest the play's popularity, this may well have been a revival. At all events, it provides a *terminus ad quem*. In the other direction, Maria's reference to the "new Map" may well refer to that appended to Hakluyt's *Voyages* in 1599; but it might have been termed "new" for the following year or two. The publication of "O Mistress Mine" in 1599 may signify only that the song antedates the comedy. More important is the evidence of Feste's role, which was clearly written for Robert Armin, who joined the Company in the late spring or early summer of 1600.[2] As Shakespeare was composing the part of Touchstone in *As You Like It* for him between then and August, one infers that *Twelfth Night* must have come somewhat later; and the name Orsino supports such a theory, for, at that time, Virginio Orsino, Duke of Bracciano and one of the foremost gentlemen of Europe, was Florentine ambassador at the English court, and Elizabeth entertained him royally on Twelfth-Night Eve, January 1601.[3] Thus the date of composition would seem to be the preceding fall or early winter. Internal evidence of versification and style approximately confirms this date. The proportion of prose does not differ greatly from that of *As You Like It* and *Much Ado About Nothing*,

---

[1] J. Q. Adams, *Life of Shakespeare* (New York, 1925), p. 292.

[2] T. W. Baldwin, "Shakespeare's Jester," *M.L.N.*, XXXIX, 447 *et seq.*

[3] G. Sarrazin, "Chronologie von Shakespeares Dichtungen," *Shakespeare Jahrbuch*, XXXII, 168.

which are generally placed about this time; the number of pentameter lines, to be sure, is somewhat high; but the percentage of feminine endings agrees with *As You Like It*, and does not greatly differ from *Much Ado* or *Hamlet*. The amount of enjambment is somewhat less than in these three plays, but the greater number of speeches ending within the line offsets this difference. In short, *Twelfth Night* would seem immediately to precede *Hamlet*; and, if one divides Shakespeare's work into four periods, it would be the final piece (should one say the *climax*?) of his second, or comic, period, which includes *Much Ado About Nothing, As You Like It*, and, somewhat earlier, the Falstaff plays. For all its wit and roistering, the significance of its theme, the close structure of its plot, and the finesse of its character portrayal make it a natural transition from comedy of manners to a great tragedy of Renaissance court intrigue and dynastic crisis such as *Hamlet*. The interpretation of the play as mere senseless reveling makes it incongruous in Shakespeare's dramatic evolution.

As in *A Midsummer Night's Dream*,[4] the action seems to take place in May. When Maria warns Feste that the Countess may turn him off because of his long absence, he flippantly replies: "for turning away, let summer bear it out";[5] and this suggests a setting in May or June, for otherwise summer would hardly mitigate his dismissal. Fabyan's facetious remark at Sir Andrew's entrance with the challenge, "More matter for a May morning,"[6] definitely implies the month of May; and Sir Toby's mention of the sign of the zodiac, Taurus,[7] suggests a date shortly before the twenty-first of that month. May, furthermore, was a sanguine time of the year,[8] appropriate to three love affairs and to Olivia's casting aside of mourning. The title of the play, therefore, would seem to refer, not to the time of year it represents but more probably to the occasion of

[4] J. W. Draper, "The Date of *A Midsommer Nights Dreame*," *M.L.N.*, Vol. LII, p. 266 *et seq.*

[5] *Twelfth Night*, I. iv. 21.

[6] *Ibid.*, III. iv. 145.

[7] *Ibid.*, I. iii. 129.

[8] Sir Thomas Elyot, *Castell of Helth* (London, 1541), leaf 71 v.

its original performance—the Queen's Twelfth Night entertainment to regale the living Duke Orsino.[9]

But for one major inconsistency, the time analysis of the comedy presents no difficulties.[10] When the play opens, Olivia's father has been dead a year, her brother, almost as long;[11] and the Captain of Viola's vessel has been absent from Illyria for a month.[12] For over a month, Orsino has been suing for the Countess' hand; and Sir Toby has just brought Sir Andrew to Olivia's house, and in the third scene introduces him to Maria. Sometime, perhaps even before the father and the brother died, Maria has hinted to Malvolio that Olivia "did affect" him;[13] and her own angling for Sir Toby has been going on long enough so that Feste and Sir Toby himself are shortly cognizant of it.[14] In short, three of Olivia's wooers began their efforts before the curtain rose; and Maria also had made up her mind. Only the Viola-Orsino and the Viola-Sebastian-Olivia love affairs are shown completely on the stage. But, apparently little of importance happened in the preplay, for, at the rising of the curtain, neither Maria nor any of Olivia's wooers has advanced in their several suits, and the first scene shows Orsino still sighing and still repulsed.

In Act I, scene ii, Viola has just been shipwrecked; she decides to seek service with Orsino; she goes to the Captain's house, is outfitted in men's clothes, proceeds to the Duke's palace, and has been there three days before the opening of scene iv.[15] The time between these two scenes must, therefore, be at least four days and cannot be much more. In scene i, Orsino heard Curio's report on his bootless embassy; in scene iv, he sends Viola in hopes of better success; and, in scene v, Viola arrives, pleads his cause, and inadvertently inspires Olivia's love. Even if one suppose that her journey to the house of the

---

[9] One wonders whether the play could possibly have been written with an oblique diplomatic purpose. Could Olivia's refusal of Orsino express Elizabeth's refusal of some suit of the real Orsino?

[10] Cf. P. A. Daniel in *Transactions of the New Shakespeare Society* (1877–79), p. 173.

[11] *Twelfth Night*, I. ii. 41.   [12] *Ibid.*, I. ii. 33 *et seq.*   [13] *Ibid.*, II. v. 25–26.

[14] This is the point of Sir Toby's making Sir Andrew "accost" Maria (I. iii. 51, *et seq.*). See also I. v. 26 *et seq.* and II. iii. 173–74.

[15] *Ibid.*, I. iv. 4.

Countess requires only an hour or two, one can hardly imagine that Act I consumes less than four days, and not more than five or six. Meanwhile, Sir Toby and Sir Andrew are still carousing in Olivia's hall, supposedly pressing the latter's suit. In Act I, scene iii, Sir Andrew is persuaded to stay "a month longer"; but, as he was easily subject to persuasion, this does not prove that Act V, during which he appears still lingering at Olivia's, must be within a month of Act I, scene iii.

In Act II, Sebastian, having been saved by Antonio from the shipwreck, has been sojourning with his rescuer, is apparently at the latter's house near the seashore; and, in scene i, they both set out for Orsino's court—or at least, for the city where he resides. This must take place about the time of Viola's embassy to Olivia, for, in the scene that follows, Malvolio overtakes the returning Viola and tries to return the ring. In Act I, scene v, Olivia had told Viola to come back soon and report on Orsino's acceptance of the rejection; and, therefore, Viola's return in Act III, scene i can hardly be more than a day later, and therefore Act II cannot take up at the most more than some twenty-four hours.

The low-life scenes give additional evidence of this rapid course of action. In Act II, scene iii, the revelers in Olivia's hall come into open conflict with Malvolio. This is the evening of the day of Viola's embassy (I.v), for Maria remarks that the Countess, as a consequence of Viola's visit, is "much out of quiet." This scene starts the plan to gull Malvolio who seemingly finds the letter the next day (II. v), and would, of course, change at once into the absurd garb that he thought his lady wished, so that his appearance in this panoply (III. ii, and III. iv) seems to come within twenty-four hours of that in II. iii and on the same day as II. v. Also in Act III, scene iv comes the first part of Sir Andrew's duel, interrupted by the zealous Antonio. In Act IV, scene i, the duel continues; and Sir Toby gets a broken head, which is bound up during the final scene of the play. Thus the duel episode proves that the latter part of Act III and all of Acts IV and V must take place within two or three hours or even less. In short, some four days elapse during Act I; and the rest of the action must follow within a day or two. In fact, Antonio declares that Act II, scene i and Act V take place on the same day.[16]

This seems beautifully consistent; and the play could easily be contained within any one of the first three weeks of May, but two statements in Act V disagree flatly with all of it. Antonio says that he has known Sebastian for "three months"; and, as their acquaintance seems to have begun when he saved the youth from the shipwreck, this statement places a three-month interval between Act I, scene ii, and the conclusion of the comedy. The Duke, moreover, mentions Viola's having served him for "so long"; and this clearly implies a period of more than four days since she came to his court. All this reminds one of the conflicting evidence on Hamlet's age;[17] and scholars have found no solution to the difficulty, unless one accept the theory of double time duration.[18] The linking of the scenes and the placing of at least the first three acts in May incline one to accept the shorter interval for the action. Of course, Shakespeare's audience would not work out the time schedule of the piece; and the playwright may have mentioned three months merely to make more probable Antonio's affection for Sebastian and Orsino's growth of love for Viola. In short, though Shakespeare does not designate hours or days of the week or month, as he does in *Romeo and Juliet*,[19] yet he seems to have conceived the comedy as compressed within a few days' time and as taking place, quite aptly, in the merry month of May.

[16] *Ibid.*, V. i. 97.

[17] J. W. Draper, The *"Hamlet"* of Shakespeare's Audience (Durham, N.C., 1938), pp. 193 *et seq.*

[18] See A. C. Sprague, *Shakespeare and the Audience* (Cambridge, Mass., 1935), pp. 47 *et seq.*

[19] See J. W. Draper, "Shakespeare's 'Star-Crossed Lovers,'" *R.E.S.*, XV, 16 *et seq.*

Appendix B

"SEBASTIAN OF MESSALINE"

SEBASTIAN and Viola in Shakespeare's *Twelfth Night* are twice mentioned as coming from "Messaline"; and, therefore, this name can hardly be an error of the text, nor can the dramatist have introduced it without some sort of purpose. Sebastian tells Antonio (II. i. 15): "My father was that Sebastian of Messaline whom I know you have heard of"; and, in the last act, Viola, answering Sebastian's questions concerning her identity, declares herself "Of Messaline: Sebastian was my father." As the former of these quotations implies, the elder Sebastian of Messaline must have been a person of note; he seems to have been acquainted with the Duke Orsino (I. ii. 28–29); and the Duke himself vouches for the noble status of the family (V. i. 256). The father of Viola and Sebastian, therefore, was apparently the feudal lord of Messaline—presumably a place within reach of Illyria (Croatia) by sea. Illyria was an actual locality noted in contemporary geographies, and the Orsini were (and still are) a noble Italian family, but editors and critics seem to agree that "There is no such town" as Messaline. This is surprising, for London was full of men who knew Italy, and Shakespeare took some pains with his Italian local color.

In Lombardy, just north of the Æmelian Road some five miles east of Modena is the old town of Manzolino. With this spelling, it appears in the 1612 edition of Ortelius' geography;[1] in a thirteenth-century life of St. Dominic[2] appears the form *Mensoline*; and thirteenth-century Latin supplies the variants *Manzolinum*, *Mansolinum*, and *Manselino*.[3] Except for the persistent -*n*- in the first syllable, two of these forms closely approach Shakespeare's *Messaline*; and, if Shakespeare

---

[1] A. Ortelius, *Theatro del Mondo* (1612), map No. 84.

[2] F. W. Manning (ed.), *The Life of Saint Dominic*, Harvard University Press (Cambridge, Mass., 1944), p. 276.

[3] *Ibid.*, p. 356.

had seen the name printed or written with this -*n*- abbreviated as a tilda (which might have been blurred or overlooked), or if he had heard a foreigner pronounce the word with the -*n*- assimilated by nasalization to the preceding vowel, he might easily have left it out. *Ergo*, perhaps his *Messaline*.

If Shakespeare seriously considered the geographical background of this play, then Viola and Sebastian might be thought of as setting out from Messaline down the valley of the Po to the Adriatic and thence crossing that sea to be shipwrecked on the Illyrian coast. Of course, they might have been bound for any Dalmatian, Greek, or south Italian port. The improbability, however, of a Roman Orsino in Slavic Croatia makes one doubt whether the dramatist really tried for geographic consistency, especially in this romantic part of the plot: probably he wanted merely an Italian place name for local color, and he remembered Messaline and used it; or perhaps he made it up, and had no actual place in mind.

Appendix C

SPEECH TEMPO IN ACT I

THE proper tempo of Shakespeare's lines not only is basic to their oral interpretation but also furnishes a clue as to the emotion and the character of the speaker. Obviously, moreover, tempo throws light on the use of other modes of emphasis, sound-volume, and inflection; for, if Shakespeare points up a certain emphatic speech or phrase by a change in tempo, he is less likely to depend heavily on other means. Tempo is a guide to matters not only of style but also of character. In Act I of *Othello*, for example, the weakness and uncertainty of Roderigo give his speech a hesitancy expressed in its somewhat nervous staccato;[1] whereas Othello's deliberate utterance expresses his unhurried self-possession; and Cassio's courtly training leaves him rarely at a loss for the quick and apt *mot juste*, and his talk is consequently lively but *legato*. The oral interpretation of Shakespeare has been all too subservient to the caprice of actors and the box-office sense of coaches and directors; and so the playwright's own intentions have been ignored—as if the greatest dramatist of modern times hadn't enough sense of "theater" to know the most effective use of his materials!

A composer, by writing expression marks such as *presto* or *accel.* on his score, indicates tempo to the performers; and Shakespeare, likewise, by five different sorts of evidence has indicated rather clearly the proper speed for most passages. The first and most important of these types of evidence consists of slurrings or syncopations made apparent by the meter. In verse, such evidence is the commonest; but it does not apply to prose. One must, moreover, take into account differences in pronunciation and speech habits between the Elizabethans and

---

[1] J. W. Draper, "Speech-Tempo in Act I of *Othello*," *West Virginia University Bulletin, Philological Papers*, V (1947), 49–58.

ourselves. For example, the line, "Methinks I feel this youth's per|fec|ti|ons"[2] is a perfect blank-verse line with the last word pronounced in four syllables; and the Elizabethans in slow speech commonly rendered -*tion* and -*sion* in two syllables. Thus, the slurring of these endings into one syllable would indicate at least some speed; and their full pronunciation in two (as in this passage) implies slow tempo. The same sort of argument fits "de|ni|al" (I. v. 250), which must be slow, and "gra|cious" (I. v. 246), which must be fast. Likewise, the different treatment of the inflectional ending in "recom|pensed" (I. v. 237) and "contemnèd" (I. v. 254) supports the theory that somewhere between lines 246 and 250 the tempo slows down considerably. But to understand just how much a given slurring implies speed or the lack of it shows deliberation of address, one must know which form was nearer the norm in the speech habits of the age: the forms -*èd* and -*ci*|*ous*, for instance, were somewhat unusual, and so would imply a definitely slow speech, whereas the slurred forms in this case would not prove very great rapidity.

The second test for tempo is also slurring, but apparent not so much in the meter as in the spellings and apostrophes used in the First Folio. Such forms presumably arose less from Shakespeare's manuscript or from the actor's usage, than from the compositor who set the type; for Elizabethan printers varied the spellings of words to "justify" the right-hand margin of their text (i.e., to make the lines come out even). But lines of verse would rarely need to be justified, for very few of them reach to the right-hand margin. Some unusual word forms such as "in't" (I. v. 180) must surely have arisen from the playwright's purpose and actor's pronunciation rather than from the printer's caprice; and " 'tis" (I. v. 182) and "question's" (for "question is") are almost as certain. Such abbreviations were the rule only in books intended for oral or dramatic delivery, and, therefore, they may be taken as probable indications of speed.

[2] See *Works* (ed. Aldis Wright), I. v. 280. Cf. I. i. 49. The references in this Appendix are to the Wright edition.

The third form of evidence is ellipsis, the omission of some grammatically essential part. Such an omission would generally imply speed; but Elizabethan grammar and word order were looser than ours, and some idioms, such as the omission of the relative pronoun introducing a restrictive clause, or the use of an auxiliary verb without the infinitive that should follow, were commoner than they are in present-day speech. Consequently, they are less expressive of haste. Even so, such evidence has some value. For example, Feste omits both the subject and the verb of the first short sentence of his speech: "Apt, in good faith; very apt" (I. v. 24). He seems to be talking so fast that one even wonders whether "in" should not be slurred to *i'*. Again the verb has fallen out of the aphorism that he attributes to "Quinapalus": "Better a witty fool than a foolish wit." Curio omits "to" before the infinitive "hunt" (I. i. 16); and Sir Toby leaves out the object of the verb "let" (I. iii. 57). In short, the inclusion or omission of such words, not only in verse, but also in prose, implies the intended speed of the passage.

The fourth evidence of tempo is the line-length of the verse, especially overlong lines of twelve syllables or more. Of course, this test depends on the assumption that a speaker tends to reduce a longer line to the normal speech-length by hurrying it. Act I of *Othello* bears out such an assumption; but irregularities of this sort are rarer in the earlier style of *Twelfth Night*. Probably the most interesting example is the transition between fast and slow in the passage:

I'll be sworn thou art;

Thy tongue, thy face, thy limbs, actions and spirit,
Do give thee five-fold blazon: not too fast: soft, soft!
Unless the master were the man. How now!
E | ven so quickly may one catch the plague?
Methinks I feel this youth's perfec | ti | ons . . . . . (I. v. 275–80)

"I'll," "actions," and probably "spirit," and also the twice-omitted "thy," all suggest speed in the first two lines, a speed that doubtless carries over through "blazon." Thus, the first

266

seven syllables of the overlong line in question must be fast; but "E|ven" and "perfec|ti|ons," which follow are certainly slow; and, even in the latter part of the twelve-syllable line itself, the marked pauses after "blazon," "fast," and "soft," suggest that this slowing up must have started in the latter part of the line "Do . . . . soft." In short, this particular twelve-syllable line, though it begins at a rapid pace, can hardly have been said in as short a time as a normal ten-syllable line. Better examples of speeding in an overlong line are to be found in a few lines broken between two speakers (I. ii. 1–2, and 17–18; I. v. 238 and 283). In the first three of these examples, adjacent slurs imply speed; and, in the last, the haste with which Olivia is calling Malvolio to run after Viola demands rapidity. This type of evidence, of course, applies only to metrical passages, and by itself is not too certain even there.

The foregoing types of evidence—slurrings, ellipses, and overlong lines—are all indications of fast rather than slow tempo; but their conspicuous omission where longer forms are substituted—the use of *I will* instead of *I'll*, for instance—suggest slow speech; and, occasionally, another type of phraseology indicates that the speaker must have been obliged to enunciate with marked deliberation. Shakespeare's verse generally flows (as he says) so "trippingly on the tongue" that it easily runs *prestissimo*; but occasionally a line contains such a combination of consonants and heavy vowels that it cannot be said fast, as for example: "A brother's dead love which she would keep fresh" (I. i. 31). Its ten syllables contain cacophonic combinations such as *rsd*, *t∫∫*, *dk*, and *pfr*. The pronunciation, moreover, of "re|mem|br|ance" in four syllables in the following line (Capell even spells it with an extra *-e-*) is further evidence of the slow delivery of the passage. "Methinks I feel this youth's perfec|ti|ons" (I. v. 280) seems also a clear case; "What else may hap to time I|will commit" (I. ii. 60) falls in the same category, and perhaps also Sir Toby's prose, "O knight, thou lackest a cup of canary . . . ." (I. iii. 76), and Malvolio's "Madam, yond young fellow swears he|will speak with you" (I. v. 131–32). All these lines contain not only consonantal combinations that do not lend themselves to speed but also other evidences of slow delivery.

Although the act is about two-thirds prose and the first and fourth types of proof apply only to verse, yet there is an average of about two items of evidence in every five lines; and this should constitute a considerable indication of tempo. As in Act I of *Othello*,[3] most of the evidence points to speed: in scenes i and ii, the ratio is more than five to one; in scene iii, eight to one; in scene iv, about five to one; and in scene v, over three to one. A priori, one might expect the prose scenes to be faster because they are more colloquial; and, of the two scenes that are chiefly prose, one has the greatest rapidity, but the other the least: one judges that scene v must have been very *rubato*, with great and sudden variations of speed. Even here, however, the general norm of speech was fast, as one might expect from the intimacy of the Elizabethan theater, from Hamlet's advice to the players, and from Shakespeare's own description of *Romeo and Juliet* as "two hours' traffic of our stage." Shakespeare, therefore, seems to have reserved his slower tempo for emphasis; and these slow passages will bear special scrutiny. The Duke Orsino and the Countess Olivia, like Brabantio, often speak with a deliberation that accords with their exalted stations; but one does not find the halting uncertainty of the callow Roderigo. Apparently, slower speech is not consistently used here to set off one character from another.

Most of the slower passages are short and seem to take their tempo from a character's momentary feeling, from the need of contrast, or from the need of the exposition to emphasize the passage. For instance, Olivia's vow of mourning must be made clear at once to the audience, especially the veil that she has assumed; and Valentine, therefore, after having rapidly begun the report of his tender mission (note especially seven in I. i. 26), slows down his speech as he continues: "But like a cloistress, she | will veilèd walk . . . . sad re | mem | br | ance." Here the slow rhythm arises from the needs of dramatic exposition.

[3] J. W. Draper, "Patterns of Humor and Tempo in *Othello*," *English Studies* (Groningen), XXVIII, 65 *et seq.*

In scene ii, Viola, in the midst of a rapid dialogue, as she thinks out her plan, suddenly diminishes her speed (I. ii. 55 *et seq.*):

> I'll serve this Duke:
> Thou shall present me as an | eunuch to him:
> It may be worth | thy pains; for I can sing,
> And speak to | him in many sorts of music
> That | will allow me very worth his service.
> What else may hap to time I | will commit . . . .

In quick contrast, the Captain replies with "I'll." In scene iii, Sir Toby, with slow-spoken mockery, summarizes Sir Andrew's rapid-fire passage at arms with Mistress Mary: "O knight, thou lack | est a cup of canary; when | did I see thee so put down?" And Sir Andrew replies, also in moderate tempo, with "Ne | ver," "I | have," and "I | am." Then follows a resumption of badinage *accelerando*. The slow passage, including two lines of Sir Toby and four of Sir Andrew, seems to be there for contrast. Elsewhere Sir Andrew boasts of his beautiful uniqueness, with fit, slow emphasis: "I am a fellow . . . ." (I. iii. 105)—in striking differentiation from the abbreviations and slurrings that precede and follow. Shortly after, Sir Toby—doubtless half-strangled from inward laughter—encourages Sir Andrew to dance with the unslurred emphasis of "Is it," "it was," "What shall," "were we not," and "it is"—all in contrast to Sir Andrew's interlarded " 'tis" and "that's." Such a momentary contrast of tempo between speakers in a dialogue appears also in the slow replies of Othello to Brabantio and Iago when the magnifico comes to arrest the general. The requirements of exposition and of contrast seem to explain these changes to slower rhythm.

In scene iv, the Duke, with great insistence orders Viola to go "un | to" Olivia and remain there with "fixèd foot"; and Viola, who does not relish this errand, replies with as much emphasis as a courtier might use in speaking to a Duke: "she ne | ver will admit me." The tempo seems clearly expressive of the situation and the reaction of each character to it and to each other. Such subtle effects are the very stuff of drama.

Scene v starts slowly with Maria and the Clown; but Feste's short soliloquy that follows indicates speed; and the ensuing dialogue with the Countess is somewhat rubato: Olivia uses "you're" and "I'll," and Feste follows with "that's," then changes to "it will not" and "there is," and then accelerates again in "beauty's a flower" and "that's as much as to say." Olivia's displeasure, and also her grieving mood, are softening under the fool's pseudo-logic and sharp wit, and she lightly says, "I'll bide your proof." The Clown then, assuming a mock-clerical seriousness, starts to catechize her, and she answers, both speaking in slow tempo with "mourn|est" and "soul|is." This tempo probably continues through Feste's "Sir Toby|will." Maria, when she enters, talks fast, and Olivia slowly, thus making an effective contrast. Sir Toby here is also rapid, and slurs his words because he is either drunk or pretending to be; and, at his exit, Olivia and Feste hold a brief, rapid colloquy with "What's," "o'my," and "He's." Malvolio returns from his errand and speaks with a measured dignity that is his natural reaction from Viola's offensive sauciness at the gate; but soon he relaxes to "he's." For some fifty lines, Olivia has, without success, been trying to find out about the "gentleman" who wishes to see her. Perhaps her curiosity is piqued. At last, she asks with emphasis: "What manner of | man?" When Viola finally enters, the talk at first seems slow and formal, except for one swift parenthesis, "That question's out of my part." With Viola's speech that begins "Most certain," the dialogue quickens, though with slow intervals, chiefly in Olivia's speech— perhaps an expression of her rising emotion and uncertainty. Toward the end, Viola also varies her tempo: "continued" is followed by "even," "reverberate," and "Olivia," and they in turn by "the | elements." Olivia's soliloquy at Viola's exit starts fast with "I'll" and "actions," and then slows down as she realizes that she has fallen in love and considers this new embarrassment. "Well, let it be," she says; and, having made up her mind, she rapidly orders Malvolio to overtake Viola, and when he is gone finishes her speech with an uneven rhythm (compare "flatterer" and "do | not") that expresses her sharp emotions.

Just as in a Beethoven symphony the composer's expression marks cannot show all the finer shades, so the similar signs in Shakespeare—slurrings, ellipses, and the rest—cannot indicate all the finesses of tempo that a truly artistic rendering of the lines demands; but they are at least signposts along the way, and any interpretation that runs counter to them must be suspect. Such evidence, of course, deals directly only with tempo; but, to the artist in the speaking voice, the tempo often implies inflection and volume of tone: obviously, for example, a very fast passage can hardly be shouted or roared. Tempo also furnishes a clue to the interpretation of a character or a scene: if rhythmic variation be any criterion, Olivia's part is the most dramatically interesting in Act I of *Twelfth Night*, and runs the widest emotional gamut with the finest subtlety; and this supports the contention of the present writer that she is the real heroine, structurally and otherwise, of the play. The tempo of this act is never very slow; in fact, it is a delicate pattern of very fast contrasting with somewhat slower; and probably this was usual in Shakespeare: his rhythms seem to be shadings and nuances, which should be studied and mastered before attempting an oral interpretation of his text.

❧ Index

GENERAL INDEX

273

274

277

INDEX BY ACTS AND SCENES